DIETRICH BONHOEFFER AND
A THEOLOGY OF THE EXCEPTION

T&T Clark New Studies in Bonhoeffer's Theology and Ethics

Series editors
Jennifer McBride
Michael Mawson
Philip G. Ziegler

DIETRICH BONHOEFFER AND A THEOLOGY OF THE EXCEPTION

Kevin O'Farrell

LONDON • NEW YORK • OXFORD • NEW DELHI • SYDNEY

T&T CLARK
Bloomsbury Publishing Plc, 50 Bedford Square, London, WC1B 3DP, UK
Bloomsbury Publishing Inc, 1385 Broadway, New York, NY 10018, USA
Bloomsbury Publishing Ireland, 29 Earlsfort Terrace, Dublin 2, D02 AY28, Ireland

BLOOMSBURY, T&T CLARK and the T&T Clark logo are trademarks of Bloomsbury Publishing Plc

First published in Great Britain 2024
Paperback edition published 2025

Copyright © Kevin O'Farrell, 2024

Kevin O'Farrell has asserted his right under the Copyright, Designs and Patents Act, 1988, to be identified as Author of this work.

For legal purposes the Acknowledgments on p. vii constitute an extension of this copyright page.

Cover image: Dietrich Bonhoeffer (1906–45) photographed in the late 1930s
Photo by ullstein bild via Getty Images

All rights reserved. No part of this publication may be: i) reproduced or transmitted in any form, electronic or mechanical, including photocopying, recording or by means of any information storage or retrieval system without prior permission in writing from the publishers; or ii) used or reproduced in any way for the training, development or operation of artificial intelligence (AI) technologies, including generative AI technologies. The rights holders expressly reserve this publication from the text and data mining exception as per Article 4(3) of the Digital Single Market Directive (EU) 2019/790.

Bloomsbury Publishing Plc does not have any control over, or responsibility for, any third-party websites referred to or in this book. All internet addresses given in this book were correct at the time of going to press. The author and publisher regret any inconvenience caused if addresses have changed or sites have ceased to exist, but can accept no responsibility for any such changes.

A catalogue record for this book is available from the British Library.

A catalog record for this book is available from the Library of Congress.

Library of Congress Cataloging-in-Publication Data

Names: O'Farrell, Kevin (Theologian), author.
Title: Dietrich Bonhoeffer and a theology of the exception / Kevin O'Farrell.
Description: London ; New York : T&T Clark, 2024. |
Series: T&T Clark new studies in Bonhoeffer's theology and ethics |
Includes bibliographical references and index.
Identifiers: LCCN 2023023861 (print) | LCCN 2023023862 (ebook) |
ISBN 9780567709394 (hardback) | ISBN 9780567709448 (paperback) |
ISBN 9780567709400 (pdf) | ISBN 9780567709431 (epub)
Subjects: LCSH: Bonhoeffer, Dietrich, 1906-1945. | Christian ethics. | Political theology.
Classification: LCC BX4827.B57 O33 2024 (print) | LCC BX4827.B57 (ebook) | DDC 241–dc23/eng/20231020
LC record available at https://lccn.loc.gov/2023023861
LC ebook record available at https://lccn.loc.gov/2023023862

ISBN: HB: 978-0-5677-0939-4
PB: 978-0-5677-0944-8
ePDF: 978-0-5677-0940-0
eBook: 978-0-5677-0943-1

Series: T&T Clark New Studies in Bonhoeffer's Theology and Ethics

Typeset by Deanta Global Publishing Services, Chennai, India

For product safety related questions contact productsafety@bloomsbury.com.

To find out more about our authors and books visit www.bloomsbury.com and sign up for our newsletters.

CONTENTS

Acknowledgments	vii
List of Abbreviations	viii

INTRODUCTION	1
The Exception in Moral and Political Theology	2
Is It Appropriate to Speak of the Exception in Bonhoeffer?	5
History and the Exception	8
Outline of the Book	10

Chapter 1
BONHOEFFER AND THE EXCEPTION IN CONTEMPORARY THEOLOGY 13

Reading Bonhoeffer's Life and Thought for Today	14
Tyrannicide and the Question of Continuity	19
Lutheran and Anabaptist Readings of Bonhoeffer's Resistance Thought	24
The Free Venture of a Responsible Individual or a Fanatic	32
Conclusion	37

Chapter 2
READING BONHOEFFER'S LIFE AND THOUGHT:
HERMENEUTICAL QUESTIONS 39

Reading Bonhoeffer's Life and Thought	40
The Fragmentariness of Bonhoeffer's Life	43
The Fragmentariness of Bonhoeffer's Thought	47
A Hermeneutic for Reading the Exception in Bonhoeffer's Life and Thought	56

Chapter 3
BONHOEFFER ON HISTORY AND THE MOMENT 61

Bonhoeffer's Early Account of History and the Moment	62
The Undoing of History and Ethics in Revelation	69
Divine Voluntarism and Creation in the Exception	72
The Moment of Temptation	76
Coda: The Relation of History to Political Orders in Bonhoeffer	80

Chapter 4
READING THE EXCEPTION IN "HISTORY AND GOOD [2]" — 83
- Responsible Action in the Exception — 85
- The Logic and Tension of *Necessitá* — 88
- Distancing from *Necessitá* — 94
- Emphasizing History in "History and Good [2]" — 98
- Narrating the Exception in "History and Good [2]" — 104
- Conclusion — 110

Chapter 5
THE POLITICS OF EXTRAORDINARY FREEDOM — 111
- The Annihilation of Freedom in Totalitarianism — 112
- Adventitious Liberation and Undetermined Political Freedom — 116
- Undetermined Freedom Is Not Arbitrary — 123
- The Conspiracy as Repentance — 132

Chapter 6
THE DISMANTLING, RECONCILIATION, AND FUTURE OF THE LAW — 135
- The Beginning, the Law, and the Moment of Exception — 135
- Reconciliation in the Borderline Case — 145
- Imagining Politics after the Exception — 157

CONCLUSION — 163
- Responding to Hermeneutic Questions in the Discourse on the Exception — 164
- Can One Speak of the Exception in Bonhoeffer? — 167

Bibliography — 171
Index — 182

ACKNOWLEDGMENTS

There are many colleagues who supported this project since its origin as a doctoral dissertation at the University of Aberdeen. Michael Mawson encouraged its vision from the beginning until its final published form. I am thankful for his generous guidance at every stage of the process. Brian Brock provided decisive supervision of the project, offering support in the most perilous of times. Ted Smith and Philip Ziegler both offered essential guidance in preparation for its publication. There are a number of forums where I presented on book chapters. These have been indispensable in the formation of this project. I presented an early draft of Chapter 4 at the weeklong "Early Career German-American Bonhoeffer Network" seminar in Berlin in 2017 led by Clifford Green, Christiane Tietz, and Michael DeJonge. I presented a condensed version of Chapter 5 at the Joint Research Seminar in Practical Theology and Theological Ethics at the University of Aberdeen in 2020. And I presented an overview of the project at the Pre-Congress Bonhoeffer Graduate Colloquium in Volmoed South Africa in 2020. My colleagues' questions and pushbacks sharpened the argument of the project in each instance. I am thankful for these various opportunities.

There are many friendships that added depth and joy in the writing of this project: Daniel Patterson, Jacob Marques Rollison, Michael Morelli, Marty Phillips, Topher Endress, Julie Land, Daniele and Angelika Bocchetti, Declan Kelly, Travis and Hannah Cory, and Jon and Mim Goossen. A special note of gratitude to my family, who have always encouraged my ministry and research. Your support and generosity are abundant. Above all, I am thankful for Chrissy and Clare. You are truly exceptional. We have braved many crises together, finding joy in the midst of consistent transition and turmoil. While Clare was only born in the final stages of this journey, Chrissy has been ever-present in friendship, support, and encouragement. This book would not be without your exceptional love and support. This book is for you.

ABBREVIATIONS

CD   Karl Barth. *Church Dogmatics*. 4 vols. Edited by Geoffrey W. Bromiley and T. F. Torrance. New York: T&T Clark, 2009.
DB-ER   Eberhard Bethge. *Dietrich Bonhoeffer: Theologian, Christian, Contemporary*. Translated by Eric Mosbacher et al. London: Collins, 1970.
DBW   Dietrich Bonhoeffer. *Dietrich Bonhoeffer Werke*. Edited by Eberhard Bethge et al. 17 vols. Munich: Kaiser/Gütersloher Verlagshaus, 1986–99.
DBWE   Dietrich Bonhoeffer. *Dietrich Bonhoeffer Works*. Edited by Victoria Barnett, Wayne Whitson Floyd Jr., and Barbara Wojhoski. 17 vols. Minneapolis: Fortress Press, 1996–2013.
LW   Martin Luther. *Luther's Works*. Edited by Jaroslav Pelikan and Helmut T. Lehmann. 56 vols. Philadelphia: Fortress Press; St. Louis: Concordia Publishing House, 1955–86.
ZN   Dietrich Bonhoeffer. *Zettelnotizen für eine "Ethik."* Edited by Isle Tödt. Gütersloh: Kaiser, 1993.

INTRODUCTION

> In human life, the truth is something foreign, something unusual, an exception.[1]

The broad consensus among commentators is that Dietrich Bonhoeffer was an exceptional individual who acted exceptionally in exceptional circumstances. He stood apart from his contemporaries as a rare individual who not only perceived the reality of the Nazi regime with intense clarity but also opposed it in speech and deed. Perhaps the most famous aspect of Bonhoeffer's legacy is his participation in a high-level military conspiracy against Hitler. Bonhoeffer, of course, had no more than a minor role in the Canaris-Oster conspiracy upon his return to Germany in 1939. His task was to use his ecumenical contacts to seek Allied support for a post-National Socialist government. While the truth of his role deflates popular "Bonhoeffer the assassin" depictions, this should not minimize the conviction with which he participated. Bonhoeffer told several contemporaries that if it fell to him, he would personally "carry out the deed" against Hitler.[2] Nor should Bonhoeffer's relatively inconsequential role minimize the risks he undertook during these years. From his subterfuge as an *Abwehr* agent to his participation in Operation Seven, Bonhoeffer risked imprisonment and execution, which is precisely the fate that befell him, culminating in his untimely death in April 1945.

While almost everyone agrees that Bonhoeffer was an exceptional individual who lived an exceptional life, his understanding of the idea of the exception has been much more hotly contested. Despite their shared etymology, there is an important distinction to be observed between the exceptional and the exception. The exceptional is an intensifier that reflects the rarity and magnitude of an entity in a comparative mode, thus narrating the exceptional on a spectrum comparable to "ordinary" persons, acts, and events. The logic of the exceptional belongs inside a prevailing frame of reference. By contrast, the exception acknowledges shared frames of reference precisely by throwing them into question from the outside. The exception differs from the exceptional by its exclusion from or inability to belong to the rule or order. It is not only rare and remarkable but is alien and singular.

---

1. DBWE 11:467.
2. DB-ER, 656.

The exception resists reduction to an immanent frame.[3] This book reflects on the exception in the theology of Dietrich Bonhoeffer.

The Exception in Moral and Political Theology

Bonhoeffer certainly was not the first person to reflect on the exception. The concept predates Bonhoeffer, and contemporary discourse on the exception continues largely outside of Bonhoeffer scholarship. One reason that the exception remains a topic of discussion is its continuing public relevance. The world brims with crises that simultaneously captivate and confound onlookers, calling for unprecedented action in the midst of rapid social and political transformation. This was true when Bonhoeffer was alive and it remains true today. Indeed, Adam Tooze has recently described our contemporary moment as one of "polycrisis" whereby multiple crises—each with their own origin and scale—amplify and accelerate one another with the sum effect being greater than any single crisis.[4] According to Tooze, one of the challenges of polycrisis is that it disarms typical forms of response, since they are inadequate to overcome the combined threat of polycrisis. The alleviation of one crisis through conventional methods often exacerbates the others. The polycrisis subsequently calls for urgent and imaginative forms of collective action, bursting the forms of established practice and law.[5] In reflecting on such crises, the exception becomes a heuristic to deliberate on responsible and effective action that may exceed the rule and order so as to meet the demands of the moment.

While the broader discourse on the exception is wide-ranging and diverse, commentators typically engage the exception in either a moral or a political sense. Commentators who engage the exception in a moral sense reflect on situations when one feels constrained to transgress or act beyond moral norms or rules in hard cases, prompting the question of whether there are "commendable exceptions" to moral principles.[6] Those who argue that there are commendable exceptions take various routes to reach their conclusions. Some narrate the exception as a transgression of a particular moral rule on the basis of a foundational moral

---

3. Ted A. Smith, *Weird John Brown: Divine Violence and the Limits of Ethics* (Stanford: Stanford University Press, 2015), 35–9.

4. Tooze employs polycrisis to describe the climate emergency, the ongoing Covid-19 pandemic, the various military conflicts that destabilize regions, looming global recession, the emergence of national populism, and other crises. While Tooze has recently popularized the concept, it is a "found concept" he received from Jean-Claude Juncker, though originating with Edgar Morin. Adam Tooze, *Shutdown: How Covid Shook the World's Economy* (New York: Viking, 2021), 6, 279–88.

5. Ibid.

6. Paul Ramsey, "The Case of the Curious Exception," in *Norm and Context in Christian Ethics*, ed. Gene H. Outka and Paul Ramsey (London: SCM Press, 1968), 67.

norm.⁷ In this situation, one is guilty of transgressing the moral precept, but the transgression is justifiable on the basis of a higher obligation. Others argue that the seeming transgression is no transgression at all, but rather paradoxical obedience to the moral rule in a peculiar situation, thus deepening one's understanding of the moral rule.⁸ Narrations of the exception in this vein do not speak of it as a singular or novel occurrence, since the discourse centers on kinds of moments that require certain kinds of actions, which belies its generic and repetitious character. As Oliver O'Donovan concludes: "Exceptions to rules are themselves rules."⁹ To speak of an exception is thus to engage in formulating exception-making criteria that clarify cases of the nonapplicability of a rule or it speaks to the exceptionality of situational features that clarify how a rule is to be applied. The exception thereby remains attached to a moral system and finds explication on its terms. Conversely, those who speak of the moral exception as a singular or novel phenomenon explicate the exception as exceeding a moral framework in part or absolutely. The origin of this deed can be, for instance, a situation when God commands a particular exception to biblical commands or moral norms, leading to a singular act of obedience beyond ordinary description.¹⁰ One glimpses in this rendition the specter of Kierkegaard's *Fear and Trembling* and his account of the teleological suspension of the ethical. Kierkegaard perceived that for an act to supersede the ethical, it must exceed moral categorization, remaining utterly singular to the point of resisting vocalization.¹¹ The knight of faith must undergo the exception in silence. Articulations of the exception in a moral sense divide on whether the exception exceeds delineation on moral terms or not.

When commentators explicate the exception in a more directly political idiom, they reflect on situations of dire necessity that require action beyond the law for the sake of the polity, echoing the ancient maxim *necessitas legem non habet* (necessity has no law).¹² It is in this frame that political theologians often invoke

---

7. Ramsey reads Bonhoeffer in this vein. See Paul Ramsey, *Deeds and Rules in Christian Ethics* (New York: Scribner, 1967), 118-19.

8. Oliver O'Donovan, *Resurrection and Moral Order: An Outline for Evangelical Ethics*, 2nd ed. (Grand Rapids: William B. Eerdmans Publishing Company, 1994), 183-97.

9. Oliver O'Donovan, *Finding and Seeking* (Cambridge: William B. Eerdmans Publishing Company, 2014), 227.

10. For a reading of Barth's ethics of war in this vein, see Richard Hays, *The Moral Vision of the New Testament* (San Francisco: Harper, 1996), 225-39. For a decisive critique of this reading of Barth, see Matthew Puffer, "Taking Exception to the *Grenzfall's* Reception: Revisiting Karl Barth's Ethics of War," *Modern Theology* 28, no. 3 (2012): 478-502.

11. Søren Kierkegaard, *Fear and Trembling* and *Repetition*, ed. and trans. Howard V. Hong and Edna H. Hong (Princeton: Princeton University Press, 1983).

12. See Agamben's discussion of the history of this maxim which originates with Gratian. Giorgio Agamben, *State of Exception*, trans. Kevin Attell (Chicago: University of Chicago Press, 2005), 24-31. Three varying approaches to the theme of necessity are Thomas Aquinas, *Summa Theologiae* IaIIae, ed. Thomas Gilby (Cambridge: Blackfriars,

Carl Schmitt's concept of the state of exception (*Ausnahmezustand*).[13] Schmitt famously describes the state of exception as an emergency situation when the sovereign suspends the entire juridical order through decision for the sake of the polity. There is no legal precedent or criterion that authorizes the decision; the sovereign decides on the exception through his own authority beyond law. The exception is not merely effective political action for Schmitt, bypassing the inefficiencies of seeking consensus through legal means in moments of extremity. The exception is also revelatory insofar as it resists the reduction of the state to a legal order by demonstrating that at the origin of the political is not the law that authorizes the sovereign, but the sovereign who decides upon and authorizes the law. Just as a norm does not contain the terms of its application, so, too, the law does not contain the terms of its enforcement. It requires an impetus from outside for its authorization in political life, which for Schmitt is the decision of the sovereign.[14] Schmitt's account presses the question of whether the exception precedes law or whether it can be inscribed within or explicated through law.

The discourse on the exception likewise asks the corresponding question of whether one can speak of "legal" resistance or a legitimate right to resistance. The different senses of law run through discussions about the right to resistance, since some affirm this right not through constitutional or legal precepts, but through a "higher" law or natural law upon which the juridical order, including public law, finds authorization and is held accountable.[15] For example, notions of tyrannicide allow in the exception that it is licit to judge political authority on the basis of a

---

1966), q. 96, art. 6; John Locke, *Two Treatises of Government*, ed. Peter Laslett (Cambridge: Cambridge University Press, 1960), chap. 14, §60; Niccolo Machiavelli, *The Prince*, trans. and ed. Peter Bondanella (Oxford: Oxford University Press, 2005), ch. 18.

13. Carl Schmitt, *Political Theology: Four Chapters on the Concept of Sovereignty*, trans. George Schwab (Chicago: University of Chicago Press, 2005). Recent works that engage Schmitt on the exception include Agamben, *State of Exception*; Giorgio Agamben, *Homo Sacer: Sovereign Power and Bare Life*, trans. Daniel Heller-Roazen (Stanford: Stanford University Press, 1998); Paul W. Kahn, *Political Theology: Four New Chapters on Sovereignty* (New York: Columbia University Press, 2012); Smith, *Weird John Brown*; Robert A. Yelle, *Sovereignty and the Sacred: Secularism and the Political Economy of Religion* (Chicago: Chicago University Press, 2019); Jacques Derrida, *The Beast and the Sovereign*, 2 vols, ed. Michel Lisse, Marie-Louise Mallet, and Ginette Michaud, trans. Geoffrey Bennington (Chicago: University of Chicago, 2009); Ryan Bartholomew, *Kierkegaard's Indirect Politics: Interludes with Lukács, Schmitt, Benjamin and Adorno* (Amsterdam: Brill, 2014); Marc de Wilde, "Violence in the State of Exception: Reflections on Theologico-Political Motifs in Benjamin and Schmitt," in *Political Theologies: Public Religions in a Post-Secular World*, ed. Hent de Vries and Lawrence E. Sullivan (New York: Fordham University Press, 2006), 188–200.

14. One cannot overlook the reference to Kierkegaard's *Repetition* by Schmitt in developing this point. Schmitt, *Political Theology*, 15.

15. Aquinas, IaIIae q., 90–7.

higher law and through that law justify the violent removal of the tyrant. Such action is just, since it adjudges the tyrant to be an abuser of law, who has forfeited political authorization before the tribunal of law.

There are obvious overlaps between discussions of the exception in moral and political theology and there can be no strict separation between them. This remains true in debates concerning Bonhoeffer's resistance biography insofar as any discussion of the political justification for the coup d'état also includes questions about the (im)moral means of its fulfillment. Put differently, the overthrow of Hitler not only raises questions about the nature and limits of political authority and law but also raises questions about the nature and limits of the fifth and eighth commandments. Bonhoeffer also seems to speak of moral and political exceptions in his discussions on the character of political resistance[16] as well as his discussions on situations when one appears to break the eighth commandment.[17] The two senses converge most obviously in Bonhoeffer's unfinished manuscript "History and Good [2]" where he describes the moment of *ultima ratio* when one must break positive law and even God's commandment for the sake of the law and human life.[18] Commentators reflect with singular concentration on Bonhoeffer's theology of the exception in this manuscript, prompting sharp debate and a myriad of interpretive conclusions.

Is It Appropriate to Speak of the Exception in Bonhoeffer?

One may question whether it is appropriate to reflect on the exception in Bonhoeffer's theology given that he does not speak explicitly about the exception (*Ausnahme*) in the texts most associated with the concept. While there is a single reference in "The 'Christian' and the 'Ethical' as a Topic" to "necessary emergency situations" (*notwendige Ausnahmezustände*), the usage belongs to a discussion not frequently associated with the exception.[19] This is because Bonhoeffer describes this situation as an emergency discourse within a community rather than an individual venture beyond or against the law.[20] Bonhoeffer instead speaks most frequently of the borderline case (*Grenzfall*), *ultima ratio*, and *necessitá* in the texts associated with the exception. Reading the exception in Bonhoeffer's theology thus risks distorting his thought, since it centers on a term largely alien to his works. One way to respond to this challenge is to affirm that reflecting on the exception in Bonhoeffer's theology does not entail an absolute commitment to the language of exception. It is

---

16. DBWE 16:514–17; DBWE 12:361–73.
17. DBWE 6:278–9; DBWE 16:601–8.
18. DBWE 6:272–4.
19. DBWE 6:368.
20. Hence I follow the critical edition translation of "necessary emergency situations" rather than "states of exception."

instead a way to enter into a particular discourse within which commentators employ the language of exception and its cognates (e.g., extraordinary demands, extreme deed, and emergency act) to summarize aspects of Bonhoeffer's thought and action.[21] The exception thus becomes shorthand for a litany of questions and themes associated with the concept that emerge in the reading of Bonhoeffer's corpus with focused attention on texts where the exception is most frequently identified, such as Bonhoeffer's 1942 Christmas letter "After Ten Years,"[22] the unfinished *Ethics* manuscripts "History and Good [2]"[23] and "Natural Life,"[24] the 1941 essay "A Position Paper on State and Church,"[25]

---

21. Scholars who speak explicitly of the exception in Bonhoeffer include Larry Rasmussen, *Dietrich Bonhoeffer: Reality and Resistance* (Nashville: Abingdon Press, 1972); Clifford Green, "Pacifism and Tyrannicide: Bonhoeffer's Christian Peace Ethic," *Studies in Christian Ethics* 18, no. 3 (2005): 31–47; Jean Bethke Elshtain, *Sovereignty: God, State, and Self* (New York: Basic Books, 2008), 116–17; Petra Brown, "Bonhoeffer, Schmitt, and the State of Exception," *Pacifica* 26, no. 3 (2013): 246–64; Petra Brown, *Bonhoeffer: God's Conspirator in a State of Exception* (Cham: Palgrave MacMillan, 2019); Jeremy K. Kessler, "Bonhoeffer on Law Breaking: A Reassessment on the Ethical Exception to the Divine Command," in *Ontology and Ethics: Bonhoeffer and Contemporary Scholarship*, ed. Adam Clark and Michael Mawson (Eugene: Pickwick Publications, 2013), 102–17; Matthew Puffer, "The 'Borderline Case' in Bonhoeffer's Political Theology," in *Dem Rad in die Speichen fallen: Das Politische in der Theologie Dietrich Bonhoeffer | A Spoke in the Wheel: The Political Theology of Dietrich Bonhoeffer*, ed. Kirsten Bush Nielsen, Ralf Karolus Wüstenberg, Jens Zimmermann (München: Gütersloher Verlagshaus, 2013), 257–69. Other scholars speak of cognates of the exception, using language like the "exceptional case" (Ulrik B. Nissen, "Dietrich Bonhoeffer: A Journey from Pacifism to Resistance," in *Christianity and Resistance in the 20th Century: From Kaj Munk and Dietrich Bonhoeffer to Desmond Tutu*, ed. Søren Dosenrode (Leiden: Brill, 2008), 155), "the teleological suspension of the ethical" (Matthew Kirkpatrick, "Bonhoeffer, Kierkegaard, and the Teleological Suspension of the Ethical," in *Ontology and Ethics*, 86–101), the "emergency situation" (Heinz Edward Tödt, *Authentic Faith: Bonhoeffer's Theological Ethics in Context*, ed. Ernst-Albert Scharffenorth, trans. David Stassen and Isle Tödt (William B. Eerdmans Publishing Co: Cambridge, 2007), 68), the responsible act "characterized by urgency, novelty, and disconnection from established practice" (Robin W. Lovin, "Becoming Responsible in Christian Ethics," *Studies in Christian Ethics* 22, no. 4 (2009), 395), "extraordinary demands of the situation" (DB-ER, 700), "an emergency situation . . . that forces Christians to go against established orders" where one "breaks divine laws" (Jens Zimmermann, *Bonhoeffer's Christian Humanism* (Oxford: Oxford University Press, 2019), 218), actions that "stand outside of the moral framework that justifies any action" (Michael DeJonge, *Bonhoeffer on Resistance: The Word Against the Wheel* (Oxford: Oxford University Press, 2018), 156).
22. DBWE 8:37–52.
23. DBWE 6:246–99.
24. DBWE 6:171–218.
25. DBWE 16:502–28.

and the unfinished 1943 manuscript from prison "What Does It Mean to Tell the Truth."[26]

This book provisionally accepts that Bonhoeffer reasons about exceptions in these key texts in order to engage the discourse while remaining open to the possibility that one must ultimately relinquish the term in preference for another. Bonhoeffer performed a similar task by developing the language of the mandates over the more prominent concepts of divine orders or Luther's three estates. The analogy is imperfect since Bonhoeffer explored the language of the mandates less because of a theological deficiency in the other terms and more because of the unhelpful baggage they acquired through their use.[27] The benefit of this analogy is in affirming Bonhoeffer's recognition that the language employed in theological discourse is never static but is ever open to new forms of speech that better capture the reality and work of God in history.

Another response to the question of whether it is appropriate to reflect on the exception in Bonhoeffer's theology is to affirm that Bonhoeffer speaks explicitly of the exception in a lesser-known writing that can help frame the reading of texts associated with the exception. In his 1932 sermon on John 8:32, Bonhoeffer claims that "in human life, the truth is something foreign, something unusual, an exception (*Ausnahmehaftes*)."[28] Bonhoeffer reasons that the truth is extraordinary and radically contingent. The happening of the truth is an exception that stands in relation to but remains apart from the ordinary and necessary. It is, as Bonhoeffer illustrates, the fool in ridiculous dress who stands among the princes and knights in the courtroom, neither blending in nor belonging, "but every court needed an exception (*Ausnahme*)."[29] The fool, while out of place, is indispensable to the court, speaking the truth that no one else can speak. The truth is ugly and unseemly; it is rejected by the world, but liberating in every sense—"the truth will set you free" (Jn 8:32). It seizes a person without warning, overcoming them in its strangeness, inducting those who undergo its liberation into the company of the "very few true revolutionaries."[30] Such events have their own origin and rationale, arising within but originating beyond the historical and political context. The exception is the truth in the order of miracle, eliciting reflection on the eventuality of the truth—"now the *truth happens*."[31] It is only in the exception as an event that one is set free, since it is only by first undergoing the event that "destroys and illuminates" that one can reflect upon the truth in the mode of exception.[32] Only in light of the event can one probe into the character of ethics, politics, and the meaning of free action, since persons would otherwise isolate themselves from the truth through

---

26. DBWE 16:601–8.
27. DBWE 6:389–90.
28. DBWE 11:467.
29. DBWE 11:466.
30. DBWE 11:465.
31. DBWE 11:469. Emphasis original.
32. DBWE 11:468.

the political and moral lies they tell themselves.³³ Bonhoeffer's diatribe against the pervasive lies of human life captures that apart from a divine inbreaking, ethics and politics are determined by the machinations of sin. Persons await a gracious incursion that liberates them and reality, setting all things in a different light. "The human being who loves because [he] has been made free by God's truth is the most revolutionary human being on earth. He is the overturning of all values; he is the explosive material in human society; he is the most dangerous human being." This one, Bonhoeffer concludes, "is the knight of truth and love."³⁴

History and the Exception

The impulse of Bonhoeffer's sermon is that the exception is principally an event that has moral and political implications. Bonhoeffer speaks of the exception initially not within the binaries of rule/exception or law/decision but as an event that befalls human life and reality, inflecting upon the meaning of individual action, ethics, and politics. If one takes seriously Bonhoeffer's claim that the exception names the initial encounter with truth as a moment in history, then it will reframe how one reads Bonhoeffer's political theology and ethics. I engage the exception in its full temporality at each juncture of this book, specifying the ways it generates a new relation between individual human action and the law in its various senses. What is distinctive about this approach is that it emphasizes human passivity insofar as the exception *befalls* human life, changing the tenor of discussions about the exception by decentering the individual and their interpretive relationship to the law and the moment.

There is a textual warrant for this program in Bonhoeffer's late resistance theology. Bonhoeffer reflected on the character of temporality and history in various writings from the conspiracy era and from prison.³⁵ It is also an often overlooked theme crucial to the unfinished *Ethics* manuscript "History and Good [2]," which is the writing most often associated with the exception in Bonhoeffer. At various junctures in this manuscript, Bonhoeffer reflects upon the meaning and character of history and how it impinges upon a narration of human action, particularly in the passage most often associated with the exception in Bonhoeffer's theology: "In thus giving up the appeal to any law, indeed only so, is there finally a surrender

---

33. DBWE 11:467–8.
34. DBWE 11:471.
35. DBWE 6:103–33; DBWE 6:219–45; DBWE 6:246–98; DBWE 8:46, 69–74, 98, 181, 303–4, 418–21; the theme of providence preoccupies Bonhoeffer in prison as well (DBWE 8:83, 358–9, 417, 517; Dietrich Bonhoeffer and Maria von Wedemeyer, *Love Letters from Cell 92*, ed. Ruth-Alice von Mismarck and Ulrich Kabitz, trans. John Brownjohn (London: HarperCollins Publisher, 1994), 64, 221). On the day after the failed plot (July 21, 1944), Bonhoeffer wrote to Bethge: "May God lead us kindly through these times, but above all, may God lead us to himself" (DBWE 8:486).

of one's own decision and action to the divine guidance of history."[36] How one explicates history, temporality, and eventuality becomes increasingly important in a reflection upon the exception in a moral and political key in Bonhoeffer's theology. I develop the claim that any consideration of the exception will require "some kind of deliberation about the meaning of history."[37]

When I engage the exception in its historicity, this does not imply that I read the exception through Bonhoeffer's biography or the details of the conspiracy. This is, in part, because there is little need for another biographical text when there are already plenteous well-researched texts on Bonhoeffer's resistance activity.[38] I engage this literature when appropriate, recognizing that this book benefits from its insights and prior historical research. I also resist reading the exception through Bonhoeffer's biography or historical context because Bonhoeffer resists this program himself. As I argue in this book, Bonhoeffer consistently affirms that the impetus and meaning of the exception exceeds the nexus of historical cause and effect. The historical or biographical context does not explain the exception as much as the exception explains one's historical context. Following the language of Claude Romano: "an event . . . illuminates its own context, rather than in any way receiving its meaning from it. It is not a consequence of this context that could be explained in light of preexisting possibilities, but it reconfigures the preexisting possibilities that precede it and signals the advent of a new world."[39] This does not deny the historicity of the exception or that one's historical context influences free action; it instead confesses that the historical context contributes to one's understanding of and response to the event, but that the origin and meaning of the event and one's free action therein ultimately exceeds them.

Following my reference to Claude Romano's phenomenological account of the event, another important clarification is to delineate how my approach differs from phenomenology. This gains further importance in light of how I draw upon the insights of phenomenology at various points in the book, though this is often relegated to the footnotes. One may question this employment, particularly

---

36. DBWE 6:274.
37. Smith, *Weird John Brown*, 177.
38. DB-ER; Sabine Dramm, *Dietrich Bonhoeffer and the Resistance* (Minneapolis: Fortress Press, 2009); Christiane Tietz, *Theologian of Resistance: The Life and Thought of Dietrich Bonhoeffer*, trans. Victoria J. Barnett (Minneapolis: Fortress Press, 2016); Charles Marsh, *Strange Glory: A Life of Dietrich Bonhoeffer* (New York: Alfred A. Knoft, 2014); Ferdinand Schlingensiepen, *Dietrich Bonhoeffer, 1906–1945: Martyr, Thinker, Man of Resistance*, trans. Isabel Best (London: Bloomsbury, 2009); John A. Moses, *The Reluctant Revolutionary: Dietrich Bonhoeffer's Collision with Prusso-German History* (Oxford: Berghahn Books, 2014).
39. Claude Romano, *Event and World*, trans. Shane Mackinlay (New York: Fordham University Press, 2009), 38.

when Heideggerian resonances lay close at hand.[40] To be as clear as possible: this book does not attempt to create a synthesis between phenomenology and theology, nor does it read Bonhoeffer as a committed phenomenologist, let alone a Heideggerian.[41] It instead recognizes a resonance between phenomenology and theology insofar as both reflect upon the eventuality of human life as well as the potentiality of moments to upset one's framework for living in the world. While the starting points and methodology of theology and phenomenology differ dramatically and possess their own integrity, a discourse on the exception becomes a point of convergence in that both describe the passivity of human life undergoing an event that transforms a person and their relation to the world.[42] In this sense, the employment of phenomenological vocabulary is ad hoc by how it provides a language that communicates my intuitions in a reading of the exception in Bonhoeffer's theology.

Outline of the Book

The first two chapters critically engage the discourse on Bonhoeffer and the exception in order to develop a hermeneutic approach for reading the exception in Bonhoeffer's life and thought. Chapter 1 summarizes the prevailing discourse on Bonhoeffer's theology of resistance more broadly and his theology of the exception in particular, and in so doing it likewise rehearses the primary motifs and texts that commentators employ when interpreting the exception in Bonhoeffer, such as the resistance rationale outlined in "The Church and the Jewish Question," the "pacifism" of *Discipleship*, and Bonhoeffer's reflections in *Ethics* on the free venture, responsibility, and the mandates. Through this summation, I identify key hermeneutic decisions that contribute to the varying readings of Bonhoeffer's theology in the discourse on the exception.

---

40. A number of interlocutors I engage are directly downstream of Heidegger and thus remain within his orbit: Giorgio Agamben, Hannah Arendt, Claude Romano, Jean-Luc Marion, Jacques Derrida, and Hans-Georg Gadamer.

41. Bonhoeffer, however, is influenced more by Heidegger than commentators often admit. For an article that attends to Heidegger's influence on Bonhoeffer, see Josh de Keijzer, "Revelation as Being: Bonhoeffer's Appropriation of Heidegger's Ontology," *The Journal of Religion* 98, no. 3 (2018): 348–70.

42. Ola Sigurdson, "'Theology in the Middle of Things': Existential Preconditions of Systematic Theology," *International Journal of Systematic Theology* 22, no. 4 (2020): 473–93. On the relationship of phenomenology and theology, see Emmanuel Falque, *Crossing the Rubicon: The Borderlands of Philosophy and Theology*, trans. Reuben Shank (New York: Fordham University Press, 2016); Dominique Janicaud et al., *Phenomenology and the "Theological Turn": The French Debate*, trans. Bernard G. Prusak (New York: Fordham University Press, 2000).

Chapter 2 centers on the question of how to read the exception in Bonhoeffer's life and thought. By attending to Bonhoeffer's late resistance and prison writings, I argue that Bonhoeffer's life and decision-making (including the decision to join the resistance) are marked by fragmentation and the experience of rupture. I also argue that Bonhoeffer's late resistance texts present multiple rationales about the exception, opening differing avenues for how to read the exception in Bonhoeffer's thought. The presence of multiple rationales entails that no attempt is made in this book to identify and coalesce the varying rationales into "Bonhoeffer's account of the exception." Since Bonhoeffer puts forward multiple rationales on the exception, I instead venture to develop a "Bonhoefferian" account of the exception. The benefit of this approach is that it makes explicit the need for judgment and discernment in a narration of the exception in Bonhoeffer, which entails at points reading against Bonhoeffer with Bonhoeffer.

Chapters 3 and 4 shift to read the exception through the lens of history in Bonhoeffer's theology. Chapter 3 attends to Bonhoeffer's early reflections on history and the moment, articulating how Bonhoeffer's reflections on these themes preserve space for a particular moment in history whereby moral and political resources are inadequate to direct action, leaving one utterly dependent on God's Word for which one must decide. Bonhoeffer thereby echoes Kierkegaard's *Fear and Trembling* and the theology of crisis. This culminates with Bonhoeffer's 1938 "Bible Study on Temptation," which explicates in a biblical idiom a fallen moment in history when one cannot employ ethical or political resources to overcome its threat, and one can only decide for or against God's Word in simple obedience.

Chapter 4 performs a close reading of the manuscript "History and Good [2]." Instead of emphasizing Bonhoeffer's employment of the Machiavellian concept of *necessitá*, which figures prominently in many readings of the exception in Bonhoeffer, I argue that there are good theological reasons to diminish this employment: it introduces a subtle account of self-justification, it skews and encourages the manipulation of reality in seeking to defend one's necessary action, and it denies the unity of the Christ-reality by asserting conflict, division, and the necessity of violence into responsible action. I argue that it is preferable instead to read the exception through Bonhoeffer's theologically inflected account of history in the manuscript. In this frame, the exception is a divine incursion beyond good and evil that liberates human action from the determinations of law for free action in responsiveness to God and neighbor. This reading of the exception allows for a differing narration of responsible action that is simultaneously free and bound to the neighbor in self-giving love.

The final two chapters reflect on the implications of the exception for a narration of freedom and law in Bonhoeffer's moral and political theology. Chapter 5 develops an account of undetermined free action oriented to the formation of political life in Bonhoeffer's theology. Such undetermined free action is epitomized by Bonhoeffer's concept of simple obedience. I anticipate and combat the critique that such free action necessarily becomes arbitrary and private, insisting that freedom undetermined by law nevertheless remains in relation to the law, affirming the intelligibility and public character of individual free action. It is responsive and oriented to God's action in history, maintaining space for discerning reflection in the Christian life. The chapter concludes by describing Bonhoeffer's conspiracy activity as repentance, capturing the simplicity and secondary character of political action in responsiveness to God's liberating action in history.

Chapter 6 reflects on the boundedness and continuity of the law in light of the exception, resisting the charge that the exception destroys and neglects everyday life. Through a reading of Bonhoeffer's unfinished commentary on Psalm 119, I argue that the exception does not entail the destruction (*Zerstörung*) of law or creation, but the dismantling of false receptions of the law that obscure God's present command that forms human life. I then engage a series of relationships in Bonhoeffer's theology that are prominent in narrations of the borderline case—the relationship between church and world, the relationship between the mandates, and the relationship between politics and ethics. Whereas common narrations of Bonhoeffer's theology read these relationships as necessarily conflicting in the borderline case, I propose that these relationships appear in a different light when framed by the reality of reconciliation, affirming their unity and coordination before God in the borderline case. At the end of Chapter 6, I reflect upon Bonhoeffer's attempts to imagine politics after the exception, considering what it means to grasp after the future in a moment that disrupts ordinary attempts to anticipate the future in action. While Bonhoeffer could not reasonably plan for the future, I suggest his action still had an important though unintended effect on the younger generations, and this reflects the nonlinear and emergent causality of political action.

Chapter 1

BONHOEFFER AND THE EXCEPTION IN CONTEMPORARY THEOLOGY

Readings of Dietrich Bonhoeffer's life and thought are as varied as they are numerous. This is, in part, because Bonhoeffer's legacy is contested territory with narrations of his life and thought being employed to champion disparate theological movements. As Stephen Haynes describes in the opening passage of his influential work, *The Bonhoeffer Phenomenon*:

> Interpreters continue to claim Bonhoeffer as a "true" radical, liberal, or conservative. He is invoked as a champion of orthodoxy, neo-orthodoxy, the theology of secularity, political and liberation theologies, religious pluralism and postmodernism. In fact, one can find Bonhoeffer's name attached to virtually every mainstream theological movement that has flourished during the past three decades.... This is no less true today.[1]

The numerous readings of Bonhoeffer's conspiratorial activity likewise reflect this broad variation. Any contemporary attempt to narrate Bonhoeffer's late resistance life and thought will do well first to comprehend these varying approaches and readings before venturing their own. And beyond merely understanding what these various scholars have said about Bonhoeffer's late resistance thought, it is further beneficial to discern the hermeneutic dispositions and contexts that contribute to the formation of their readings.

To this end, the purpose of this chapter is twofold. First, it is to lay out the prevailing discourses and issues that surround readings of Bonhoeffer's theology of resistance more broadly and his theology of the exception in particular. The chapter performs a survey albeit selectively. It does not engage every commentator who discusses Bonhoeffer on the exception but instead engages thinkers who display prominent strains of thought on the topic, placing them in conversation with one another to elicit key hermeneutical decisions at play in reading Bonhoeffer's theology. This sets up the discussion on how to read Bonhoeffer's

---

1. Stephen R. Haynes, *The Bonhoeffer Phenomenon: Portraits of a Protestant Saint* (Minneapolis: Fortress Press, 2004), 10.

life and thought in Chapter 2. The second purpose is to highlight key texts and concepts in Bonhoeffer's theology that predominate discussions concerning his resistance thought, and how these texts and concepts interplay in each theologian's reading of Bonhoeffer. By explicating the various readings in this chapter, the most frequently invoked concepts and texts in narrating the exception in Bonhoeffer are summarized.

The chapter has four sections, each drawing on two readings of Bonhoeffer's life and resistance thought. The first section engages the "popular Bonhoeffer" of American readings in conversation with the South African reception of Bonhoeffer. Their differences raise the question of how one can speak of Bonhoeffer as a "contemporary," and in what ways (if at all) one can draw parallels between Bonhoeffer's historical context and one's own. Put differently, it raises the question of how to read Bonhoeffer for today. The second section engages the prominent work of Clifford Green and Larry Rasmussen, who agree that Bonhoeffer's account of the exception is best summarized as tyrannicide but disagree on whether Bonhoeffer intentionally developed a theology of tyrannicide or if it is a later imposition. They also disagree on whether Bonhoeffer's resistance theology is characterized by continuity or discontinuity with his earlier texts. The third section puts Michael DeJonge's Lutheran reading of Bonhoeffer in conversation with the Anabaptist readings of Stanley Hauerwas and Mark Nation. I observe that while their disagreements are stark and often heated, there are striking similarities between their readings, thus raising the question of whether Bonhoeffer's theology is "traditioned," systematic, and consistent. The final section centers on Bonhoeffer's account of the individual venture by engaging the reading of Robin Lovin, who reads Bonhoeffer as a Christian realist, and the reading of Petra Brown, who reads Bonhoeffer as a religious fanatic. Their respective readings raise the question of whether Bonhoeffer's venture in the exception is best characterized by discernment or decision and whether it is rational.

Reading Bonhoeffer's Life and Thought for Today

In recent years, many Americans have claimed that a "Bonhoeffer moment" has emerged, which requires decisive resistance.[2] Stephen Haynes describes the concept as a "clarion call" that identifies a "cultural *Kairos*" summoning disciples to resist in a manner that parallels Bonhoeffer's own resistance.[3] It is a way to narrate the character of a contemporary situation in terms analogous to Bonhoeffer's own situation, and it is a way to advocate for acts that are said to parallel Bonhoeffer's

---

2. For a genealogy of this claim, see Stephen R. Haynes, *The Battle for Bonhoeffer: Debating Discipleship in the Age of Trump* (Grand Rapids: Eerdmans, 2018).

3. Ibid., 5.

own resistance.⁴ The point of reference in Bonhoeffer's life often leads to a vastly different vision of contemporary resistance. When persons appeal to Bonhoeffer's pacifism and early resistance writings, they often envision contemporary responses marked by civil disobedience and nonviolent political activism.⁵ When others appeal to his participation in the coup d'état, these evoke a clear-cut decision for or against a political order, sometimes terminating in fanatical violence.⁶ In a similar manner, the parties that invoke the phrase are just as varied—there are American "liberals" and "conservatives" as well as academics and popular pundits.⁷ Appeals to the Bonhoeffer moment increased with the 2016 US presidential election, with varying figures decrying both presidential candidates as resembling Hitler. Karen Bloomquist labeled Donald Trump "our homegrown Hitler,"⁸ while Eric Metaxas suggested that a vote for Trump is a vote against the tyranny of Hillary Clinton.⁹ Metaxas' best-selling biography¹⁰ on Bonhoeffer has drawn the ire of the Bonhoeffer academic guild for the way it creates hasty parallels between Bonhoeffer's context and the American context in order to bolster a predetermined course of action.¹¹ Bonhoeffer, critics assert, is forced into the mold of an American evangelical, and Metaxas violently appropriates Bonhoeffer's life and thought for political ends.

---

4. Making analogies between Bonhoeffer's time and the present context is not a new phenomenon. For instance, Raymond Mengus, "Dietrich Bonhoeffer and the Decision to Resist," *The Journal of Modern History* 64 (December 1992): S134–46.

5. For example, David French, "How Should One Resist the Trump Administration?" *New York Times*, published February 14, 2017, https://www.nytimes.com/2017/02/14/opinion/how-should-one-resist-the-trump-administration.html. Others make an explicit connection and analogy between the resistance of Bonhoeffer and the resistance of Martin Luther King Jr. Reggie Williams, "Bonhoeffer and King: Christ the Moral Arc," *Black Theology* 9, no. 3 (2011): 356–69; Willis Jenkins and Jennifer M. McBride, eds., *Bonhoeffer and King: Their Legacies and Import for Christian Social Thought* (Minneapolis: Fortress Press, 2010).

6. Haynes, *The Bonhoeffer Phenomenon*, 169–76.

7. For an incisive commentary and survey of proponents of the Bonhoeffer moment, see Joshua T. Mauldin, "Interpreting the Divine Mandates in a Bonhoeffer Moment," *Political Theology* 20, no. 7 (2019): 574–94.

8. Karen L. Bloomquist, "Radicalizing Reformation and Today's Crises, in the Spirit of Bonhoeffer," in *Luther, Bonhoeffer, and Public Ethics: Reforming the Church of the Future*, ed. Michael P. DeJonge and Clifford J. Green (New York: Lexington Books, 2018), 87.

9. Eric Metaxas, "Should Christians Vote for Trump," *Wall Street Journal*, published October 12, 2016, https://www.wsj.com/articles/should-christians-vote-for-trump-1476294992.

10. Eric Metaxas, *Bonhoeffer: Pastor, Martyr, Prophet, Spy* (Nashville: Thomas Nelson, 2010).

11. For a paradigmatic example of this criticism, see Lori Brandt Hale and Reggie L. Williams, "Is this a Bonhoeffer Moment?" *Sojourners*, published February 2018, https://sojo.net/magazine/february-2018/bonhoeffer-moment.

One paradigmatic response to the Bonhoeffer moment phenomenon is to assert the distance and foreignness of Bonhoeffer's context and thought to the present calls and paradigms into which Bonhoeffer seemingly fits. The charge is that commentators impose particularly American understandings of resistance upon a German theologian (no less a bourgeois German Lutheran) while misconstruing both Bonhoeffer's context and the present context in order to force a historical analogy. The retort is well-heeded and necessary but risks overstatement. The problem is that this retort can become truncated insofar as it can diminish a basic presupposition of historical study: the belief that past events and forms of thought can offer a crucial perspective that sheds light on the present. It thus misses, echoing Gadamer, that to ask what someone meant is a way to consider what they mean for today.[12] The question that the discourse surrounding the Bonhoeffer moment thus raises is: How does one read Bonhoeffer's life and thought for today without performing a violent appropriation? In a broader lens, it raises the question of what differentiates a responsible hermeneutic from a violent hermeneutic in reading and responding to history.[13]

The South African reception of Bonhoeffer offers an illuminating counterpoint in developing a provisional answer to these questions, since it, too, has an orientation to public theology and political action for today while largely, if not entirely, avoiding the violent appropriations paradigmatic of Bonhoeffer's "popular" reception in the United States.[14] Indeed, the strength and uniqueness of the South African reception compared to the "popular" Bonhoeffer is its corresponding activity of reflecting continually on the character of responsible reception and appropriation of Bonhoeffer for the present context.[15] At the forefront of developing this hermeneutic is John de Gruchy, who has described his life as a dialogue with Bonhoeffer, which aims not at a mere regurgitation of Bonhoeffer's thought but in the articulation of a theology that contributes to and

---

12. Hans-Georg Gadamer, *Truth and Method*, trans. Joel Weinsheimer and Donald G. Marshall (London: Bloomsbury Publishing, 2013).

13. Odo Marquard, *Farewell to Matters of Principle: Philosophical Studies* (Oxford: Oxford University Press, 1989), 120–4.

14. For a recent self-conscious approach for reading Bonhoeffer in South Africa, see Nico Koopman and Robert Volsoo, eds., *Reading Bonhoeffer in South Africa after the Transition to Democracy: Selected Essays* (Berlin: Peter Lang, 2020). I am not suggesting in this section that Americans are incapable of instantiating a self-conscious approach. For instance, see Larry Rasmussen, *Dietrich Bonhoeffer: His Significance for North Americans* (Minneapolis: Fortress Press, 1990).

15. Robert Vosloo, "Interpreting Bonhoeffer in South Africa? The Search for a Historical and Methodological Responsible Hermeneutic," in *Bonhoeffer and Interpretive Theory: Essays on Methods and Understanding*, ed. Peter Frick (Frankfurt am Main: Peter Lang GmbH, 2013), 119–42.

bolsters faithful action in one's context.[16] The best way to perform this task, de Gruchy asserts, is "by not canonizing [Bonhoeffer's] theology but using it critically in attempting to understand the Scriptures and Christian faith in our context."[17]

De Gruchy develops his hermeneutical approach by suggesting that a dialogue with Bonhoeffer proceeds on three levels:

> The first level is that at which we critically investigate Bonhoeffer's theology in its own context; the second level is that of theological reflection on and analysis of our own historical situation; and the third level is that of reflective participation, obedient discipleship, or *praxis*. It is at the third level that the integration takes place, or, to use the language of H. G. Gadamer, "the horizons are fused."[18]

An important clarification to de Gruchy's approach is that the three levels do not represent a linear methodology that begins with the objective meaning of the texts in their historical context and ends with an application of its contents in the present action. The three levels are rather interconnected and correspond to the so-called "hermeneutical circle." Action, for de Gruchy, is not a *terminus*, but the *telos* of interpretation insofar as action is constitutive of the interpretive process. It has a hermeneutic function that clarifies Bonhoeffer's witness in a form of life, which reflects and deepens readings of Bonhoeffer's texts. It also discloses the impetus for reading Bonhoeffer, which is a faithful appropriation of Bonhoeffer's witness in politically generative action.

One could suggest, however, that there is a similarity to the violent appropriations of the Bonhoeffer moment in de Gruchy's account since both "employ" Bonhoeffer for the sake of contemporary action. As de Gruchy notes, drawing parallels between situations often serves a "moral purpose."[19] This raises the question of whether the Bonhoeffer reception in South Africa is merely a more self-conscious iteration of a violent appropriation. One retort to this charge is that the first two levels of the dialogical task display the distance between Bonhoeffer and the present, thus generating a necessary pause in making historical analogies. The benefit of this claim is that Bonhoeffer's voice remains alien to the present, preserving its ability to undercut the parochial wisdom of today. De Gruchy bolsters this claim by emphasizing the contemporaneity of Bonhoeffer's living voice that is ever capable of surprising and new insights that shed light on the present. This puts the reader in an initially passive relation to Bonhoeffer's address, thus emphasizing the vulnerability of the present interlocutor to Bonhoeffer's

---

16. John de Gruchy, *Bonhoeffer's Questions: A Life-Changing Conversation* (Minneapolis: Fortress Press, 2019).

17. John de Gruchy, *Bonhoeffer and South Africa: Theology in Dialogue* (Grand Rapids: Eerdmans Publishing, 1984), 34–5.

18. Ibid., 35.

19. Ibid., 39.

contemporary claim as a prerequisite to any historical analogy posited between Bonhoeffer's time and today.

Robert Vosloo deepens this account of Bonhoeffer's contemporariness in his excellent article, "Bonhoeffer, Our Contemporary?"[20] Vosloo frames his article around "the uncanny experience" of Bonhoeffer speaking a language for which one desperately sought, with this disclosure becoming an event for the recipient— an event when the past surges forth into the present, making an unforeseen claim upon the listener. This experience presents Bonhoeffer as a contemporary who not only speaks into the present but becomes present to the reader. Vosloo draws upon Bonhoeffer's own articulations in "The Essence of Christianity" where Bonhoeffer describes this experience in the following terms: "We experience contemporaneity with historical events only where we perceive the claims of history, that is, where we accept or reject those claims and allow ourselves to be touched by them in our most profound existence."[21] It is within this experience that history—like textuality—always possesses a latency that affects the present, demanding reflection upon what this experience discloses about temporality and the relation of past to present.[22]

When Vosloo shifts to unpack what it means for Bonhoeffer to be a contemporary, he paradoxically speaks of Bonhoeffer as *untimely*. Drawing on Agamben's notion of the contemporary, Vosloo describes Bonhoeffer as one who is formed by his context in culture, language, and so on, but remains anachronistic to it insofar as he participates in a different modality of time, which for Agamben is Messianic Time and for Bonhoeffer is eternity. This provides a critical distance that enables the contemporary to perceive and speak into the fault lines and breaking points of the times they inhabit. The contemporary, in Bonhoeffer's idiom, is akin to the prophet who speaks decisively into the moment as one "who wrestled with God and with their own age, an age in which everything was out of joint."[23] Vosloo further extends this account to argue that the contemporary not only identifies the fault lines of the moment but also makes the fault lines a meeting place hospitable for intergenerational discourse.[24] The contemporary speaks directly to

---

20. Robert Vosloo, "Bonhoeffer, our Contemporary? Engaging Bonhoeffer on Time, the Times, and Public Theology," *The Bonhoeffer Legacy: An International Journal* 5, no. 2 (2018): 19–36.

21. DBWE 10:346.

22. Vosloo further reflects on temporality and narrating history in the following pieces: Robert Vosloo, "The Feeling of Time: Bonhoeffer on Temporality and the Fully Human Life," *Scriptura* 99 (2008): 337–49; Robert Vosloo, "Time Out of Joint and Future-Oriented Memory: Engaging Dietrich Bonhoeffer in the Search for a Way to Deal Responsibly with the Ghosts of the Past," *Religions* 8, no. 42 (2017): 1–9; Robert Vosloo, "Dietrich Bonhoeffer's Reformation Day Sermons and Performative Remembering," *Theology Today* 74, no. 3 (2017): 252–62.

23. DBWE 10:328.

24. Vosloo, "Bonhoeffer Our Contemporary," 24.

the irregular and disjointed moment, initiating a discourse in its space that bridges the past and present in order to serve the moment. Within these disjointed times, persons experience Bonhoeffer as a contemporary who speaks decisively into the present, bolstering action for today.

The South African reception of Bonhoeffer epitomized by de Gruchy and further developed by Vosloo thus avoids the violent appropriations of the Bonhoeffer moment by attending not only to how to make "responsible" parallels between the past and the present but also by reflecting on the character of history that allows those who speak in the past to become present. This mode of reflection differs dramatically from the discourse surrounding the Bonhoeffer moment, which tends to treat history as an objective compound of "what-is-past" and the moment as a mere scenario open to casuistic reasoning. These conceptions keep history as an object susceptible to human analysis and employment, which is at the heart of violent appropriations that combat and exclude other interpretive possibilities.[25] The South African response deflects this danger by affirming the vulnerability of the reader to the claims of the past as well as the neighbor in the moment, thus maintaining the latency of both history and Bonhoeffer's texts to elicit unexpected insights and acts in response to its address. The emphasis first falls on the effect that Bonhoeffer's voice has on the present listener rather than on the original "historical" meaning or on the way it can function in contemporary political discourse. The question of meaning and function are not excluded as much as they are framed within the vulnerable experience of being addressed and invited into a dialogue.[26] It is in this sense that Vosloo describes a responsible South African hermeneutic as being irreducibly vulnerable, communal, and participatory.[27] Ultimately, what the South African hermeneutic accentuates is the need to reflect directly not only on how to make historical parallels fruitful but also on the character of history, the moment, and the experience of temporality in narrating Bonhoeffer's life and witness today. This becomes an essential aspect of the current reading of the exception as an event in Bonhoeffer's texts, and its importance will extend in informing how to read Bonhoeffer's life and thought in the next chapter.

Tyrannicide and the Question of Continuity

The embrace of Bonhoeffer's legacy was delayed in postwar Germany. People approached Bonhoeffer with reserve with his participation in the planned coup

---

25. See Thesis VI of Walter Benjamin, "Theses on the Philosophy of History," in *Illuminations*, ed. Hannah Arendt, trans. Harry Zohn (New York: Mariner Books, 2019), 198–200.

26. For an account on the necessity of experiencing historical claims in the narration of history and temporality, see David Carr, *Time, Narrative, and History* (Bloomington: Indiana University Press, 1986).

27. Vosloo, "Interpreting Bonhoeffer in South Africa," 132–42.

d'état becoming a central part of this cold reception. This was particularly true in the Federal Republic of Germany where Bonhoeffer was considered a traitor for acting illegitimately against the head of state.[28] Even if Hitler was a tyrant, it was argued, any planned coup could not receive moral vindication. Early in the 1950s, a movement led by Ernst Wolf and Hans-Joachim Iwand began to utilize the language of tyrannicide to argue that the coup was a necessary and justified act of resistance and not an act of treason against the state.[29] This is because in the tyrannicide framework there is a higher or natural law that legitimates political authority and holds it accountable, and this law subsequently becomes the basis in certain cases to violently remove tyrants who forfeit their political authorization by abusing the law. The language of tyrannicide eventually became paradigmatic of narrations of Bonhoeffer's late resistance life and thought. Two prominent theologians who represent the mature utilization of this frame in their respective works are Clifford Green and Larry Rasmussen.

Clifford Green is one of the most prominent advocates for summarizing Bonhoeffer's conspiracy rationale and activity as tyrannicide. One benefit for Green in utilizing the language of tyrannicide is how it underscores the uniqueness and distance of Bonhoeffer's context and thought from contemporary appeals by figures like George W. Bush, who appealed to Bonhoeffer's legacy in the "war on terror," and by extremists who appealed to Bonhoeffer's legacy to bolster their fanatical acts of violence. For Green, appeals to Bonhoeffer by such figures are a "serious misuse of [Bonhoeffer's] writings" and "an abuse of his example."[30] They miss how Bonhoeffer's act is a "last resort" ventured in the most extreme of times developed "against the background of an established moral tradition that allowed tyrannicide under certain strictly defined criteria."[31] As Green notes:

> Without arguing from the tyrannicide model himself, Bonhoeffer was surely aware of the Christian ethical tradition according to which killing a tyrant, under carefully constrained conditions, was analogous to the just war doctrine of legitimate defense. This immediately constricts the moral scope of the conspirators' activity, defining it more precisely. And it negates the promiscuous

---

28. Eberhard Bethge, *Exile and Martyr*, ed. John de Gruchy (New York: The Seabury Press, 1976), 11. On the reception of Bonhoeffer in Germany, see Wolfgang Huber, "Inspiration, Controversy, and Legacy: Responses to Dietrich Bonhoeffer in Three Germanys," in *Interpreting Bonhoeffer*, ed. Clifford Green and Guy C. Carter (Minneapolis: Fortress Press, 2013), 3–14.

29. Huber, "Responses to Bonhoeffer," 6. See Ernst Wolf, "Political and Moral Motives behind the Resistance," in *The German Resistance to Hitler*, trans. Peter and Betty Ross (Bristol: B. T. Batsford Ltd, 1970), 193–234.

30. Clifford Green, "Review of *Dietrich Bonhoeffer: Reality and Resistance*," *Conversations in Religion and Theology*, 6, no. 2 (2008): 156.

31. Green, "Pacifism and Tyrannicide," 41.

extrapolations of those who would co-opt Bonhoeffer's example to justify preemptive wars and to legitimate other causes of random violence.[32]

To speak of Bonhoeffer's activity and thought as tyrannicide is not an unwarranted extrapolation for Green, since he insists that this rationale is reflected clearly in Bonhoeffer's writings, particularly in the unfinished *Ethics*.[33] The heart of this discussion occurs in the unfinished manuscript "History and Good [2]" under the discussion of "The Structure of Responsible Life."[34] According to Green, the manuscript is important for Bonhoeffer as it reflects his own wrestling with what it means to participate in the coup d'état.[35] This autobiographical element is reflected in Bonhoeffer's use of *Mann* rather than the more general *Mensch* in summarizing the rationale of free responsible action: "Those (*den Mann*) who act out of free responsibility are justified before others by dire necessity; before themselves they are acquitted by their conscience, but before God they hope only for grace."[36] In this discussion Bonhoeffer enunciates most clearly the kind of resources that can sustain the free action required by those in the resistance.

This close connection to tyrannicide in the structure of responsible life is reflected in each of its four dimensions: vicarious representative action (*Stellvertretung*), correspondence to reality, freedom, and readiness to take on guilt (*Schuldübernahme*).[37] Vicarious representative action reflects Bonhoeffer's conviction that just as Christ acted on behalf of the world so also the resistance group must act on behalf of Germany and the West. Responsible action in correspondence to reality reflects Bonhoeffer's conviction that exceptional action is never ventured blind but is always appropriate to its sphere and its time. The responsible person must analyze the situation, assess the probable outcome, and deliberate on the steps required to reach the anticipated goal.[38] This aspect is for Green the heart of Bonhoeffer's ethics of tyrannicide, since it is while discussing action appropriate to statecraft that Bonhoeffer describes responsible action in extreme moments that ventures beyond law on the basis of human and political necessity. These moments

---

32. Green, "Review," 157-8. Green is correct that Bonhoeffer was aware of the tyrannicide tradition. He discusses it briefly in his lecture on Article XVI of the Augsburg Confession (DBWE 14:338). Bonhoeffer likewise describes Hitler as a "tyrant" and the "tyrannical despiser of humanity" (DBWE 6:86). There is also a reference to the "tyrants of history" in Bonhoeffer's fiction writings (DBWE 7:120).

33. Green, "Pacifism and Tyrannicide," 42. "Editor's Introduction to the English Edition," DBWE 6:11-14.

34. DBWE 6:256-89.

35. Clifford Green, *Bonhoeffer: A Theology of Sociality* (Grand Rapids: William B. Eerdmans Publishing Co., 1999), 311.

36. DBWE 6:283.

37. "Readiness to take on guilt" is Green's preferred translation for *Schuldübernahme*, since it emphasizes the active dimension to the concept. Green, *A Theology of Sociality*, 316.

38. Ibid., 314-15.

generate the *ultima ratio* of tyrannicide.[39] It is in this light that freedom—the third dimension of responsible life—is read not as a form of enthusiasm, since responsible action is always appropriate to the situation at hand. Freedom entails that the conspiracy cannot be "constrained by laws nor justified by them," since it is an act that breaks the law on behalf of others as a last resort.[40] Readiness to take on guilt emphasizes how the conspirators were ready to incur guilt and punishment in breaking the law on behalf of others. Guilt was unavoidable, but it was better to incur guilt on behalf of others rather than to sit idly and preserve one's innocence. As Green argues: "To those who asked how Bonhoeffer could become guilty by planning tyrannicide and a coup, he replied: How could he *not* do so? To fail to do so, in the face of Nazi aggression and the Holocaust, would be to incur the greater culpability."[41] Green ultimately argues that "History and Good [2]" solidifies his assertion that tyrannicide is only ventured in the most extreme of circumstances. It is "a particular exception, a singular extreme case not justified by law or principle but only as a free act of Christian responsibility done in the hope of God's mercy."[42]

Larry Rasmussen speaks in a similar idiom in his influential work, *Reality and Resistance*.[43] Rasmussen likewise suggests that tyrannicide best characterizes Bonhoeffer's late resistance activity, and he also envisions a close correspondence between Bonhoeffer's thought and activity in his late writings. Another similarity between Green and Rasmussen is that both describe Bonhoeffer's ethics as thoroughly Christological, unprincipled, and concrete, leading them both to conclude that Bonhoeffer was never a "principled" pacifist, since Bonhoeffer always maintained space for the utterly particular moment that demands violent resistance.[44]

An initial disagreement emerges between Green and Rasmussen, however, on the point of continuity. While Green reads Bonhoeffer's ethics as unified and consistent throughout the corpus, Rasmussen reads it as broadly continuous, but also containing fissures and inconsistencies. Rasmussen argues that two developments were needed between *Discipleship* and *Ethics* to make sense of active resistance via the coup d'état: Bonhoeffer needed to abandon asceticism and two-spheres thinking, since these led to passive suffering and church sectarianism.[45] Bonhoeffer needed to

---

39. DBWE 6:271–3.
40. Green, "Pacifism and Tyrannicide," 43.
41. Green, *A Theology of Sociality*, 317.
42. Green, "Pacifism and Tyrannicide," 45–6.
43. Green and Rasmussen are longtime friends who completed their doctorates on Bonhoeffer at Union Theological Seminary at the same time. *Reality and Resistance* is Rasmussen's revised doctoral thesis, and the first book length treatment on Bonhoeffer's resistance thought in English scholarship.
44. Rasmussen and Green thus disagree with Kelly and Nelson that Bonhoeffer "abandon[ed] the ways of non-violence." Geffrey B. Kelly and F. Burton Nelson, *The Cost of Moral Leadership: The Responsibility of Dietrich Bonhoeffer* (Grand Rapids: Eerdmans Publishing House, 2020), 113.
45. Rasmussen, *Reality and Resistance*, 121–4.

move from the particular to the general and from the contingent to the universal to articulate a more mature resistance rationale for the world.[46] Rasmussen and Green also disagree on the coherence of Bonhoeffer's ethical approach in *Ethics*. Green argues that Bonhoeffer articulates a singular ethic that varies according to context; there is an ethics of everyday life and an ethics of extremity when the exception arises.[47] Rasmussen argues that Bonhoeffer develops two distinct methodologies that do not necessarily cohere.[48] The primary ethic is an ethic of formation, which remains basic and more enduring within Bonhoeffer's corpus. The secondary ethic is an ethic of commandment, which is "a genuine motif, but a subordinate one." The ethic of formation simply "fits" better across Bonhoeffer's writing and thought.[49] Rasmussen argues that the lack of cohesion in the late manuscripts is because Bonhoeffer wrote under great duress and time constraints, leaving behind a series of experimental, fragmentary, and unfinished manuscripts. Bonhoeffer simply did not have time to unify his disparate thoughts and manuscripts.

This emphasis leads to a second difference between them. Rasmussen thinks Green is wrong to argue that Bonhoeffer was consciously developing his resistance account through the tradition of tyrannicide. For Rasmussen, tyrannicide is rather a framework to assess Bonhoeffer's activity and thought after the fact. While it is a foreign lens to read and narrate Bonhoeffer's activity and thought, this does not make it unjustifiable. Rasmussen emphasizes Bonhoeffer's testimony that he and his co-conspirators lacked time to reflect adequately on what to do and that they found every ethical program insufficient to direct their action. As Bonhoeffer states in his 1942 letter "After Ten Years," "Have there ever been people in history who in their time had so little ground under their feet, people to whom every possible alternative open to them at the time appeared unbearable, senseless, and contrary to life?"[50] Bonhoeffer lived in a time of perpetual crisis, and for Rasmussen this is reflected in the unfinished and provisional character of his late resistance reflections.[51] The benefit of tyrannicide is that it offers a language for which Bonhoeffer was desperately searching. It offers a lens to reconstruct Bonhoeffer's case in the most coherent and clear frame. Rasmussen thus utilizes Barth's account of tyrannicide in *Church Dogmatics* III/4 to frame Bonhoeffer's own resistance activity, since "this is Barth's reconstruction of Bonhoeffer's real case, the case for that portion of the German Resistance which plotted Hitler's death."[52] It puts together what was scattered in Bonhoeffer's provisional writings.

---

46. Ibid., 26.
47. Green, *A Theology of Sociality*, 301–27.
48. Larry Rasmussen, "A Question of Method," in *New Studies in Bonhoeffer's Ethics*, ed. William J. Peck (New York: The Edwin Mellen Press, 1987), 138.
49. Ibid.
50. DBWE 8:38.
51. Larry Rasmussen, "Response to Review of *Reality and Resistance*," *Conversations in Religion and Theology* 6, no. 2 (2008): 167.
52. Rasmussen, *Reality and Resistance*, 132–3. CD III/4, 448–50.

After the release of the second edition of *Reality and Resistance*, Green wrote a review on Rasmussen's work, which highlighted their divergences in interpretation. In his response to Green's review, Rasmussen is struck that while he finds their accounts to be "very close," Green seems to envision their accounts as stark alternatives. This troubles Rasmussen: "Why do I not see Green's as 'clearly an alternative' to my rendition rather than substantially the same, even though I focus on discontinuities?"[53] Rasmussen ventures a few possible reasons. First, Rasmussen considers that maybe their differences arise from their varying academic disciplines. Green is a systematic theologian, whereas Rasmussen is primarily an ethicist. Green sought to trace internal development and systematic consistency, whereas Rasmussen sought to analyze the ethical thought of Bonhoeffer through "an external body of moral and ethical thought . . . brought to my subject."[54] Second, Rasmussen suggests that maybe their differing contexts led to their varying emphases. Rasmussen wrote during heated debates about conscientious objection during the Vietnam War as well as during the civil rights movement, attempting to interrogate these debates through Bonhoeffer's writings. Green wrote in light of Bush's appeals to Bonhoeffer for justifying the invasion of Iraq as well as invocations of Bonhoeffer's witness by vigilantes. Green wanted to show how "these have betrayed Bonhoeffer's ethics instead of learning from it."[55] Third, Rasmussen suggests that perhaps it is because the students he teaches always ask about divergences in language between *Discipleship* and *Ethics*, and this means he is constantly responding to the question of discontinuity, which subsequently frames his interpretations.[56]

Rasmussen's reflections are important insofar as they display how differing approaches, contexts, and questions can elicit different emphases and material claims in reading Bonhoeffer's corpus. While Green and Rasmussen are very close in their readings, it is striking that their material disagreements on the question of continuity could arise through their "different academic disciplines, frameworks, and preoccupations."[57] The question of how determinative one's lens and context are for reading Bonhoeffer is brought to the surface in Rasmussen's reflections on their respective readings. The question finds intensification in the next set of interlocutors, who present vastly different accounts of Bonhoeffer's "traditioned" thought.

Lutheran and Anabaptist Readings of Bonhoeffer's Resistance Thought

The relationship between Michael DeJonge and the pacifist readers Stanley Hauerwas and Mark Nation is remarkably dissimilar from the relationship

---

53. Rasmussen, "Response," 168.
54. Ibid., 169.
55. Ibid.
56. Ibid.
57. Ibid., 168.

between Clifford Green and Larry Rasmussen. Unlike the latter interpreters, there is no broad agreement in their respective accounts, and the differences between DeJonge's Lutheran reading of Bonhoeffer and Hauerwas and Nation's broadly Anabaptist readings are obvious and stark. DeJonge has argued at length against their Anabaptist readings, stating that they are "easy" to disprove.[58] Hauerwas and Nation have made it a point to challenge DeJonge's strong claims, bolstering their own account that Bonhoeffer was a committed pacifist throughout his life.[59] The writers clearly envision their respective readings as strong alternatives. But even with this disagreement, reflection on their arguments reveals striking similarities between their accounts that warrant reading them side-by-side.

In *Performing the Faith: Bonhoeffer and the Practice of Nonviolence*, Hauerwas reads Dietrich Bonhoeffer as "an ally" of John Howard Yoder, arguing that the two theologians complement each other.[60] According to Hauerwas, Bonhoeffer, like Yoder, was a committed pacifist, who argued for the necessary visibility of the church in clear distinction from the world.[61] And Bonhoeffer, like Yoder, emphasized the importance of the church community speaking truthfully; it is a necessary condition for Christian witness and the performance of justice. The combination of peaceableness, truth-telling, and the visible distinctiveness of the church marks Hauerwas' reading of Bonhoeffer's political theology.

Discipleship is central to Hauerwas' reading, describing it as "the most political of [Bonhoeffer's] works."[62] It contains some of the clearest statements by Bonhoeffer on how the church's visibility over against the world is central to its "political ethics."[63] It also possesses some of the clearest statements by Bonhoeffer on the necessity of obedience to the Sermon on the Mount and the command to peace, such as the following: "Jesus' followers are called to peace. . . . Now they are not only to have peace, but they are to make peace. To do this they *renounce*

---

58. Michael DeJonge, *Bonhoeffer's Reception of Luther* (Oxford: Oxford University Press, 2017), 143. See also: Michael DeJonge, "How to Read Bonhoeffer's Peace Statements: Or, Bonhoeffer was a Lutheran and Not an Anabaptist," *Theology* 118, no. 3 (2015): 162–71; Michael DeJonge, "Bonhoeffer's Non-Commitment to Nonviolence: A Response to Stanley Hauerwas," *Journal of Religious Ethics* 44, no. 2 (2016): 278–94.

59. Mark Thiessen Nation and Stanley Hauerwas, "'A Pacifist and Enemy of the State': Bonhoeffer's Journey to Nonviolence," published April 19, 2018, https://www.abc.net.au/religion/a-pacifist-and-enemy-of-the-state-bonhoeffers-journey-to-nonviol/10094798.

60. Stanley Hauerwas, *Performing the Faith: Bonhoeffer on Truth and Politics* (Grand Rapids: Brazos Press, 2004), 18, 55.

61. Ibid., 34.

62. Stanley Hauerwas, "Dietrich Bonhoeffer," in *The Blackwell Companion to Political Theology*, ed. Peter Scott and William T. Cavanaugh (Maiden: Blackwell Publishing, 2004), 140.

63. "The 'political ethics' of the church-community is grounded solely in its sanctification, the goal of which is that world be world and community be community, and that, nevertheless, God's word goes out from the church-community to all the world. . . . That is the 'political' character of the church-community" (DBWE 4:261–2).

violence and strife. Those things never help the cause of Christ."[64] Hauerwas further connects the command for peacemaking to truth-telling in Bonhoeffer's political ethics, concluding that to live in obedience to Christ's command for peace is to live in a community of truthful witness.[65] This is the basis for a radical politics that witnesses to and derives from the peaceable reign of God in the world. Conversely, violence generates a false politics based on a lie that "suffocates truth and justice."[66] Whereas the world and its violence are grounded in lies and falsehood, the church's commitment to peace witnesses to the truth and reality of Christ's reign.

What is striking in Hauerwas' reading of Bonhoeffer is that there is no reference to Bonhoeffer's manuscript "History and Good [2]." While Hauerwas engages *Ethics* in his reading, he nevertheless prioritizes other manuscripts that accentuate what he considers the central convictions of Bonhoeffer's political theology. Hauerwas thinks that by too quickly reverting to questions about the conspiracy and exceptional violence in "History and Good [2]," readers miss the consistent and radical themes of Bonhoeffer's political thought that span the totality of his corpus. Such readings end up positioning Bonhoeffer's political thought alongside Niebuhrian approaches which center on "responsibility" and "taking on guilt" in performing necessary violence.[67] Hauerwas rejects these readings on the grounds that Bonhoeffer's status in the conspiracy against Hitler is ambiguous. He assumes that a narration of Bonhoeffer's life should center on what is more prominent and certain, such as Bonhoeffer's explicit testimony that the Bible and the command to nonviolence definitively shaped his life and its course.[68]

In Nation, Siegrist, and Umbel's *Bonhoeffer the Assassin?*, the authors extend Hauerwas' argument by suggesting that Bonhoeffer's commitment to pacifism reframes his "resistance" biography. Their strategy is twofold. First, the authors survey the details of Bonhoeffer's biography, arguing that Bonhoeffer's participation in the conspiracy is highly improbable, raising doubts about what one knows about Bonhoeffer's late resistance activity.[69] Second, the authors argue that from

---

64. DBWE 4:108. Emphasis original.

65. Hauerwas, *Performing the Faith*, 55–72.

66. DBWE 12:365.

67. Hauerwas admits that he does not know how to read all the elements in "History and Good [2]," since some passages sound like Bonhoeffer is plotting to kill Hitler. Stanley Hauerwas, foreword to *Bonhoeffer the Assassin? Challenging the Myth, Recovering His Call to Peacemaking* (Grand Rapids: Baker Academic, 2013), xiv.

68. Hauerwas, *Performing the Faith*, 35–6.

69. Nation et al., *Bonhoeffer the Assassin?*, 15–98. The most controversial aspect of this argument is that Nation et al. question the veracity of Bethge's narration of Bonhoeffer's conspiracy participation. Nation et al. argue that Franz Hildebrant, who was a committed pacifist, was Bonhoeffer's "most like-minded friend" and most trustworthy theological confidant instead of Bethge. See Nation et al., *Bonhoeffer the Assassin?*, 231–2. For a decisive argument against this claim, see Clifford Green, "Peace Ethic or 'Pacifism?' An Assessment of *Bonhoeffer the Assassin*," *Modern Theology* 31, no. 1 (2015): 201–8.

Bonhoeffer's "conversion" in 1932, Bonhoeffer remained a consistent pacifist to the end of his life, and this pacifism must orient readings of Bonhoeffer's *Ethics* and other texts from the era.[70] Of central importance to the authors are two letters from Bonhoeffer's time in prison. The first is Bonhoeffer's letter to Bethge from May 1944 where he claims: "I am wholly under the impression that my life—strange as it may sound—has gone in a straight line, uninterrupted, at least with regard to how I have led it."[71] This suggests the consistency of Bonhoeffer's convictions and direction even in his "conspiracy" years. The second is Bonhoeffer's letter to Bethge from July 21, 1944, where he claims that he "still stands by" *Discipleship*.[72] For Nation et al., Bonhoeffer remains a consistent, unified thinker from 1932 onwards, which includes his pacifism and his commitment to literal obedience to the Sermon on the Mount. And while there is certainly development and innovation in his thought, "Bonhoeffer's thinking over the course of his lifetime demonstrates his ability to integrate new ideas into the existing thought structures, thereby transforming them and being transformed himself."[73] Taken together, these statements suggest a radical consistency and singularity to Bonhoeffer's thought that includes his pacifism.[74] Nation et al. press the question of whether Bonhoeffer scholarship has misconstrued Bonhoeffer's late theology by de-emphasizing Bonhoeffer's explicit commitment to pacifism and by imposing the alien language of "tyrannicide" or "peace ethic" onto his thought. Nation et al. thus advocate Bonhoeffer's earlier claim that one "should not balk here at using the word 'pacifism.'"[75] The fear is that by diminishing the language of pacifism, one diminishes what is most radical in Bonhoeffer's political witness to a world dominated by violence.[76]

DeJonge's primary charge against the Anabaptist reading is that it ignores passages where Bonhoeffer describes his pacifism as provisional.[77] While Bonhoeffer's pacifism appears uncompromising in certain passages, DeJonge convincingly demonstrates this is not always the case. For instance, Bonhoeffer rejects "doctrinaire pacifism" and suggests that "a final answer to the question of whether a Christian should or should not participate [in war] must be rejected. Both answers are possible."[78] Bonhoeffer likewise writes in his 1940 manuscript, "Natural Life," that there are times when in the context of war "the killing of another's life can only take place on the basis of unconditional necessity, and then it must be carried out even against any number of other reasons, even good

---

70. DBWE 14:134–5.
71. DBWE 8:352–3.
72. DBWE 8:486.
73. Nation et al., *Bonhoeffer the Assassin?*, 102.
74. Ibid., 222–3.
75. DBWE 12:367.
76. Nation et al., *Bonhoeffer the Assassin?*, 222–3.
77. DeJonge, "Bonhoeffer's Non-Commitment to Nonviolence," 380–1.
78. DBWE 14:766.

ones."⁷⁹ And in a letter from 1939 to George Bell, Bonhoeffer qualifies his inability to perform military service in a manner that leaves open the possibility in the future: "I am thinking of leaving Germany sometime. The main reason is the compulsory military service to which the men of my age (1906) will be called up this year. It seems to me conscientiously impossible to join in a war under the present circumstances."⁸⁰ The key phrase "under the present circumstances" leaves open the possibility that the circumstances could change, and participation would be plausible. In short, DeJonge identifies a range of statements that make allowances for the possibility of Christian participation in war, undercutting a picture of Bonhoeffer as a committed pacifist.⁸¹

When considering the imbalanced reading of Hauerwas and Nation et al., DeJonge suggests that their failure is reading Bonhoeffer through the wrong tradition and the wrong "hermeneutical framework."⁸² Where pacifist readers accuse others of reading Bonhoeffer through a Niebuhrian lens, DeJonge accuses them of reading Bonhoeffer through an Anabaptist lens.⁸³ DeJonge chastises them not for reading Bonhoeffer through a particular tradition but for reading him through the wrong tradition.⁸⁴

For DeJonge, to read Bonhoeffer's theology well is to read him as a Lutheran.⁸⁵ That Bonhoeffer's theology has a Lutheran character does not mean it is exclusively Lutheran. DeJonge is careful to note that Bonhoeffer's thought is more creative and wide-ranging than that. Nevertheless, DeJonge asserts that Bonhoeffer's thought is irreducibly Lutheran and that a failure to appreciate this leads to misunderstanding Bonhoeffer's resistance thought. One can emphasize the same key phrases in Bonhoeffer's theology but miss the crucial theological sense they hold when read through the wrong tradition—an error which DeJonge laments in many contemporary appeals to Bonhoeffer's resistance legacy.⁸⁶ There is a particular sense of tradition running through DeJonge's reading that extends to his narration of Bonhoeffer's resistance thought. DeJonge implies that the Lutheran tradition is a comprehensive, consistent, and unified narration of reality and its constituent parts, having an integrity that belies sharp boundaries that demarcate it from others. And traditions generate cohesive and far-reaching systems of thought that illuminate various elements of the world in light of the whole.⁸⁷ Hence any accurate

---

79. DBWE 6:185.
80. DBWE 15:159.
81. DeJonge, *Bonhoeffer's Reception of Luther*, 177.
82. Ibid., 149.
83. DeJonge further accuses them of not considering Yoder's own suggestion that Bonhoeffer and his own pacifist positions do not cohere. See ibid., 149–54.
84. DeJonge, "Bonhoeffer was a Lutheran not an Anabaptist," 163.
85. DeJonge, *Bonhoeffer on Resistance*, 6.
86. Ibid.
87. It is in this sense that Mawson recently argues that DeJonge's account of tradition is very similar to Alasdair MacIntyre's account. Michael Mawson, "Lutheran or Lutherish? Framing Bonhoeffer's Reception of Luther," *Modern Theology* 35, no. 2 (2019): 1–8.

understanding of Bonhoeffer's thought entails grasping its Lutheran character if one is to avoid violently appropriating his ideas. The upshot is that when someone enters into the tradition, they discern Bonhoeffer to be a remarkably consistent, systematic, and coherent thinker whose earlier writings frame his later writings.

There is a sense that Bonhoeffer not only affirms and creatively engages the Lutheran tradition throughout his career but that his thought mirrors the structure, consistency, and systematicity of the Lutheran tradition. As DeJonge argues regarding Bonhoeffer's resistance thought:

> Bonhoeffer has a systematic, differentiated, and well-developed vision of political activity and resistance. To a degree rarely recognized, Bonhoeffer's resistance thinking is systematic. It considers a variety of resistance scenarios according to situation, agent of resistance, and means of resistance. The systematic character of his resistance thinking is easy to miss because Bonhoeffer scatters the various components of this system throughout his corpus and presents some of them only in passing. But these components can be gathered up to present a systematic picture of political resistance.[88]

Further, any developments in Bonhoeffer's thought are "an extension of that conceptual framework" first developed in Bonhoeffer's earlier thought.[89]

The consistency and development of Bonhoeffer's Lutheran resistance thought comes through in DeJonge's focused attention on Bonhoeffer's 1933 essay, "The Church and the Jewish Question," since the germ of Bonhoeffer's systematic account of resistance is contained therein.[90] DeJonge identifies two distinct agents of resistance in the essay. The first is the Christian individual, who engages in direct political resistance based on their vocation and their position in society. It is the resistance of a doctor before the hospital or the citizen before the state. Individual Christians and humanitarian organizations, per Bonhoeffer, are "called ... in certain cases" to "accuse the state of 'inhumanity.'"[91] The church is the second agent of resistance. Whereas the individual reasons from law and morality, the church reasons from the Gospel. The church postpones "direct" political resistance when it can, since the church recognizes its distinct spiritual authority and task in relation to the state's temporal authority and task to create law and order.[92] This postponement is grounded in Bonhoeffer's adherence to Luther's doctrine of the Two Kingdoms, which maintains the necessary relationship between the church and the state as the two arms of God's singular rule. But when the church can no longer postpone directly resisting the state, it resists through the ministry of

---

88. DeJonge, *Bonhoeffer on Resistance*, 10–11.
89. Ibid., 11.
90. In *Bonhoeffer on Resistance*, DeJonge focuses on Bonhoeffer's 1933 essay for five consecutive chapters.
91. DBWE 12:363–4. DeJonge, *Bonhoeffer on Resistance*, 64.
92. DBWE 12:366.

the word, venturing a concrete claim and commandment on what faithful politics requires today, thereby decrying specific actions of the state.

DeJonge emphasizes the particularly Lutheran grammar to which this direct resistance belongs. When Bonhoeffer decries the introduction of the Aryan Paragraph, which denied church membership to Jewish Christians, DeJonge argues that Bonhoeffer is not primarily concerned about the plight of Jewish Christians in this essay but about the fidelity of the Gospel through proper church authority and governance; these are threatened by the Aryan Paragraph because the government oversteps the authority of the church by defining the membership of the church on a racial basis, putting preconditions to who can sit under the free proclamation of the Gospel. The issue, DeJonge argues, is not race per se, which for Bonhoeffer is an indifferent matter as *adiaphoron*, but the overreach of government in defining church membership on the basis of race. The church must speak directly against the state in this extraordinary moment of *status confessionis*, commanding the state not to overstep its authority and task through the Aryan Paragraph.[93] When commentators insist that race is at the center of Bonhoeffer's ecclesiology and late resistance activity, DeJonge insists they impose contemporary understandings of race upon Bonhoeffer's Lutheran logic, missing Bonhoeffer's unique witness for today.

In Bonhoeffer's later shift to active conspiracy, DeJonge asserts that such activity is not ventured in a churchly capacity but in an individual capacity, since the church never resists in the mode of violent, conspiratorial resistance. The resistance of the church terminates with its word and discipleship: "Anything more would actually be less, for it would bargain away the character of the church."[94] Bonhoeffer's late resistance, then, must be performed in an individual capacity, becoming an extension of the individual resistance identified in "The Church and the Jewish Question."[95] The uniqueness to Bonhoeffer's late resistance is that this

---

93. The Lutheran logic emerges in Bonhoeffer's appeals to *adiaphoron* and *status confessionis* (DBWE 12:370–3). See Michael DeJonge, "Race is an *Adiaphoron*: The Place of Race in Bonhoeffer's 1933 Writings," *Evangelische Theologie* 80, no. 4 (2020), https://doi.org/10.14315/evth-2020-800406.

94. DeJonge, *Bonhoeffer on Resistance*, 138.

95. The connection for DeJonge between individual resistance in the coup and "The Church and the Jewish Question" stems from the testimony of Gaetano Latmiral who was in prison with Bonhoeffer. In a letter to Leibholz, Latmiral recounts Bonhoeffer answering a question about how he could participate in the conspiracy as a pastor in the following terms which echo the 1933 essay: "He said that as a pastor he considered his duty not only to console or to take care of the victims of exalted men who drove madly a motorcar in a crowded street, but also to try to stop them." Gaetano Latmiral, "Letter to Professor Gerhard Leibholz, June 3, 1946" in *Dietrich Bonhoeffer Yearbook/Jahrbuch 2003* 1:30. This echoes Bonhoeffer's famous quote in "The Church and the Jewish Question": "The third possibility [of resistance] is not just to bind up the wounds of the victims beneath the wheel but to seize the wheel itself" (DBWE 12:366).

action against state authorities commences only once all other forms of resistance prove ineffective for restoring law and order and when the state no longer listens to the church's proclamation. DeJonge is at pains to emphasize that this final stage of resistance cannot be a churchly act of resistance. By refusing to allow the church to overstep its unique role and limits, the church's unique witness is not compromised but re-enforced in the final stage of resistance.

While the readings of DeJonge and the Anabaptist readers display sharp differences, there are also striking similarities between them. These writers all emphasize the continuity of Bonhoeffer's theological structure and commitments, reading Bonhoeffer's later texts as building upon and reflecting what was established in Bonhoeffer's early writings; they all emphasize the important distinction between the church and world or, at least, between the church and state in narrating Bonhoeffer's political theology and account of resistance; they all argue that Bonhoeffer's radical political witness is dissimilar from many contemporary renderings of Bonhoeffer's account of resistance and that this radicality is closely tied to Bonhoeffer's account of the church's speech; and, finally, they all read Bonhoeffer (whether explicitly or implicitly) as reflecting a particular theological tradition that illuminates the writings under discussion.

The convergence of these elements in their readings raises important questions that must remain in the foreground of the reading developed in this book. First, there is the question of whether Bonhoeffer's thought is inherently systematic and cohesive like these authors maintain. Second, there is the question of whether traditions operate in the manner that DeJonge suggests as well as the question of how determinative traditions are for reading Bonhoeffer. A positive answer raises the corresponding question of which tradition one should read Bonhoeffer through, given the existence of a wide range of studies that read Bonhoeffer in relation to differing figures and intellectual traditions.[96] Finally, there is the question of whether one should read Bonhoeffer's late theology through the lens of his earlier theology or whether such an approach stifles the fecundity of Bonhoeffer's late "fragmentary" texts? These questions are taken up directly in Chapter 2.

---

96. A nonexhaustive but indicative list of full-length treatments of influences on Bonhoeffer's theology includes: David S. Robinson, *Christ and Revelatory Community in Bonhoeffer's Reception of Hegel* (Tübingen: Mohr Siebeck, 2018); Andreas Pangritz, *Karl Barth in the Theology of Dietrich Bonhoeffer*, trans. Barbara and Martin Rumscheidt (Grand Rapids: William B. Eerdmans Publishing Company, 2000); Matthew Kirkpatrick, *Attacks on Christendom in A World Come of Age: Kierkegaard, Bonhoeffer, and the Question of "Religionless Christianity"* (Eugene: Pickwick Publications, 2011); DeJonge, *Bonhoeffer's Reception of Luther*; Reggie L. Williams, *Bonhoeffer's Black Jesus: Harlem Renaissance Theology and an Ethic of Resistance* (Waco: Baylor University Press, 2014); Peter Frick, ed., *Bonhoeffer's Intellectual Formation: Theology and Philosophy in His Thought* (Tübingen: Mohr Siebeck, 2008).

The Free Venture of a Responsible Individual or a Fanatic

In the manuscript "History and Good [2]," Bonhoeffer narrates responsible action as radically free in the borderline case. It is a "free venture" unconstrained by yet breaking the law in its various senses, thus incurring guilt while surrendering that decision to God's judgment.[97] Whenever one writes on Bonhoeffer's late resistance thought, the theme of the free venture is unavoidable, raising the question of how one should narrate the individual's action in the exception. Two scholars whose reflections center on the individual venture in Bonhoeffer's late resistance texts are Robin Lovin and Petra Brown.

Robin Lovin reads Bonhoeffer as a theologian who epitomizes Christian Realism. While Bonhoeffer did not utilize the concept, his late resistance writings nevertheless display its primary characteristics, and the individual venture epitomizes its *ethos*. For Lovin, Bonhoeffer was a "realist" because he never acted on the basis of abstract ideology but attended to the concrete moment and acted toward proximate political goods for the benefit of others through the conspiracy; and Bonhoeffer was "Christian" because his realist political and moral program is funded by the belief in Christ's reconciling activity and future eschatological judgment.[98] In the mire of the historical present, Bonhoeffer ventured risky decision in seeking concrete historical good in anticipation of God's final judgment and vindication.

Lovin grounds Bonhoeffer's Christian Realism in Bonhoeffer's account of the mandates, the ultimate and penultimate, and responsible action. For Lovin, Bonhoeffer's late reflections on the mandates are central for narrating the meaning and structure of human political life and action. As an extension of Luther's doctrine of the three estates (*Stände*), Bonhoeffer explicates the mandates as the places where God's commandment directs human life to attend and respond to God and neighbor, affirming the distinctions, intersections, and mutual limitations that each mandate presents to the others; it is through the fourfold structure of government, church, work, and family that one hears and responds to their vocation in responsible action. As Bonhoeffer says in "Christ, Reality, and the Good": "The practice of the Christian life can be learned only under these four mandates of God."[99] Lovin insists that apart from the mandates, human action becomes a baseless gamble that is rendered senseless to others, and this is particularly true in the conspiracy. "We mistake the whole idea of the venture of responsibility," Lovin continues, "if we think that the conspirators were saying to themselves, 'Let's kill Hitler and see what happens then.' They had confidence in the underlying structures of their society, and Bonhoeffer understood those

---

97. DBWE 6:274.

98. Robin Lovin, *Christian Realism and the New Realities* (Cambridge: Cambridge University Press, 2008), 1–18.

99. DBWE 6:69.

structures as the framework within which the command of God can be heard."[100] Even so, the mandates exist within a fallen world, which means they stand in tension against one another and often present real conflicts for concrete human life and decisions. These tensions and conflicts are irreducible aspects of modern life which Bonhoeffer experienced in his late resistance activity, since he could not fulfill the demands of the mandates in the conspiracy, leaving him under judgment.[101]

The relationship between the penultimate and ultimate in Bonhoeffer's theology helps narrate this experience of conflict between the mandates.[102] The experience of conflict reveals that the mandates are penultimate goods. While they promise historical good, they are finite historical entities that cannot deliver the ultimate justice and eschatological good for which humans long; the mandates as penultimate are prone to distortion and conflict in the present age. The penultimate awaits the ultimate. In the meantime, the ultimate provides the basis for the substantive critique of the mandates and human action therein. The ultimate exposes where the penultimate falls short, enabling persons to critique the mandates, calling them to a greater approximation of justice today. The ultimate, however, does not deauthorize the penultimate. The mandates as penultimate goods are still good, since Christ has reconciled all of reality to himself. One cannot reject the mandates, since God is present there, exercising authority.[103]

This emphasis on the conflicted demands of the mandates and the relationship between the ultimate and penultimate frames Lovin's discussion of the individual venture of responsible action. Lovin describes how responsible action is often ventured in the face of irreducible conflicts between the mandates in the murkiness of the historical present. Humans are called to act for the good of the human community, but they find that the decisions before them are ambiguous, and moral purity is unachievable. Lovin quotes "History and Good [2]" at this point: "Responsible action must decide not simply between right and wrong, good and evil, but between right and right, wrong and wrong."[104] The relationship between the ultimate and penultimate offers orientation in this situation. The ultimate reminds the person that their action can never accomplish the final victory of absolute justice. This frees human action to attend only to the penultimate. Responsible action thus seeks proximate, penultimate goods that serve human life today.[105] This is true even in extraordinary times when the mandates "are ineffective, damaged or corrupted," losing their ability to direct responsible action. In fact, such moments are revelatory for Lovin, since the nature of responsibility emerges most

---

100. Robin Lovin, "The Mandates in an Age of Globalization," in *Ontology and Ethics*, 24.
101. Lovin, *Christian Realism and the New Realities*, 15, 181, 202.
102. DBWE 6:146–70.
103. DBWE 6:197–203.
104. DBWE 6:283.
105. Lovin, "Becoming Responsible in Christian Ethics," 394–5.

perspicuously when the mandates deteriorate: "we see our responsibility before God best when there is no law to tell us what to do, or when our situation has changed so dramatically that the wisdom of the past no longer makes any sense."[106] In such moments, the lonely human decides without guidance *for* the benefit of humans and *for* the restoration of the law and the mandates; the individual seeks realistic goals that are a consequence of their action (penultimate) while praying for God's action and guidance of history (ultimate).

There is an ambiguity in Lovin's narration insofar as he can speak simultaneously of the reasonableness and irrationality of the responsible venture. When discussing the mandates, Lovin decries narrations of Bonhoeffer's conspiracy participation as a "blind leap,"[107] yet when describing the individual venture, Lovin can narrate Bonhoeffer and the conspirators' actions as "more like a leap in the dark" that hopes for the ultimate.[108] The former description emphasizes the reasonableness of the decision and the predictability of the consequences pursued; the latter emphasizes the utter risk of one's action and the unpredictability of what it will produce. The issue at stake is whether to describe the action as discernment or decision. Does the individual *discern* the right action on the basis of necessity and the mandates? Or does the individual *decide* in freedom without guidance?[109]

Petra Brown's reading further probes this tension, declaring Bonhoeffer's late resistance thought untenable and dangerous, lending itself to religious violence that has become all too common.[110] According to Brown, Bonhoeffer describes the disciple as one who decides in an immediate suprarational relationship to Christ whether violent action is necessary in a "state of exception." This decision is not open to public scrutiny since it occurs in one's private relationship to God, thus becoming fanatical and extremist. Brown grounds this reading by giving hermeneutic priority to Bonhoeffer's concept of the extraordinary (*außerordentliche*) in *Discipleship*, which reappears in "History and Good [2]" in his description of *ultima ratio* as the "extraordinary situation" (*außerordentliche*

---

106. Ibid.

107. Lovin, "The Mandates in an Age of Globalization," 26.

108. Robin Lovin, "Reinhold Niebuhr and Dietrich Bonhoeffer on Responsibility," in *Engaging Bonhoeffer: The Impact and Influence of Bonhoeffer's Life and Thought*, ed. Matthew D. Kirkpatrick (Minneapolis: Fortress Press, 2016), 77–8.

109. Lovin places Bonhoeffer in close proximity to the Niebuhrs. Within this ambiguity one can discern Bonhoeffer walking a tightrope for Lovin between the emphases of Reinhold Niebuhr and H. Richard Niebuhr. Bonhoeffer shares important similarities to Reinhold Niebuhr by emphasizing the individual and their risked decisions in the historical moment. Bonhoeffer shares important similarities to H. Richard Niebuhr by emphasizing how responsible action is never determined by the isolated individual, but the responsible action responds to the whole of reality. Reinhold Niebuhr focuses on the deciding agent; H. Richard Niebuhr on the responsive individual.

110. Brown, *God's Conspirator*, 190.

Situation).¹¹¹ In *Discipleship*, Bonhoeffer develops an account of the extraordinary when interpreting Jesus' command to love one's enemy (Mt. 5:43-48).¹¹² According to Bonhoeffer, what is extraordinary is that the disciple's obedience to the command is immediate, unreflective, and irrational, witnessing to the world a form of life that is inconceivable to it. The result of this extraordinary obedience is that the disciple is separated from the world and put into an immediate relationship to God.¹¹³ When Brown turns to the "extraordinary situation" in "History and Good [2]," she perceives continuity in Bonhoeffer's emphasis on the individual who acts "irrationally" apart from all law and ethics. The last resort is an action that cannot be judged before the tribunal of law. Brown also perceives a shift away from *Discipleship* in how this act now occurs in and for the world as directly political action. This shift is funded through Bonhoeffer's development of the extraordinary via Machiavelli's concept of *necessitá*, which describes how the prince is to act lawlessly in emergency situations for the sake of the polity.¹¹⁴ In this way, Brown argues that Bonhoeffer's primary referent is no longer the Sermon on the Mount, but Machiavelli, thus placing Bonhoeffer into the tradition of Thomas Hobbes, Karl Jaspers, and Carl Schmitt.¹¹⁵

Brown turns to Schmitt in particular, arguing that Bonhoeffer's account of the "extraordinary situation" shares strong conceptual overlaps with Schmitt's concept of the state of exception. Brown argues that their convergence is in conflating the situation of necessity with the individual decision. Brown identifies this error first in Schmitt where the sovereign not only discerns but decides upon and proclaims the state of exception.¹¹⁶ The exception is a situation enacted by the sovereign, since there are no juristic criteria required to decide whether the emergency has arisen. This emphasis on the individual in the extraordinary situation is troubling for Brown, since it conflates the individual with the situation thereby granting the individual unlimited authority to exert lawless violence. The exception becomes a technique.¹¹⁷

Brown argues that Bonhoeffer repeats Schmitt's error of conflation in claiming that the disciple who responds immediately to God's command is beyond the law,

---

111. Ibid.
112. DBWE 4:139-44.
113. Brown, *God's Conspirator*, 44-6; Brown, "Bonhoeffer, Schmitt, and the State of Exception," 249-50.
114. Brown, *God's Conspirator*, 58-9.
115. Brown, "Bonhoeffer, Schmitt, and the State of Exception," 251; *God's Conspirator*, 58-60, 70-3.
116. Brown observes that one can read Schmitt's famous opening line to *Political Theology* (*Soverän ist, wer über den Ausnahmezustand entscheidet*) in two senses. It can be read as "he who decides what the exceptional case is" or "he who decides what to do about the exceptional case." Brown, *God's Conspirator*, 83.
117. Brown, "Bonhoeffer, Schmitt, and the State of Exception," 253-4.

acting in a manner inaccessible to public judgment.[118] This conflation, according to Brown, has two dire consequences. First, the individual can claim that an event is exceptional without accountability, since the individual must respond without a "temporal gap" to Christ's immediate and direct Word that supersedes ethical discourse. What is particularly worrying for Brown is that the individual is not merely the sovereign of the state; the individual is any person who stands in a direct relationship to Christ.[119] The act occurs in "existential isolation" from the world, rationality, and others in response to God's "immediate" Word.[120] Second, this conflation opens a space for force outside of the law which can propagate a greater violence than is already present. Instead of alleviating the exceptional situation, it can exacerbate it by lionizing action beyond *ratio* that further extends the violence it seeks to end.[121] Brown ultimately concludes that Bonhoeffer's theology can enable Christian extremist violence.[122]

While both Lovin and Brown emphasize the risked quality of individual action, the differences between their narrations are noteworthy. Lovin presents Bonhoeffer as a responsible citizen, who acts for the law and the political community through the venture that seeks concrete proximate goods. And while this act cannot guarantee a particular outcome, Lovin narrates the act as reasonable and even necessary in the given circumstances. Brown, conversely, presents Bonhoeffer as a violent fanatic, who acts in radical isolation in response to Christ's command. The act is beyond *ratio* and is all too similar to fanatical terrorist violence. The difference between citizen and fanatic is a thin line given that both thinkers emphasize the risk, individuality, and relativity of the action in an extraordinary time.

The sources for the differences between Lovin and Brown are twofold. First, they differ on whether to emphasize the individual venture as decision or discernment. Lovin's narration emphasizes the discernment of the moment and the act—there is the discernment of an extraordinary situation of necessity and there is the discernment of what types of action will lead to certain predictable ends. This narration recognizes the risk of error but minimizes the disastrous effects it could have. Brown's picture emphasizes the subjectivity of decision that grates against public rationality and law. The individual decides that the extraordinary event has arisen and thus acts according to their own judgment. This emphasizes the subjectivity of one's perception of the moment and what action is necessary to achieve certain ends. Brown raises the point that determining what constitutes an emergency is more ambiguous than often acknowledged, thus raising the question of whether it is too simple to describe "objective criteria" that one must meet to enact the last resort as many Bonhoeffer scholars do. Second, they differ on whether the act occurs in relation to the mandates and law or if the act occurs over

---

118. Ibid., 255.
119. Brown, *God's Conspirator*, 110.
120. Ibid., 123.
121. Ibid., 91.
122. Ibid., 189.

against the mandates and law. Lovin emphasizes how the act occurs in relation to the mandates and law even in their utter deterioration. Even when these cannot offer clear direction, one still acts for the mandates and law by referring to them in deliberation. Brown emphasizes how the act occurs over against and above the mandates and law, emphasizing the radical and fanatical character of this act. Christ commands the action of the disciple, which destabilizes any account of law, rationality, and continuous political life. Lovin and Brown agree that Bonhoeffer's late resistance activity and thought should be intelligible and politically responsible, but they disagree about whether it finally meets this criterion.

This debate highlights two questions: Whether to emphasize the exception as objectively discerned or subjectively decided? And how to narrate the relationship of the exception to law, politics, and reason? How one answers these questions will be decisive for any narration of Bonhoeffer's late resistance life and thought.

Conclusion

Various questions emerged in this chapter regarding how to read the exception in Bonhoeffer's resistance life and thought. Two questions, in particular, are important to identify and address in the next chapter before shifting to the constructive reading forwarded in the next chapters. The first asks about (dis)continuity between Bonhoeffer's later thought and his earlier texts, raising the question of how to read Bonhoeffer's corpus. As displayed in the disagreement between Green and Rasmussen, there is debate about whether Bonhoeffer's conspiracy participation represents a shift (or development) in his activity and corresponding theological and ethical convictions. Discussion regarding the continuity of Bonhoeffer's theology usually centers on the relationship of *Discipleship* to *Ethics*,[123] but it also pertains to other points in the Bonhoeffer corpus. There is, for instance, the relationship between the writings that precede and follow Bonhoeffer's "conversion" in 1932, and there is the relationship between the conspiracy-era writings and Bonhoeffer's writings from prison.[124] How one negotiates the question of (dis) continuity in these various pieces has a material effect on how Bonhoeffer's account on any given subject is explicated, and this remains true for an account of the exception. The second question regards whether Bonhoeffer's resistance thought is coherent and systematic like DeJonge and the Anabaptist readers suggest or whether his resistance thought is fragmentary, possessing multiple approaches.

---

123. A recent work that reflects on this relationship is Florian Schmitz, "*Nachfolge*": *Zur Theologie Dietrich Bonhoeffers* (Göttingen: Vandenhoeck & Ruprecht GmbH, 2013).

124. The pacifist reading tends to emphasize the shift that occurs in 1932 while emphasizing continuity at the other junctures, epitomized in Nation et al., *Bonhoeffer the Assassin?* For two readings that emphasize discontinuity between *Ethics* and *Letters and Papers from Prison*, see Brown, *God's Conspirator*; and Kessler, "Bonhoeffer on Law Breaking." Green narrates continuity at each juncture in *A Theology of Sociality*.

Was Bonhoeffer's thought, particularly as articulated in his unfinished *Ethics*, coherent and consistent or does it possess false starts and contradicting ethical strands? There has always been a tension in Bonhoeffer scholarship on this second question, epitomized in Bethge's early description of Bonhoeffer's "fragmentary, yet systematic, work."[125] By addressing these questions in the next chapter, I move to develop the hermeneutic implications for reading the exception in Bonhoeffer's life and thought.

---

125. Eberhard Bethge, "The Challenge of Dietrich Bonhoeffer's Life and Theology," in *World Come of Age: A Symposium on Dietrich Bonhoeffer*, ed. Ronald Gregor Smith (Collins: London, 1967), 75.

Chapter 2

READING BONHOEFFER'S LIFE AND THOUGHT

HERMENEUTICAL QUESTIONS

The end of Chapter 1 highlighted two key questions in reading Bonhoeffer's theology: the question of how continuous Bonhoeffer's later thought is to his earlier thought and the question of how coherent and systematic Bonhoeffer's thought is. The second question can be seen as an extension of the first question insofar as a claim to discontinuity undercuts a claim to a systematic thought structure that spans Bonhoeffer's corpus.[1] The first two questions also implicate another set of questions: How should one read Bonhoeffer's life and thought, particularly in relation to the exception? In what sense does Bonhoeffer's biography relate to or determine Bonhoeffer's thought or the thought determine the biography? Are the two necessarily interlinked? This set of questions becomes important for how to answer the questions of continuity and coherence. For instance, prioritizing the biography often leads to an emphasis on discontinuity with Bonhoeffer's shift from Finkenwalde to active resistance. And prioritizing the thought often leads to an emphasis on continuity and coherence that develops throughout the corpus and informs his conspiratorial activity.

The purpose of this chapter is to engage these questions directly in order to develop a hermeneutic for reading the exception in Bonhoeffer's texts. The first section engages the question of how to read Bonhoeffer's life and thought. I argue that both Bonhoeffer's life and thought are mediated via texts, which entails that a hermeneutic for reading Bonhoeffer's life and thought must emerge from the texts themselves. This refuses to read Bonhoeffer's texts as being determined by his biography or psychological states, since these approaches assume that the reader has access to Bonhoeffer behind the texts that bear his name. The second and third sections engage Bonhoeffer's life and thought, respectively, answering the questions of (dis)continuity and coherence in Bonhoeffer's thought in its course. I argue that Bonhoeffer's life and decision-making (including the decision to join

---

1. It can also undercut the claim that Bonhoeffer's late resistance thought is itself coherent and systematic. The disparate and fragmentary *Ethics* has led some commentators to discern multiple ethical approaches to Bonhoeffer's late thought, such as Bethge arguing that Bonhoeffer's *Ethics* possesses four distinct starting points (DB-ER, 622–6).

the resistance) are marked by fragmentation and the experience of rupture and that Bonhoeffer's late resistance texts present multiple rationales about the exception, opening differing avenues for how to read the exception in Bonhoeffer's thought. This undoes the presupposition that Bonhoeffer's thought must be systematic and coherent in order for his texts to be read together. In the final section, I forward a hermeneutic for reading the exception in Bonhoeffer's life and thought, arguing that they open themselves to a constructive discourse on the character and form of the exception in a "Bonhoefferian" idiom.

Reading Bonhoeffer's Life and Thought

Since the inception of Bonhoeffer studies, interpreters remain continually impressed by the "remarkable unity" perceived between Bonhoeffer's life and thought.[2] Interpreters are often drawn to Bonhoeffer's texts because of his backstory. It is difficult to imagine Bonhoeffer's thought gaining much traction apart from his resistance to and subsequent imprisonment by the National Socialist regime. Yet these interpreters also note that Bonhoeffer's thought was central to the course of action that epitomized his life. Bonhoeffer's theological convictions inform both his ecumenical and resistance activity. Indeed, interpreters are often impressed by the remarkable correspondence of Bonhoeffer's action and convictions—a correspondence that is perceived to be all too often lacking in the lives of contemporary theologians. This tight correlation between Bonhoeffer's life and thought, Bethge argued, requires there to be no clear separation between them.[3] For many, to separate Bonhoeffer's life from his thought would obscure Bonhoeffer's full impact and witness.[4] This identification of an inseparability between Bonhoeffer's life and thought has for many become a hermeneutic principle for Bonhoeffer interpretation. The basic claim is that one cannot engage Bonhoeffer's thought apart from his biography and that his biography is only enriched and deepened by attending to his thought.

The insight is important, and I do not wish to challenge it. What is necessary is to ensure that the unity between the life and thought are properly maintained by adding the stipulation that Bonhoeffer's life and thought are read—they are not "brute facts" that stand behind the text.[5] They are textually mediated. As Markus

---

2. Haynes, *The Bonhoeffer Phenomenon*, 23.

3. Bethge, "The Challenge of Dietrich Bonhoeffer's Life and Theology," 22–88.

4. Interpreters separate them on occasion. Many popular narrations of Bonhoeffer's life center on his resistance activity *in spite of* his thought. Haynes reports that one person appreciated that Bonhoeffer's "theology did not impede his witness or work." Haynes, *The Battle for Bonhoeffer*, 133.

5. This becomes particularly true with the passing of Bonhoeffer's contemporaries. One must engage Bethge's biography and various writings, for instance, to receive a broader account of Bonhoeffer's historical context.

Franz argues: Bonhoeffer's life and thought "are to be perceived only through the language in which both are articulated and which is inseparable from them."[6] This is not to argue that Bonhoeffer is reducible to his texts or that the "real" Bonhoeffer is ahistorical. It only excludes the presumption that one can gain access to Bonhoeffer apart from those texts, using this supratextual access as the lens to identify a fundamental coherence or unity within Bonhoeffer's life and thought.

The result of prioritizing an objective and determinative entity behind the texts in reading Bonhoeffer is that it generates imbalanced and distorted readings of the actual texts.[7] This can occur, for instance, when the details of Bonhoeffer's historical context and biography become the determinative lens for reading his theology.[8] Without denying the genuine insight that these sources provide, Bonhoeffer's theological articulations are nevertheless misrepresented when they are reduced to responses to his context.[9] The creativity of Bonhoeffer's thought is reduced to a reflection of biography, stifling genuine readings of the text and the directions that they lead.[10] The "life" overdetermines Bonhoeffer's "thought." Conversely, when Bonhoeffer's resistance activity and rationale are narrated as the natural by-product of his psychological disposition, then Bonhoeffer's "thought" overdetermines his "life."[11] The danger is that one assumes they can ascertain Bonhoeffer's deeper motivations behind the text while engaging the texts themselves. Ultimately, the problem with these approaches is that they take attention away from Bonhoeffer's texts and they assume that one can encounter the "authentic" and "unified" Bonhoeffer by prioritizing something other than the texts themselves.

---

6. Markus Franz, "Inside and Beyond the 'Bonhoeffer-Archive'—Foucaultian Reflections on the Discourse of Bonhoeffer's Life and Theology," in *Bonhoeffer and Interpretive Theory: Essays on Methods and Understanding*, 28.

7. Ibid., 27.

8. Instantiating this approach is David M. Gides, *Pacifism, Just War, and Tyrannicide: Bonhoeffer's Church-World Theology and His Changing Forms of Political Thinking and Involvement* (Eugene: Pickwick Publications, 2011).

9. For a critique of this program in reading Bonhoeffer's poetry, see Hans Ulrich, "'Stations on the Way to Freedom:' The Presence of God—The Freedom of Disciples," in *Who Am I? Bonhoeffer's Theology through His Poetry*, edited by Bernd Wannenwetsch (London: T&T Clark, 2009), 151–3.

10. A more nuanced but still troubled approach to reading the biography through the text is by William Peck, who argues that the surface reading of a text opens space for a "deep" reading, which allows the biographical and historical details to rise to the surface. The benefit of Peck's approach is the centrality of the text, but his basic assumption that a *deep* reading occurs through reading events behind the text betrays the assumption that the biography directs the reflections. Ultimately, Bonhoeffer's context and activity emerges as the deep meaning of the text, which is smuggled into the theological rationale presented. See William Peck, "'The Euthanasia Text," in *New Studies in Bonhoeffer's Ethics*, 141–65.

11. For an example of this psychological determination of Bonhoeffer's theology, see Green, *A Theology of Sociality*, 140–78.

In this approach I draw on the work of Ernst Feil who argues that a hermeneutic for reading Bonhoeffer's life and thought must arise from Bonhoeffer's theology.[12] I diverge with Feil and other commentators by how they extend this argument to emphasize the continuity, coherence, and unity of Bonhoeffer's life and thought, appealing to statements made by Bonhoeffer in April 1944 in two letters to Bethge:

> I am wholly under the impression that my life—strange as it may sound—has gone in a straight line, uninterrupted, at least with regard to how I have led it. It has been a continually enriching experience for which I can only be grateful. If my present situation were to be the conclusion of my life, that would have a meaning that I believe I could understand.[13]

And:

> There are people who change, and many who can hardly change at all. I do not think I have ever changed much, except perhaps at the time of my first impressions abroad, and under the conscious influence of Papa's personality. It was then that a turning from the phraseological to the real ensued. . . . Neither of us has really experienced a break in his life. . . . Continuity with one's own past is actually a great gift.[14]

Passages like these are thus given hermeneutic priority, giving the impression that Bonhoeffer experienced his life and thought as unified, continuous, and coherent and that he could discern the meaning of his life and action.[15]

The purpose of the next two sections is to trouble the hermeneutic priority given to the claim of unity and coherence by emphasizing the fragmentary and discontinuous character of Bonhoeffer's life and thought. The route for this claim is not to deny that the foregoing quotations testify to continuity and coherence. It instead gives hermeneutic priority to other writings from Bonhoeffer's prison and conspiracy era texts that present an opposing self-description. For it is not a problem if Bonhoeffer echoes a different sentiment from different times in his late writings, since any incongruence between writings in itself challenges a claim to an inner-coherence or continuity to Bonhoeffer's thought and experience of

---

12. Ernst Feil, *The Theology of Dietrich Bonhoeffer*, trans. Martin Rumscheidt (Minneapolis: Fortress Press, 1985), 3–55.

13. DBWE 8:352–3.

14. DBWE 8:358.

15. Readers who employ these quotes toward these ends include: Ralf Wüstenberg, *A Theology of Life: Dietrich Bonhoeffer's Religionless Christianity*, trans. Douglas W. Scott (Grand Rapids: W. B. Eerdmans, 1998), 118–19; Feil, *The Theology of Dietrich Bonhoeffer*, 52–3; Nation et al., *Bonhoeffer the Assassin?*, 101–4; DB-ER, 581; Trey Palmisano, *Peace and Violence in the Ethics of Dietrich Bonhoeffer: An Analysis of Method* (Eugene: Wipf and Stock, 2016).

his life. In short, it is not troublesome if Bonhoeffer felt his life and thought was unified and continuous at a given moment and that he likewise experienced and thought of these as fragmentary and disjointed at others. Only if one assumes in advance an inner-coherence between the various writings does one require a coalescing to take place. The form of the prison writings in particular is discursive, occasional, and often unfinished, which leads to the possibility of multiple strands that do not coalesce in a unified and coherent system.[16] The form of the writings justifies the move to give hermeneutic priority to particular texts that accentuate the experience of fragmentariness, such as Bonhoeffer's poems from prison.

The Fragmentariness of Bonhoeffer's Life

On several occasions in prison, Bonhoeffer directly addresses the fragmentariness of his life. In his meditation for his godson's baptism, Bonhoeffer speaks of his life and that of his contemporaries as becoming "formless or even fragmentary."[17] And in another letter to Bethge from February 23, 1944, Bonhoeffer refers to "this fragment of life we have."[18] To speak of his fragmentary life reflects the disjointed character of his experience of time in prison. Bonhoeffer's position in prison is completely disconnected from his past life, and this—as he says in another letter—can make his time and even his life seem empty and lost, thus requiring fresh reflection in response to this disorienting experience.[19] Direct reflection on the experience of fragmentation and disorientation is a common theme in Bonhoeffer's late attempts at poetry. The poems are unique in how many are drawn directly from Bonhoeffer's impressions and experience of prison. But the poems are not merely rough sketches of what he experienced; they become the context of Bonhoeffer's own attempts to factor these into decisive theological claims about reality.[20]

One pertinent example is Bonhoeffer's 1944 poem "Who Am I?"[21] The first noteworthy quality of the poem is its context. It draws exclusively from Bonhoeffer's prison experience, reflecting on the impression that others have of him as well as his own impressions of himself. Central to the poem's structure is the dichotomy that emerges between these two perspectives. The first three stanzas reflect how

---

16. For more on this point, see Wayne Whitson Floyd Jr., "Style and the Critique of Metaphysics: The Letter as Form in Bonhoeffer and Adorno," in *Theology and the Practice of Responsibility: Essays on Dietrich Bonhoeffer*, ed. Wayne Whitson Floyd, Jr. and Charles Marsh (Valley Forge: Trinity Press, 1984), 239–51.
17. DBWE 8:387.
18. DBWE 8:306.
19. DBWE 8:181.
20. Philip Ziegler, "'Voices in the Night': Human Solidarity and Eschatological Hope," in *Who Am I?*, 143.
21. DBWE 8:459–60.

others describe Bonhoeffer. To the guards and prisoners, Bonhoeffer appears calm and self-possessed, reflecting the virtues of his bourgeois upbringing. Yet what Bonhoeffer experiences of himself subverts this external perspective.[22] To himself, Bonhoeffer appears restless and lonely, yearning for human companionship. He appears to himself short-tempered, impatient, and prayerless. The utter incoherence between the two perspectives leads Bonhoeffer to an impasse between which he finds himself ill-suited to adjudicate, since he fails to affirm one as his true self; he is unable to find solid ground through psychological self-reflection, his societal position, or in the testimony of others concerning his virtues. These only lead to a self-questioning that ultimately generates fragmentation and a vicious self-suspicion.

It is in light of this experience that Bonhoeffer shifts his language and attention to another who transcends his experience. In the final stanza, Bonhoeffer addresses God directly, turning to God as the only One who can disclose a person's true self once and for all: "Whoever I am, thou knowest me; O God, I am thine!"[23] What is noteworthy in this final shift is that Bonhoeffer takes seriously the experience of fragmentation, which leads to an inner-suspicion that unveils the instability of his position and experience. Nevertheless, Bonhoeffer does not stop with an act of suspicion, but rather shifts to the address of prayer.[24] The "answer," however, is not the practice of prayer itself.[25] For Bonhoeffer to ground his confidence in the fostering of practices only opens him anew to a hermeneutic of self-suspicion—suspicion of his motivation for prayer and suspicion regarding the efficacy of the prayers of a sinner mired in his own turmoil. Rather, the only solace is a literal turning away from oneself in expectation of a final disclosure by the One who truly knows him. Bonhoeffer's attention must be turned away from himself and his activity, and it must be turned to the One who precedes and pervades his own fragmentary experience if he is going to receive an orientation that enables him to live in the present. As Bonhoeffer wrote in a letter to Bethge on May 29, 1944: "Everything, whether objective or subjective, disintegrates into fragments. Christianity, on the other hand, puts us into many different dimensions of life at the same time."[26] To think and live within God's world is a gift of grace that is only perceptible in the provisionality of one's thought and experience, in the expectation that the true status of the world will be revealed once and for all in Christ.

---

22. See Hans D. van Hoogstraten, "Ethics and the Problem of Metaphysics," in *Theology and the Practice of Responsibility*, 225.

23. DBWE 8:460.

24. Bernd Wannenwetsch, *Political Worship* (Oxford: Oxford University Press, 2004), 290–3.

25. Contra Michael Northcott, "'Who Am I?' Human Identity and the Spiritual Disciplines in the Witness of Dietrich Bonhoeffer," in *Who Am I?*, 11–31.

26. DBWE 8:405.

This is true, further, when Bonhoeffer considers not only the question of his identity but also when he considers what his life *means* in the fragmentariness of the historical present and the passing of time. The impetus for Bonhoeffer's reflections on this topic is twofold. First, there is Bonhoeffer's experience of time in prison. In being cut off from all that characterized his past life, his experience of prison caused everything to appear empty and lost, revealing how Bonhoeffer's past life was always outside of his control and only fleetingly becomes present to him.[27] In the notes for Bonhoeffer's now lost "Essay on the Sense of Time," Bonhoeffer reflects on this loss and disorientation in one's experience of time: "continuity with the past and the future interrupted," "fantasizing, distortion of past and future," and "*! Experience of time* as experience of *separation*."[28] Second, Bonhoeffer reflects on the words scrawled in his cell by a previous inmate: "in one hundred years all will be over."[29] For the prisoner who wrote these words, the mere passage of time offers hope, since the present is vulnerable to change; nothing is secure from the contingency of time. Bonhoeffer recognizes in this statement an attempt to cope with the present experience in hope for the future. The difference with Bonhoeffer is that he finds his hope not in the mere passage of time but in the hope of an apocalyptic unveiling anticipated in the present.

This emerges in Bonhoeffer's poem "Night Voices," which was written a year later.[30] In "Night Voices," Bonhoeffer writes on his impression of prison in expectant hope of God's activity and revelation.[31] In this poem, the author holds little hope in the mere passage of time but awaits the advent of a new day. This emerges in the tenth stanza, where the author contrasts two different modes of time operative in the poem. The former mundane sense of time is that of the prison, which possesses no promise with each passing day. Faced with the meaningless shift of days marked by the clang of prison bells, the author finds that the passage of time offers no hope, and thus turns to expect and desire "to see the turning of the times" that transforms the present by bringing divine justice and human solidarity.[32]

The turning of the times is anything but mundane and immanent to the historical nexus of cause and effect. It, rather, illuminates and transforms all things. Ziegler suggests this poem is Bonhoeffer's reflection on how the experience of the present is transformed and gifted to the author "in the mode of promise."[33] Even so, the expectation of the promise is no immanent possession of the author, but it

---

27. "An essay on 'the sense of time' arose primarily out of the need to make my own past present to myself in a situation in which time could so easily appear 'empty' and 'lost'" (DBWE 8:181). Bonhoeffer reflects on this theme in his poem "The Past" as well (DBWE 8:418–21).
28. DBWE 8:70–4. Emphasis original.
29. DBWE 8:79–80.
30. DBWE 8:462–80.
31. DBWE 8:457.
32. DBWE 8:518.
33. Ziegler, "'Voices in the Night,'" in *Who Am I?*, 130.

exceeds his grasp. This partial vision exceeds full realization; it is present and is yet to come. This expectancy leads to the final chorus of the prisoners who plead to God for the unveiling of mercy and justice on the new day.[34]

Taken together, Bonhoeffer's poems and his fragments of an essay on the sense of time reflect how the experience of the present and one's self can be disorienting as well as disjunctive from all that precedes and follows after. Time can terrify and torture as well as bring new insight and joy. It can make the past present again and it can also isolate, revealing an infinite expanse that separates past seasons from one's present experience. Bonhoeffer captures that the past and one's relation to it are not primarily objects of reflection, but entities that are received by grace, pursued only in light of God's promise and presence. For Bonhoeffer, history in and of itself does not offer a lens to assess the meaning and vindication of a life; the mere passage of time does not guarantee healing, but, at best, a scarring over of wounds. The only hope is God's condescension and promise in Christ: "the unbiblical concept of 'meaning,' after all, is only one translation of what the Bible calls 'promise.'"[35]

When Bonhoeffer considered the meaning of his life from prison, he trusted neither in his own recollection of his past nor in the vindication of his life through historical progression. Both options offered no solace for Bonhoeffer, and this solidified his judgment that any self-evaluation of a life is provisional, awaiting the fulfillment of God's promises for him. There is a certain sense that Bonhoeffer negates in these poems what is often assumed in narrations of his life: namely, that Bonhoeffer's participation in the conspiracy was performed with absolute certainty of its moral vindication and justifiability. As argued in the next section, Bonhoeffer did not narrate his resistance thought in this register. He rather narrated it as disruptive and unsettling. And consistent with the conclusions of his poetry, neither did he appraise his life and actions as absolutely vindicated. When Bonhoeffer reflects on his past and his identity, Bonhoeffer views both as entities that elude his control and only come to him by grace. And when Bonhoeffer looks to his future, he recognizes that the mere turning of time offers no vindication, since history does not possess an immanent arc of progress. To speak of his life as victorious and certain can more often reflect the moral prejudices and positions of this age than Bonhoeffer's own. It obfuscates the real angst that accompanied his decisions and convictions, and it can thus "domesticate" the life and witness of Bonhoeffer.

This theme is not limited to Bonhoeffer's prison writings but finds articulation in Bonhoeffer's reflections on returning to Germany in 1939. In a diary entry from June 20, 1939, Bonhoeffer describes his decisions—including the decision to return to Germany—as often being made before he fully understood why they were made, reflecting that the reasons for his action are often hidden from himself:

---

34. DBWE 8:467–8.
35. DBWE 8:515.

With that the decision has been made. I turned it down.... For me it may mean something more than I am able to foresee at the moment. God alone knows. It is strange that in all my decisions I am never completely clear about my motives. Is that a sign of lack of clarity, inner dishonesty, or is it a sign that we are *led* beyond that which we can discern, or is it both?

Isa. 45:19: "I am the Lord who speaks of righteousness, I declare what is right."

1 Pet. 1:17: "If you invoke as Father the one who judges all people impartially according to their deeds, live in reverent fear during the time of your exile."

The Daily Text today speaks with terrible severity of God's incorruptible judgment. God certainly sees how much personal concern, how much fear is contained in today's decision, as courageous as it may appear. The reasons that one puts forward to others and oneself for an action are certainly not sufficient. One can simply give reasons for anything. In the end one acts out of a level that remains hidden from us. Because of that one can only pray that God will wish to judge us and forgive us. At the end of the day, I can only pray that God may hold merciful judgment over this day and all decisions. It is now in God's hand.[36]

Bonhoeffer's testimony to his lack of clarity about the self, his reasons for acting, and the meaning of his life significantly troubles the notion that Bonhoeffer experienced his life as continuous, unified, and coherent to himself. Significantly, this testimony spans from this 1939 diary entry through his prison writings, framing the period of Bonhoeffer's conspiracy participation.

The Fragmentariness of Bonhoeffer's Thought

The question addressed in this section is whether Bonhoeffer's late resistance thought is best characterized by coherence, singularity, and systematicity as Feil and DeJonge suggest. By attending to Bonhoeffer's texts, I argue that Bonhoeffer's resistance writings do not forward a singular, systematic rationale on the exception, but they rather present rationales. This multiplicity suggests a different approach to reading these texts, which is forwarded in the final section of this chapter. This claim to multiplicity is forwarded on three grounds: the form of Bonhoeffer's late resistance writings, Bonhoeffer's testimony to how his experience of resistance contextualized his ethical and resistance thought, and through an analysis of Bonhoeffer's late resistance writings on the borderline case (*Grenzfall*), which reveal that Bonhoeffer develops multiple rationales on the exception.

The Fragmentary Form of Bonhoeffer's Writings

The fragmentary form of Bonhoeffer's late writings is undisputed. From Bonhoeffer's unfinished *Ethics* to his occasional writings from prison, Bonhoeffer's

---

36. DBWE 15:226–7. Emphasis original.

late work possesses a fragmentary and unfinished character. Many writings from this period remain unpolished, often breaking off unexpectedly. This is particularly evident in Bonhoeffer's *Ethics*, which Bonhoeffer lamented that he could not complete to his liking.[37] To possess these writings is a gift, and the Bonhoeffer community owes much to Bethge and the many others who have diligently collated and published the corpus as we have it today. Even with this extensive work, the fragmentary character is unmistakable, becoming an essential aspect to reading Bonhoeffer's late thought. There are several strategies for negotiating this fragmentary corpus. One option is to survey the various writings in order to identify a coherent systematicity to Bonhoeffer's thought on a given topic. There is a certain textual warrant for this approach. As Bonhoeffer argued in *Act and Being*, "Thinking, including theological thinking, will always be 'systematic' by nature."[38] To think is to pursue an organization of thought on a given topic, and it is reasonable to investigate Bonhoeffer's disparate writings in seeking to identify this.[39] There is a difference, though, between an attempted systematicity in a given piece of writing and a presupposed accomplishment of systematicity dispersed across many writings. The former admits a provisional character to all thought, which can generate fissures and unintended consequences over time. As Bonhoeffer also argued in *Act and Being*, true systematicity is an eschatological gift that awaits realization, which entails that all thought in the interim gestures toward but can never achieve airtight systematicity, remaining open to disruption.[40] The latter is a metaphysical claim in which one asserts a singularity and coalescence to the thought of the author across the corpus. The writings present a system because the author who stands behind the text is presupposed to possess a unified form of thought reflected in those writings.[41] Naturally, many readers of Bonhoeffer would contest this charge by arguing that continuity and consistent systematicity is discernable in the texts themselves, and this remains a possibility. The point is rather to ensure that the continuity of the author's signature does not overdetermine the reading of these fragmentary texts in presupposing a systematic continuity between them.

---

37. DBWE 8:181.

38. DBWE 2:132.

39. DeJonge labels this as a "hermeneutical" form of thought based on the reconciliation of all of reality in Christ where all parts are reconciled in a logically prior whole. Michael DeJonge, "Bonhoeffer from the Perspective of Intellectual History," in *Interpreting Bonhoeffer*, 202–4. See also, Michael DeJonge, *Bonhoeffer's Theological Formation* (Oxford: Oxford University Press, 2012).

40. DBWE 2:89, 130–2.

41. For more on this point and the question of what it means to read a corpus, see Jacques Derrida, "Interpreting Signatures (Nietzsche/Heidegger): Two Questions," in *Dialogue and Deconstruction: The Gadamer-Derrida Encounter*, ed. and trans. Diane Michelfelder and Richard E. Palmer (New York: SUNY Press, 1989), 58–71.

Another option for reading these fragmentary texts is to view their form as an invitation to a particular mode of discourse. As Wayne Whitson Floyd Jr. has argued, the form of Bonhoeffer's fragmentary writings may give the crucial clue to the style of Bonhoeffer's theological thought from the late period.[42] By this, Floyd Jr. argues that the predominantly occasional form of Bonhoeffer's writing invites a particular mode of reading that is decidedly antisystematic. The form of the letter, for instance, "can resist and criticize the prevalent system-building propensities of western philosophy and theology" through its linguistic and communicative strategies. And the unfinished writings lend themselves to open-ended readings which generate constructive theological insight that claim contemporary attention.[43] Even if one is wary of the diatribe against systematic theology, the benefit of this mode of reading is that it keeps in the forefront the contingency and open-endedness of Bonhoeffer's texts that remain vulnerable to disruption.[44] Another benefit is that it refuses to lament the fragmentary form of Bonhoeffer's texts as something to move beyond, but rather as indicative of Bonhoeffer's late style, shaping contemporary readings of the texts. It also remains open to a plurality of readings that play off different texts. Floyd Jr. quotes Bonhoeffer's late discussion of polyphony to capture this possibility.[45] It is the form of these texts, in fact, that could in part explain the various contradicting narrations observed in Chapter 1. While this is not to imply that all readings are equal, it suggests that the disparate readings encountered may arise depending on which strands of Bonhoeffer's late thought are accentuated and which are de-emphasized. By embracing the fragmentary form, it thus brings these decisions and judgments about which strands to emphasize to the surface, drawing questions of discernment and weight to the forefront of any discussion of Bonhoeffer's late texts.

Bonhoeffer's Narration of His Thought as Fragmentary

Bonhoeffer's testimony about his experience of the resistance suggests a symmetrical fragmentariness to the content of Bonhoeffer's resistance thought. Bonhoeffer does not narrate his resistance activity as the natural outflow of his ethical and political thought; he rather describes his experience as utterly disruptive thereby requiring fresh reflection. This testimony occurs in Bonhoeffer's 1942 Christmas letter, "After Ten Years," where he reflects on the time spent in resistance—since the rise of Hitler—and what concrete time has taught him. He opens the letter:

---

42. Floyd Jr., "Style and the Critique of Metaphysics," 240.
43. Ibid., 240–1.
44. In the idiom of *Act and Being*, the system derives from the past in coherence with reason, whereas the contingent revelation of Christ transcends the system, originating from the future that determines the present (DBWE 2:111).
45. DBWE 8:405.

In the following pages I want to try to give an accounting of some of the shared experience and insight that have been forced upon us in these times, not personal experiences, nothing systematically organized, not arguments and theories, but conclusions about human experience—lined up side by side, connected only by concrete experience—that have been reached together in a circle of like-minded people.[46]

Under the first subheadings, Bonhoeffer testifies to the experience of having all ethical forms of thought, personal strengths, and practices fall short of the challenges of the moment, leaving him empty-handed in his ability to respond: "Have there ever been people who in their time, like us, had so little ground under their feet, people to whom every possible alternative open to them at the time appeared equally unbearable, senseless, and contrary to life."[47] Bonhoeffer was responding to what he considered unprecedented thereby requiring fresh ethical thought. It is unsurprising, then, if his late resistance thought possesses tensions not easily resolved, particularly in relation to the borderline case. Bonhoeffer's testimony is that all ethical forms of thought were inadequate, which emphasizes the exploratory and provisional character of his writings on the exception. To narrate Bonhoeffer's action as if he knew what to do before the situation even arose is to discredit this testimony, minimizing in advance the various directions that his late resistance thought could take.

Establishing Multiple Rationales in Bonhoeffer's Late Resistance Thought

Bonhoeffer engages the concept of the borderline case at various times in his late resistance writings, and these engagements reflect different emphases and rationales that sit uneasily next to each other. In his unfinished *Ethics* alone, the concept arises on a number of occasions with each occurrence varying in context as well as vocabulary employed to describe the phenomenon.[48] In his late 1940 to early 1941 manuscript "Natural Life," Bonhoeffer speaks of the "borderline case" (*Grenzfall*) that emerges when human rights, which are prepolitical realities grounded in the Natural and perceivable by reason, conflict with one another.[49] These conflicts are destined to arise as a result of the fall, and Bonhoeffer negotiates these conflicts through a casuistic rationale that draws on Catholic moral theology.[50] One particular example is the scenario where a plague breaks out

---

46. DBWE 8:37.

47. DBWE 8:38.

48. For more on the borderline case in *Ethics*, see Matthew Puffer, "The 'Borderline Case,'" in *Dem Rad in die Speichen fallen*, 257–69.

49. There are three places where potential borderline cases arise in this essay (DBWE 6:195, 212, 198–202).

50. On casuistry, Bonhoeffer wrote on January 20, 1941: "In my work I am just coming to the question of euthanasia. The more I am able to write, the more the material engages

on a ship at sea with half of those onboard infected. According to Bonhoeffer, this presents a borderline case when the rights to bodily life conflict, and the question remains open regarding whether the healthy could kill the infected to preserve their own lives.[51] In his 1943 manuscript, "The 'Christian' and the 'Ethical' as a Topic," Bonhoeffer speaks in a different idiom about the "boundary event" (*Grenzereignis*) that emerges within political life and threatens to disintegrate it.[52] The event threatens to destabilize the community's form of life by questioning the norms that undergird it. The boundary event is when the norms of a community, which Bonhoeffer calls the "Ethical," become a topic of discussion that requires a decision for or against them. It is an event when one reestablishes or demolishes what is otherwise assumed in the freedom of day-to-day life.[53] Unlike "Natural Life," this discourse is authorized not by reason but by determinate relationships of authority within the community, showing the political orientation and constitution of this boundary event and its overcoming.[54] Bonhoeffer speaks also of the borderline case in the 1942 manuscript "History and Good [2]" when he explicates the account of *necessitá*. The difference from "The 'Christian' and the 'Ethical' as a Topic" is that while this, too, is a political phenomenon, its resolution is not through political discourse, but through the individual venture that cannot be justified or explicated on political, natural, or ethical grounds.[55] It breaks both the "explicit law" of the government as well as God's command in seeking the restoration of just governance and law in its various senses.[56]

To observe this diversity does not necessarily entail a lack of coherence between the manuscripts as much as it demonstrates the varied contexts and language that Bonhoeffer utilized to explore the borderline case. Any consideration of the exception needs to keep this diversity of writings in view. In order to demonstrate substantive developments and incongruences between the manuscripts that pertain to the exception, attention to specific texts and their rationales is required. Matthew Puffer's work on Bonhoeffer's *Ethics* is helpful in this regard. In his article, "Election in Bonhoeffer's *Ethics*: Discerning a Late Revision," Puffer argues there is a shift in theo-logic from Bonhoeffer's mid-1942 manuscript "History and Good [2]" to his late 1942 manuscript "God's Love and the Disintegration of the World" and that this shift leads Bonhoeffer to develop a differing rationale on the exception distinct from "History and Good [2]," Bonhoeffer's most famous text

---

me. I find Catholic ethics in many ways instructive and more practical than ours. Up to now we have always dismissed it as 'casuistry.' Today we are grateful for much—precisely on the topic of my present theme" (DBWE 16:126).

51. DBWE 6:195.
52. DBWE 6:368.
53. DBWE 6:368–75.
54. DBWE 6:375.
55. DBWE 6:278–9.
56. DBWE 6:273–4.

on the exception.[57] Puffer argues that Bonhoeffer's reading of the galley proofs for II/2 of Barth's *Church Dogmatics* is decisive in spurring Bonhoeffer's substantive developments in "God's Love and the Disintegration of the World." According to Puffer, Barth's account of ethics in II/2 leads Bonhoeffer to shift the locus of his ethics from the doctrine of justification in "History and Good [2]" to the doctrine of election in "God's Love and the Disintegration of the World."[58]

---

57. Matthew Puffer, "Election in Bonhoeffer's *Ethics*: Discerning a Late Revision," *International Journal of Systematic Theology* 14, no. 3 (2012): 255–76. Puffer extends this argument in a later article, Matthew Puffer, "Three Rival Versions of Moral Reasoning: Interpreting Bonhoeffer's Ethics of Lying, Guilt, and Responsibility," *Harvard Theological Review* 112, no. 2 (2019): 160–83. I perform an in-depth reading of "History and Good [2]" in Chapter 4 and of "God's Love and the Disintegration of the World" in Chapter 5.

58. In a letter to Barth dated May 13, 1942, Bonhoeffer notes that he received the galley proofs for the "new *Dogmatics* volume" and that he "would like to work through at least the second part of [the] volume" (DBWE 16:266–77). In a letter to Ernst Wolf from September 13, 1942, Bonhoeffer states: "I have read the second main section of the new *Dogmatics*; I've not yet had a chance to read the first" (DBWE 16:359). According to the editors of the critical edition of *Ethics*, Bonhoeffer wrote "History and Good [2]" in the third phase of his *Ethics* writing, thus dating the manuscript in the first half of 1942 (see DBWE 6:424, 472); Bonhoeffer wrote "God's Love and the Disintegration of the World" in the fourth stage of his *Ethics* writing, dating the manuscript in the second half of 1942—sometime between September and December 1942 (DBWE 6:445–6, 472).

The importance of this dating of this essay is twofold. First, the essay "God's Love and the Disintegration of the World" was previously dated between 1939 to 1940, which suggested that "History and Good [2]" was a later and more mature attempt at the ethical question than "God's Love and the Disintegration of the World." The new dating questions the claim that "History and Good [2]" is paradigmatic of Bonhoeffer's ethical approach. Second, the new dating supports the suggestion that Bonhoeffer wrote "God's Love and the Disintegration of the World" *after* reading the galley proofs for CD II/2. See Puffer, "Election," 258–62 for more on the issue of dating "God's Love and the Disintegration of the World." Of course, further argumentation is needed to support the suggestion that "God's Love and the Disintegration of the World" is written in response to Bonhoeffer's reading of Barth. As Puffer observes, Barth's language of election is not unique to CD II/2 and it is conceivable that Bonhoeffer draws on this language elsewhere. And while there is substantive overlap in themes addressed in "God's Love and the Disintegration of the World" and CD II/2 (self-examination, conscience, moral discernment, the command as event, etc.), mere correspondence only suggests a relationship but does not confirm one. As Puffer states: "A more explicit connection must be demonstrated for one to assert Bonhoeffer's dependence upon a specific work of Barth's" (Puffer, "Election," 266). Puffer convincingly argues that this connection is found in Bonhoeffer's discussion of knowing and doing God's will in "God's Love and the Disintegration of the World," which draws

At critical junctures in "History and Good [2]," Bonhoeffer considers whether particular actions are justifiable in light of the relativity of fallen history, which eludes clear-cut ethical judgments. There are moments, per Bonhoeffer, when every possible action is exposed to judgment before others and before God.[59] At such times, Bonhoeffer suggests that the incursion of guilt is inevitable (*Schuldübernahme*), and this is particularly true for those who act responsibly on behalf of others. Puffer argues that the underlying moral rationale of *Schuldübernahme* centers on the justifiability of a given act even when the typical grounds to justify an act are no longer in effect. This emphasis on accepting guilt takes precedence in Bonhoeffer's discussion of the moment of *ultima ratio* when someone breaks the law on behalf of the other. While this act incurs guilt, it is nevertheless necessary and is in a certain sense "justified before others by dire necessity."[60] There is a Christological logic to this guilt-inducing act. Bonhoeffer argues that just as Jesus broke the law out of real love for human beings, so humans

from Barth's small text section on testing (*prüfen*) God's will (CD II/2, 636–41). To quote Puffer at length: "Bonhoeffer presents a discussion outlining the necessity of a renewed mind in order to discern God's will (Rom. 12:2). In the context of his argument, Bonhoeffer translates the term *ta diapheronta*, found in two of these verses (Rom. 2:18 and Phil. 1:10) as 'the various situations' (*die verschiedenen Situationen*). The translation itself is of limited importance for Bonhoeffer's understanding of election. Of the utmost import is that the translation is not original to Bonhoeffer but matches exactly the translation from an excursus in the second half of CD II/2. Barth's translation of this term appears in the context of a strikingly similar discussion about discerning (*prüfen*) the will of God. Closer examination shows not only that Barth provided Bonhoeffer with the translation but also that the excursus in CD II/2 references the same seven verses as does Bonhoeffer.... Here, in what was to serve as Bonhoeffer's introduction to his magnum opus, Bonhoeffer is incorporating Barth's material from a small-print section 130 pages into Barth's 270-page chapter on 'The Command of God' in CD II/2. This discovery indicates that Bonhoeffer was not simply familiar with the ethical portion of Barth's doctrine of God at this time, earlier than the generally acknowledged *Phase 5* of *Ethics*, but that he was intently reading and incorporating the ethics in CD II/2 at the very beginning of *Phase 4*.... What is most significant about finding such dependence in this particular chapter, however, is that it shows Bonhoeffer's response to reading Barth's general ethics in CD II/2 coincides precisely with his decision to write this new introduction to his own theological ethics" (Puffer, "Election," 266–7). The Bible references that Bonhoeffer engages that are also utilized by Barth are Rom. 2:18, 12:2; 2 Cor. 13:5; Gal. 6:4; Eph. 5:8; Phil. 1:10; and 1 Thess. 5:21. See CD II/2, 639–40 and DBWE 6:320, 322, 325. Further strengthening the connection is how Bonhoeffer quotes 2 Cor. 13:5 and Gal. 6:4 in discussing self-examination (DBWE 6:325), which is the same theme Barth is engaging when he quotes those verses (CD II/2, 640).

59. DBWE 6:284.
60. DBWE 6:282.

break the law for others.⁶¹ Bonhoeffer is insistent that one cannot deny that guilt is incurred in such moments, but nevertheless one must choose responsible action over personal innocence. This is epitomized by Bonhoeffer's famous statement: "Those who act responsibly become guilty without sin."⁶²

Bonhoeffer speaks in a very different register in "God's Love and the Disintegration of the World." There is no further engagement with the concept of incurring or accepting guilt, and the inevitability of ethical conflicts in the murkiness of history is missing. Bonhoeffer rather speaks of the simplicity of Christian action that does not know the good or bad of one's action—it eludes self-judgment.⁶³ Bonhoeffer further argues that any consideration of ethical conflicts stems from a denial of God's election in Christ. In ethical conflicts, humans attempt to be the subject of election instead of God, thus positioning themselves as the ones who elect and subsequently judge human action on the basis of the postlapsarian division of good and evil.⁶⁴ This division of good and evil leads to the emergence of "tragic" ethical conflicts and the necessity of ethical reflection that works on the basis of this disunity. Bonhoeffer asserts that Christian action must proceed on a completely different basis that overcomes this disunity: the election of God. Jesus epitomizes this differing mode of action by responding with simplicity to God's will. Instead of breaking the Sabbath law, Bonhoeffer narrates Jesus as living in freedom from the law "that is not even bound by the law of logical alternatives."⁶⁵ Jesus never breaks God's commandments, and he never considers whether he incurs guilt through his actions, since he never decides between countless possibilities; Jesus obeys God's will in simplicity.⁶⁶ This simplicity of action highlights what is missing in this manuscript from "History and Good [2]": the concept of *Schuldübernahme*. Bonhoeffer drops this language entirely in this manuscript, seemingly because it contradicts the form and origin of simple Christian action in response to God's will. It is further telling that after "History and Good [2]" the phrase is never used again by Bonhoeffer.⁶⁷

---

61. DBWE 6:278.

62. DBWE 6:282.

63. If one does judge, it is only on the basis of God's election in Christ, and this becomes the basis of any self-examination or act of judging (DBWE 6:316–17).

64. DBWE 6:302.

65. DBWE 6:312.

66. DBWE 6:313.

67. Puffer, "Election," 274. There is a question about whether the concept is utilized after "History and Good [2]." In "After Ten Years," for instance, Bonhoeffer states: "There is clearly no historically significant action that does not trespass ever again against the limits set by those laws. But it makes a decisive difference whether such trespasses against the established limit are viewed as their abolishment in principle and hence presented as a law of its own kind, or whether one is conscious that such trespassing is perhaps an unavoidable guilt that has its justification only in that law and limit being reinstated and honored as

The importance of these remarkably different formulations on Christian ethics is not to suggest that Bonhoeffer is an incoherent author whose formulations bear no resemblance to one another. When interpreters discern strong continuities in the Bonhoeffer corpus as well as between these two manuscripts, it is because there are real and important continuities that emerge in any close reading of the texts. Even so, the differing articulations between the manuscripts are not inconsequential. They reflect differing moral logics that reframe key aspects of Bonhoeffer's ethical reflection in "History and Good [2]." "God's Love and the Disintegration of the World" is not necessarily developing upon the themes of "History and Good [2]," and it may represent a reframing of crucial themes in *Ethics*. This point is strengthened when one considers that "God's Love and the Disintegration of the World" was probably intended to be the introductory essay for *Ethics*, further highlighting how "God's Love and the Disintegration of the World" could reframe what was written up to that point.

Puffer bolsters his argument by displaying the consistency of this shift in theologic when he considers the strong discontinuity in how the borderline case of lying is handled between "History and Good [2]" and Bonhoeffer's 1943 essay, "What Does It Mean to Tell the Truth?"[68] In both pieces, which mirror reflection on the exception in a moral sense, Bonhoeffer considers Kant's musings on a scenario where a murderer comes to one's home, inquiring about the whereabouts of one's friend in order to kill them.[69] Kant reasons that he would feel obliged to disclose the whereabouts of his friend in maintaining truthfulness. Bonhoeffer disagrees with Kant in both pieces, arguing that one must misdirect the murderer so not to disclose the whereabouts of the friend. Bonhoeffer's reasoning about the case, however, is markedly different between the two pieces. In "History and Good [2]," Bonhoeffer argues one must lie in "violating the principle of truthfulness for the sake of my friend." Bonhoeffer thinks that there is no avoiding that one has lied thereby incurring guilt.[70] In "What Does It Mean to Tell the Truth?," Bonhoeffer argues that such misdirection cannot be a lie: "If one characterizes this sort of behavior as a lie, then lying receives a moral consecration and justification that contradicts its meaning in every respect."[71] Rather, the misdirection of the murderer is paradoxically an act of truth-telling, since the "false" statement remains in accordance with reality by remaining true to his friend. There is no incursion of guilt in this scenario, since any statement that is in accordance with reality is an

---

quickly as possible" (DBWE 8:46). Outside of this instance, however, the concept of actively incurring guilt is notably absent.

68. DBWE 16:601–8.

69. Immanuel Kant, "On a Supposed Right to Lie from Philanthropy," in *Practical Philosophy*, ed. and trans. Mary J. Gregor, *The Cambridge Edition of the Works of Immanuel Kant* (Cambridge: Cambridge University Press, 1996), 605–15.

70. DBWE 6:280.

71. DBWE 16:607.

act of truth-telling.[72] In fact, the only one who lied in this instance is the murderer who inquires about the whereabouts of one's friend, since the murderer acts against reality through their illegitimate question. What is important to recognize in "What Does It Mean to Tell the Truth?" is that Bonhoeffer continues after "God's Love and the Disintegration of the World" to diverge from the language of taking on guilt by affirming the unity of one's action to God's will and reality. As Puffer states: "Speaking falsely to Kant's 'criminal' is understood differently from the previous account in three respects. It is neither a lie, nor guilt-incurring, nor a violation of God's law."[73] And this reflects the differing moral rationales at play in this particular borderline case, evidencing further how Bonhoeffer continued to speak in a different idiom that diverges from the earlier articulations in "History and Good [2]."

In summary, the reading forwarded by Puffer questions the common claim that "History and Good [2]" is paradigmatic and determinative for Bonhoeffer's mature ethics. It instead suggests that Bonhoeffer's articulations in "History and Good [2]" are exploratory and discursive, which permits readings that identify how Bonhoeffer's later articulations shift from what comes before, lending themselves to different narrations of the exception. Furthermore, it brings to the fore the need for discernment in order to know which aspects of Bonhoeffer's theology are to be emphasized and which are to be diminished in a particular reading of the exception in Bonhoeffer's larger theology, since different emphases and rationales emerge between various essays and the larger corpus. This is what Puffer's analysis draws out.

A Hermeneutic for Reading the Exception in Bonhoeffer's Life and Thought

In this final section, I develop the hermeneutic implications that follow from Bonhoeffer's fragmentary life and thought for reading the exception in his texts. This program follows the early judgment of Ernst Feil, who argued that Bonhoeffer's texts have direct hermeneutic implications for reading his theology. It diverges from Feil by emphasizing the hermeneutic implications that follow from Bonhoeffer's testimony to the experience of his life as fragmentary and illusive. It also diverges from Feil in emphasizing the hermeneutic implications that follow from the multiplicity of Bonhoeffer's fragmentary thought rather than its systematicity and coherence. The result is that a differing narration of unity and coherence in Bonhoeffer's life and thought emerges, which accepts their multiplicity and fragmentariness as an advantage in a constructive reading of Bonhoeffer's texts within a discourse on the exception.

---

72. DBWE 16:606–7.
73. Puffer, "Election," 271.

2. Reading Bonhoeffer's Life and Thought

Hermeneutic Implications of Bonhoeffer's Life

One of the more radical implications of Bonhoeffer's narration of the self who eludes self-appropriation is that Bonhoeffer does not encounter an ego who externalizes the self in thought, but an ego that narrates the self as a stranger. This troubles the common claim that Bonhoeffer's thought and action were synchronized and evident to Bonhoeffer himself.[74] The result is that both the testified motivations for a decision, such as the decision to enter the conspiracy, and the professed knowledge of the unity and continuity of one's life are tempered by the instability and hiddenness of the self. It further captures how any given narration of the self is selective and opaque insofar as the communication of oneself varies on account of place, time, and the other to whom one is giving an account of oneself.[75] This explains in part the starkly different self-narrations of Bonhoeffer's life from prison that diverge with regard to its unity, coherence, and meaning. The crucial danger in narrating the continuity and coherence of Bonhoeffer's life is less that it ontologizes the signature, then that it presents Bonhoeffer as one so self-possessed as to make perspicuous to himself and others a narration of the meaning of his life and action. The result is that the conspiracy becomes a culmination to the "inner course"[76] of Bonhoeffer's life, thus diminishing the testimony that bookends the late period of his life (1939–45) to the passivity, fragmentation, and hiddenness of the self that awaits God's eschatological disclosure. Indeed, the emphasis on continuity and coherence tends to give the impression that Bonhoeffer's actions were so self-possessed as to externalize his very self and thought, thus bolstering attempts to articulate the undergirding systematic and coherent thought that spans Bonhoeffer's occasional and often fragmentary writings.

Two options that both emphasize this passivity of the self emerge for reading Bonhoeffer's life at this juncture. The first option is reductively to narrate Bonhoeffer's testimony as determined by historical context. The unity of the life is determined by what happens to him in a given time and place. This option is discarded, since, as I argue in Chapter 5, it reduces Bonhoeffer to a reflexive marionette, excluding Bonhoeffer as an actor altogether and thus diminishing any substantive account of Christian freedom. The second option is to explicate the unity of the self *coram Deo*, thus emphasizing that the self is not an immanently accessible ego but is gifted in every instance. This emphasis appears in Bonhoeffer's poem "Who Am I?" and finds early articulation in *Act and Being* where "all ontological definitions remain bound to the revelation of God," which includes "such 'creaturely' categories as individuality, being in history, in nature, being and becoming," and

---

74. As Marion suggests, "the *cogito* supposed to appropriate me to myself as a *myself*, expels me from myself and defines me by this very exile." Jean-Luc Marion, *In the Self's Place: The Approach of Saint Augustine*, trans. Jeffrey L. Kosky (Stanford: Stanford University Press, 2012), 63.

75. Judith Butler, *Giving an Account of Oneself* (New York: Fordham University Press, 2005).

76. Bethge, "The Challenge of Dietrich Bonhoeffer's Life and Theology," 58.

so on.[77] The primary point in these texts is that the "I" is continuous and unified insofar as it is held in divine activity,[78] and it is disclosed (externalized) to oneself in revelatory encounter with God and neighbor (and even the self as another).[79] The result is that one does not narrate the unity of Bonhoeffer's life through the lens of his self-understanding nor his biography, but as external to the self—an externality epitomized in the textual mediation of Bonhoeffer's life and thought. The hermeneutic result is that the continuity and development of Bonhoeffer's life can no longer be posited as immanently available to Bonhoeffer and others but only grasped in faith through the reading of Bonhoeffer's fragmentary texts. This further entails that the unity of the life is not centered in Bonhoeffer's activity but God's activity to which Bonhoeffer testifies.[80]

Hermeneutic Implications of Bonhoeffer's Thought

The assertion that Bonhoeffer's thought is fragmentary in form and forward multiple rationales on the borderline case is to affirm the unsystematic character of Bonhoeffer's resistance thought. Bonhoeffer did not imagine his thought to form an airtight system, nor does the form of his writings display such systematicity. While this does not foreclose the possibility of a systematic explication of Bonhoeffer's texts, it asserts that such systematicity is developed after the fact, coalescing and framing the disparate writings into a systematic presentation. The denial that Bonhoeffer's thought is systematic does not imply that there are no essential continuities and resonances between the various writings, and it does not deny that Bonhoeffer's disparate texts should be read together as a corpus. It is rather to affirm that these texts belong to a particular discourse initiated by Bonhoeffer, which displays both continuities in idiom and themes as well as noteworthy discontinuities and tensions. The unity of Bonhoeffer's thought, in short, is not in its systematicity and inner-coherence, but in its continuation of a discourse that spans his corpus—a discourse that contemporary interlocutors enter into and around which they frame their interpretive discussions. This discursive quality provides a clue for reading Bonhoeffer's late resistance writings

---

77. DBWE 2:152–3.

78. "To be placed into truth before God means to be dead or to live; neither of these can human beings give themselves. They are conferred on them only by the encounter with Christ in *contritio passiva* and faith" (DBWE 2:141).

79. DBWE 2:135.

80. Hans Ulrich captures this well in his reading of Bonhoeffer's late poem from prison, "Stations on the Way to Freedom" (DBWE 8:512–14). "In Bonhoeffer's case, we are confronted not only with a biographical story but with a life-story, which is the genuine subject of his writing, as it is the case with many biblical texts and authors. What Bonhoeffer articulates in his writings is the life of a human being in patient and attentive expectation of God's action, ready to surrender to God's will and plan—which makes him a disciple." Ulrich, "'Stations on the Way to Freedom,'" in *Who Am I?*, 150–1.

in relation to the exception. The reading generated here makes forthright the need for explicit judgment and discernment in the constructive reading of these texts. There is no illusion that "Bonhoeffer's account of the exception" will emerge through this book, since there is no singular account that needs to be identified nor for which one must argue as native to Bonhoeffer's texts. Rather, this book attends to Bonhoeffer's particular theological emphases and modes of thought by thinking alongside him in the constructive reading of these texts within the discourse on the exception. In this sense, it performs a "Bonhoefferian" reading of the exception that engages critically with the various rationales in his texts, rather than crystallizing "Bonhoeffer's view" on the exception.[81]

This discursive approach to reading the exception recognizes that Bonhoeffer's texts are not identical to the discourses that relate to those texts. The interpretive frameworks associated with the texts are helpful as well as unavoidable, since one cannot excise themselves from the discourses already set in motion. But these discourses do not determine absolutely any given reading of the texts, and the multiplicity of Bonhoeffer's texts remains potent in their ability to disrupt a given discourse, showing a breach in understanding that requires a renewed attentiveness to the texts. The reading of texts within a given discourse can always throw a given narration or synthesis into question, bringing fresh insights to the surface which were otherwise obfuscated in the prevailing modes of discourse. As Bonhoeffer wrote from prison: "In a conversation something new can always happen."[82]

In Chapters 3 and 4, I argue that the theme of history in Bonhoeffer's texts allows one to gain a critical purchase in the discourse on the exception, leading to a differing narration of the exception. Indeed, the theme of history is latent, but underdeveloped, in the prevailing discourse on the exception in Bonhoeffer. For instance, when the theme of the "Bonhoeffer moment" comes under consideration, there is much debate about how to read Bonhoeffer's life, theology, and historical context, but there is little interrogation of what one means when talking about the moment. The assumption is that the moment is the sort of thing that is uncontested, whereas the debate lies in the application of ethical and political concepts. But the character of history and the moment is never straightforward or perspicuous, and sustained reflection on the theme is necessary when speaking of a moment that "demands" the exception.[83] Bonhoeffer understood this himself, reflecting at length on the nature of history in the most famous manuscript associated with the exception: "History and Good [2]." Likewise, Bonhoeffer

---

81. One must admit with de Gruchy that the appellation "Bonhoefferians" is "a tongue twister." De Gruchy, *Bonhoeffer in South Africa*, 33.

82. DBWE 8:453.

83. For a helpful recounting of various approaches to history, see Karl Löwith, *Meaning in History* (Chicago: The University of Chicago Press, 1949). For a more recent account that draws on Löwith's work on this theme, see Louis Dupré, *The Enlightenment and the Intellectual Foundations of Modern Culture* (New Haven: Yale University Press, 2004), 187–228.

reflects at many junctures in his corpus on the relationship between history, the moment, and temporality, connecting them with other crucial theological themes that relate to the exception: the nature and limits of ethics and politics, the doctrine of God, the character of individual action, and so on. By engaging the concept of history as a lens to read the texts most often associated with the exception, I argue that different possibilities emerge for narrating the exception in Bonhoeffer.

Chapter 3

BONHOEFFER ON HISTORY AND THE MOMENT

This chapter attends to Bonhoeffer's early reflections on history and the moment. The purpose of this task is twofold. First, it is to display the centrality of history for Bonhoeffer's thought, identifying how it consistently arises throughout his corpus and articulating how it connects to other crucial doctrines that relate to the exception, such as the doctrines of God, creation, and sin. Second, it is to display how Bonhoeffer's account of history preserves space for a particular moment whereby moral resources are proven inadequate to offer guidance. While such a moment is not identical to what could be called a moment of the exception, it certainly relates to it in important ways, thereby safeguarding the possibility of an exception in history. The concepts developed in this chapter undergird the reading of the exception forwarded in Chapter 4 through Bonhoeffer's *Ethics* manuscript, "History and Good [2]."

In the first section, I engage Bonhoeffer's early articulations on history and the moment of decision in *Sanctorum Communio*, observing how his reflections on the moment have strong Kierkegaardian resonances that echo *Fear and Trembling*. Next, I engage Bonhoeffer's writings from Union Theological Seminary to elicit how divine revelation undoes both history and ethics, requiring re-narration in the light of grace. I then elucidate Bonhoeffer's voluntaristic doctrine of God through *Creation and Fall* in responding to the common criticism that the divine exception is arbitrarily destructive. Bonhoeffer's account, I suggest, maintains the possibility of a divine exception that remains faithful to the promises of God established in creation. In the final section, I perform a reading of Bonhoeffer's 1938, "Bible Study on Temptation," which explicates a moment characterized by the determinations of sin, which disarms the person who undergoes it of all moral and natural resources thereby calling for decision for or against God's Word. By attending to these diverse writings, I argue that Bonhoeffer consistently maintains that there are moments within history whereby the individual is encountered by a demand which relativizes both ethics and fallen creation to offer moral guidance, leaving one utterly dependent on God's Word for which one must decide.

Bonhoeffer's Early Account of History and the Moment

Bonhoeffer first develops many of his most famous theological concepts in *Sanctorum Communio*, such as ecclesiology, vicarious representative action, and responsibility. This is likewise true for Bonhoeffer's articulations on history and the moment, which inflects on a theology of the exception. The theme of history is a crucial but often underappreciated theme in *Sanctorum Communio*. The concept arises at various junctures of Bonhoeffer's dissertation, becoming prominent in his accounts of personhood and community which are at the center of the project. Personhood, community, and history are mutually implicating concepts for Bonhoeffer insofar as personhood and community are determined by their relation to the dialectic of history: "The concepts of person and community, for example, are understood only within an intrinsically broken history, as conveyed in the concepts of primal state, sin, and reconciliation. Neither concept can be understood theologically 'in itself,' but only within a real historical dialectic—not a dialectic of concepts."[1] Both personhood and community are determined by their position in history, revealing that there is no ahistorical conception of either.[2]

Bonhoeffer describes history in two senses in *Sanctorum Communio*. First, he describes history as originating with the fall and subsequently being marked by the determinations of sin.[3] This entails that for Bonhoeffer history is not intrinsically meaningful or perspicuous. History likewise does not have an infinite duration nor does it contain an inherent process that drives it toward its culmination or goal. Bonhoeffer can, therefore, exclaim that history "is incapable of bringing the ultimate solution. It further follows that the meaning of history cannot consist in a progressive development, but that 'every age is in direct relationship with God' (Ranke)."[4] Bonhoeffer thereby positions fallen history as remaining in an irrevocable relation to the suprahistorical events of creation and eschaton. It originates in its severance from the event of creation and will cease with the final event of Christ's eschatological judgment. Second, Bonhoeffer describes history as redeemed in Christ, becoming the time of God's revelatory encounter. The Christ-

---

1. DBWE 1:62.

2. For an argument for this reading, see Michael Mawson, *Christ Existing as Community* (Oxford: Oxford University Press, 2018). How the community relates to history and time distinguishes it from the society and the mass. The community has a purpose that exceeds the bounds of history, whereas society's purpose finds its limit at the end of history. The community is eschatologically oriented, whereas the society is historically oriented (DBWE 1:101). Contrastingly, the mass is constituted only in "the temporally limited, the temporal 'moment,' which draws isolated individuals through a 'mechanical stimulus'" (DBWE 1:95–6).

3. ". . . death as the wages of sin (Rom. 6:23) first constitutes *history*" (DBWE 1:146). Further, history "in the true sense only begins with sin and the fate of death that is linked with it" (DBWE 1:63).

4. DBWE 1:282.

event disrupts the historical process "not empirically, but objectively"[5] reorienting it around Christ, who is "the hidden center of world history"[6] and represents the "whole history of humanity in his historical life."[7] There is a careful distinction between the historicity of revelation and the suprahistorical source of revelation in this assertion. Christ's revelation is actualized in history, since revelation must be historical if it is revelation. Nevertheless, the source of revelation is outside of time, encountering persons from without and overwhelming time by its presence.[8] "Revelation," Bonhoeffer insists, "enters into time not just apparently but actually, and precisely by so doing it bursts the form of time."[9] History is therefore an effect of the fall, but it is also the time of revelation whereby Christ encounters and claims history and persons for himself, reorienting them to and for his presence and purposes.[10]

This dynamic of history and revelation that "bursts the form of time" comes to the fore in Bonhoeffer's discussion of the moment (*Augenblick*). Bonhoeffer describes the moment as a historical encounter with another person, who makes a demand that cannot be bypassed or mitigated through rationalization. It is an irreducible demand that is elicited by the Holy Spirit through another person, and this encounter determines both the historical moment and the encountered-I by demanding decision:

> At the moment of being addressed, the person enters a state of *responsibility* or, in other words, of decision. By person I do not mean at this point the idealists' person of mind or reason, but the person in concrete living individuality. This is not the person internally divided, but the one addressed as a whole person; not one existing in timeless fullness of value and spirit, but in a state of responsibility in the midst of time; not one existing in time's continuous flow, but in the value-related—not value-filled moment. *In the concept of the moment, the concept of time and its value-relatedness (Wertbezogenheit) are co-posited.* The moment is not the shortest span of time, a mechanically conceived atom, as it were. The "moment" is the time of responsibility, value-related time, or, let us say, time related to God; and, most essentially, it is concrete time. Only in concrete time is the real claim of ethics effectual; and only when I am responsible am I fully

---

5. DBWE 1:147.
6. DBWE 1:211.
7. DBWE 1:147. As Bonhoeffer says in a sermon on Rom. 12:11: "The Lord of the ages is God. The turning point of the ages is Christ. The true spirit of the age (*Zeitgeist*) is the Holy Spirit" (DBWE 10:531).
8. Bonhoeffer deepens this point in his seminar paper, "The Church and Eschatology" (DBWE 9:310–24), which was written in preparation for *Sanctorum Communio*. See also DBWE 14:416–18.
9. DBWE 1:143.
10. "Because of the eschatological character of community, which it shares with history, the deepest significance of history is 'from God to God'" (DBWE 1:101).

> conscious of being bound to time. . . . I enter the reality of time by relating my concrete person in time and all its particularities to this imperative—by making myself ethically responsible.[11]

The moment is not determined by what precedes it in the nexus of historical cause and effect but is determined by divine encounter—it is "time related to God." This encounter determines time for the person, since it transforms one's understanding of and relation to time by being confronted by the "absolute demand" of the other.[12] In a real sense, time does not precede encounter but encounter precedes time (or, at least, reflection upon time). Yet the encounter only occurs in the full historicity of the moment and its contingencies; the encounter is not a private phenomenon but occurs in and through the neighbor in one's concrete locale, eliciting the call for responsibility.[13] As Bonhoeffer notes later, the moment of divine encounter does not break the historical process "empirically," only "objectively."[14] But even here, the divine prerogative is primary and determinative of the encounter. What generates the revelatory encounter in the moment is not the neighbor or one's experience of the neighbor but only the divine will that meets the human will through the neighbor.[15]

Bonhoeffer's narration of the moment dispels both the objective and idealist views of history. It dispels the objective view which asserts there is a "singular, real" history that is verifiable through historical investigation of the facts. With the proper methodology, the investigator in this view can ascertain the meaning and character of history. Bonhoeffer's narration of the moment, contrastingly, accounts for the disarming of the self to an encounter that refuses objectification, since the meaning and character of the moment exceeds the limits of historical methodology and refuses reduction to historical facts. In a similar vein, it dispels what Bonhoeffer describes as the idealist view, which relegates the movement of time to the atemporality of the mind's intuition. According to Bonhoeffer, idealism asserts that persons have at their disposal reality epistemologically, possessing the resources necessary to address all ethical demands through a "timeless way of thinking."[16] Bonhoeffer asserts that the idealist view is inadequate because it cannot account for the disruption of the moment and its "absolute demand," which neutralizes all attempts to grasp it and put it under the control of human reflection.

---

11. DBWE 1:48.
12. DBWE 1:49.
13. For a sustained reading of Bonhoeffer's theology of responsibility in this vein, see Esther Reed, *The Limit of Responsibility: Dietrich Bonhoeffer's Ethics for a Globalizing Era* (London: Bloomsbury T&T Clark, 2018).
14. DBWE 1:146.
15. "God or the Holy Spirit joins the concrete You; only through God's active working does the other become a You to me from whom my I arises. In other words, every human You is an image of the divine You" (DBWE 1:54–5).
16. DBWE 1:47.

3. Bonhoeffer on History and the Moment

The critique is that idealism cannot understand the moment's disruptive character, which issues a concrete demand that overwhelms the person, moving them into a new relation to reality and time through decision.[17] Against both the objective and idealist views, Bonhoeffer is ultimately asserting the primacy of an encounter that disrupts one's paradigms and methods for understanding history as well as deliberating on human action, and this necessarily leads to differing narrations of history and ethics.

Kierkegaardian Resonances in der Augenblick

This reading of Bonhoeffer's account of the moment and history certainly adjudges his account as broadly Kierkegaardian, which is not an unfounded claim since Bonhoeffer notes this explicitly.[18] There is a strong Kierkegaardian influence that permeates *Sanctorum Communio* as a whole.[19] The influence of Kierkegaard's *Fear and Trembling* is particularly noticeable in the passage where Bonhoeffer distances the Christian concept of personhood from idealism:

> Idealism has no appreciation of movement (*Bewegnung*). The movement of the dialectic of mind was abstract and metaphysical, while that of ethics is concrete. Further, idealism has no understanding of the moment in which the person feels the threat of absolute demand (*absoluten Forderung*). The idealist ethicist knows what he ought to do, and, what is more, he can always do it precisely because he ought. Where is there room, then, for distress of conscience, for infinite anxiety (*unendliche Angst*) in the face of decisions?[20]

The three terms that echo *Fear and Trembling* most clearly are "movement" (*Bewegnung*), "absolute demand" (*absoluten Forderung*), and "anxiety" (*Angst*), which are all central concepts within Kierkegaard's text.[21]

---

17. Idealism also cannot understand the disruptive origins of time with the introduction of sin (DBWE 1:48).

18. DBWE 1:57. For an account of Kierkegaard's understanding of time, the moment, and history, see Arne Grøn, "Time and History," in *The Oxford Handbook of Kierkegaard*, ed. John Lippitt and George Pattison (Oxford: Oxford University Press, 2013), 273–91.

19. Bonhoeffer is heavily influenced by Kierkegaard in this early period and this extends throughout his corpus, particularly evident in *Discipleship* as well as in early lectures and writings that follow after *Sanctorum Communio*. For more on the influence of Kierkegaard on Bonhoeffer, see Kirkpatrick, *Attacks on Christendom*.

20. DBWE 1:49.

21. Bonhoeffer has the following edition of *Fear and Trembling* listed in the bibliography of *Sanctorum Communio*. "Kierkegaard, S. *Furcht und Zittern* (Gesammelte Werke, hg. V. H. Gottsched und C. Schrempft Bd. 3), Jena ²1909" (DBW 1:301). The translation of *Fear and Trembling* that Bonhoeffer used consistently translates "movement" as *Bewegnung*. The language of *absoluten Forderung* for "absolute duty," admittedly, is lacking from the

In the famous account of the teleological suspension of the ethical, Kierkegaard argued that Abraham's sacrifice of Isaac is only praiseworthy in the particularity of his relationship to God.[22] For if the act is narrated on the basis of the ethical, it can only elicit damnation, since the ethical cannot mediate or express the absolute demand of God. The ethical, which echoes the Hegelian concept of *Sittlichkeit*, is utterly dissimilar to the particularity of the absolute demand, since it is universal in character and thus applies to everyone without exception.[23] For Abraham's action to be praiseworthy, he must stand in an absolute relation to God which places him above the universal and thereby suspends the demand of the ethical.[24] The export of this concept, according to Evans, is that "if there is then to be an absolute duty to God, Johannes believes that the duty must be essentially nonmoral in character; the knight of faith acts in a sphere 'beyond good and evil.'"[25] It cannot be expressed or mediated by the ethical since the demand suspends the ethical. This movement also cannot be mediated through human language or thought "for all mediation occurs precisely by virtue of the universal."[26] The inaccessibility of the absolute demand to language captures how Kierkegaard's understanding of language is intimately tied to the concept of the universal. For Kierkegaard, language is the externalization of the universal, which includes the ethical. Abraham therefore cannot communicate the absolute demand to anyone. He must bear it alone in silence: "Abraham *cannot* speak, for

---

translation, using instead the language of *absolute Pflicht*. "Anxiety" is translated as *Angst*. Kierkegaard does not describe "infinite anxiety" in *Fear and Trembling* which most obviously echoes Søren Kierkegaard, *The Concept of Anxiety: A Simple Psychologically Orienting Deliberation on the Dogmatic Issue of Hereditary Sin*, ed. and trans. Reidar Thomte (Princeton: Princeton University Press, 1980). The concept of the "infinite," though, is prominent in the infinite movement of resignation, which is translated as *unendliche* or *Unendlichkeit*. One might assume that Bonhoeffer draws from *The Concept of Anxiety* rather than *Fear and Trembling* in this passage, since the concept of the moment is most explicitly employed in the latter. Kirkpatrick is right to spot strong similarities between *The Concept of Anxiety* and Bonhoeffer's discussion of movement and the moment in *Sanctorum Communio*, but he does not address why Bonhoeffer left *The Concept of Anxiety* out of the bibliography of *Sanctorum Communio*. See Kirkpatrick, *Attacks on Christendom*, 92–4. It is for this reason that reading this passage in light of *Fear and Trembling* is a safer route.

22. Of course, Johannes de Silentio is the listed author for *Fear and Trembling*, indicating a particular Kierkegaardian form of argumentation.

23. C. Stephen Evans, Introduction to *Fear and Trembling*, trans. Sylvia Walsh (Cambridge: Cambridge University Press, 2011), xix–xxvi.

24. This becomes the topic of the second problem. See Kierkegaard, *Fear and Trembling*, 68–81.

25. C. Stephen Evans, "Is the Concept of an Absolute Duty toward God Morally Unintelligible?" in *Kierkegaard's Fear and Trembling: Critical Appraisal*, ed. Robert L. Perkins (Eugene: Wipf and Stock Publishers, 2009), 142.

26. Kierkegaard, *Fear and Trembling*, 56.

he cannot say that which would explain everything (i.e. so that it is intelligible), that is a trial, of a sort, mind you, in which the ethical is the temptation."[27] The trial of silence elicits "distress and anxiety," revealing that attempts to rationalize the decision to others becomes a temptation rather than an aid.[28] Abraham's only hope is for God's deliverance in the face of infinite anxiety, believing that God will be faithful, even though his act is incomprehensible and damned if judged on the basis of the ethical.

When Bonhoeffer thus speaks of the "absolute demand" that invokes "infinite anxiety" and exceeds one's ability to anticipate and respond to the moment, one can hear resonances of *Fear and Trembling*. While Bonhoeffer's account of the moment does not entail that every moment of decision would invoke infinite anxiety on the basis of the absolute demand, the language that Bonhoeffer employs leaves room for such an absolute demand in the moment. This reading is strengthened when considering Bonhoeffer's understanding of language in *Sanctorum Communio*, which performs a similar function to language in *Fear and Trembling*. Language, for Bonhoeffer, is the exteriorization of objective spirit within a community—it is the objectification of the past in speech that is determinative of social being and exerts pressure on future acts. As Bonhoeffer notes, objective spirit is *"the historical-social turning point between past and future"* as well as *"the connection between historical and communal meaning, between the temporal and spatial intentions of a community. Objective spirit is will exerting itself effectively on the members of the community."*[29] And this spirit, certainly, is reflected in the language of the community: "Thus, with language, a *system of social spirit* has been built into human beings; in other words, '*objective spirit*' has become effective in history."[30] This account of language is utterly finite and cannot comprehend or communicate an absolute demand that is generated in relation to God, since God transcends all the languages formed by human communities.[31] The absolute demand thus isolates the individual in such moments from the objective spirit of the community, entailing that one must decide before God.[32] There are limits to speech and objective spirit that emerge in revelatory moments.

This contention is strengthened when considering that Bonhoeffer describes ethics elsewhere as originating with the fall and the knowledge of good and evil.[33] Ethics is

---

27. Ibid., 115.
28. Ibid., 113.
29. DBWE 1:99. Emphasis original.
30. DBWE 1:70. Emphasis original.
31. When Bonhoeffer explicates the nature of the church's objective spirit, he is sure to distinguish it from the Holy Spirit in the community (DBWE 1:193–9).
32. Within *Sanctorum Communio*, there are moments where one must act alone and cannot rely on the community for overcoming the moment's challenge. Two examples are suffering and death (DBWE 1:181).
33. DBWE 1:108; DBWE 3:87–8.

a reflective discipline that emerges with the incursion of sin; it attempts to categorize particular human actions as good or evil.[34] This postlapsarian form of ethics belongs to the language of Adam. Ethics, in other words, is part of a fallen community's objective spirit, reflected and externalized in ethical discourse. Bonhoeffer reflects this understanding in his 1928–9 lectures, "Basic Questions of a Christian Ethic," where he states: "Ethics is a matter of blood and a matter of history. It did not simply descend to earth from heaven. Rather, it is a child of the earth, and for that reason its face changes with history as well as with a renewal of blood, with the transition between generations."[35] Whereas ethics attempts to anticipate and categorize the good action in advance, the reconciled person "must rather always establish anew [one's] own immediate relationship with God's will."[36] The Christian, Bonhoeffer suggests, does not act on the basis of previously articulated ethics or norms but acts in freedom before God and in response to God's will, which may supersede the language of ethics.[37]

One could challenge this reading of the moment by noting how in *Sanctorum Communio* personhood is ethical, whereas for Kierkegaard the absolute demand suspends the ethical and cannot be described on the basis of ethics. While there is a genuine tension that arises with this observation, the different senses of the ethical within Kierkegaard's texts as well as within Bonhoeffer's own early works alleviate it. Kierkegaard describes the ethical in varying senses throughout his extensive corpus with perhaps the most famous relating to the three "stages" or "spheres" of existence: the aesthetic, the ethical, and the religious.[38] While in *Fear and Trembling*, the ethical is a moral system realized in social life, Kierkegaard also describes the ethical in different terms, such as an orientation to life or as a mode of existence manifest in decision.[39] Bonhoeffer, likewise, employs varying senses of ethics and the ethical. Whereas Bonhoeffer can describe ethics as the fallen attempt to categorize and explicate human action, he describes the ethical in *Sanctorum Communio* as denoting the genuine encounter that constitutes the person in responsive decision. Importantly, Bonhoeffer also understands the ethical person in Kierkegaard in this sense, though critiquing Kierkegaard for

---

34. "Sicut deus—the creator-human-being who lives on the basis of the divide between good and evil" (DBWE 3:113).

35. DBWE 10:360.

36. DBWE 10:365.

37. DBWE 10:367.

38. The differences relate to their pseudonymous authors as well. Judge William, for instance, understands the ethical as a path of life through ethical commitment. See Søren Kierkegaard, *Either/Or II*, ed. and trans. Howard V. Hong and Edna H. Hong (Princeton: Princeton University Press, 1987). For a brief summary of the varying uses of ethical in Kierkegaard, see C. Stephen Evans and Robert C. Roberts, "Ethics," in *The Oxford Handbook on Kierkegaard*, 211–18.

39. Kirkpatrick, *Attacks on Christendom*, 112.

narrating the "ethical decision" of the person as "self-established rather than being established by a You."[40]

When considering the varying senses of ethics and ethical in Kierkegaard, one can read the moment of decision in Bonhoeffer in the following terms: in the moment of encounter, God gives a command that exceeds the historical language of ethics. The demand of the moment cannot be communicable in the language of good and evil, but nevertheless a decision is required from the individual, since this demand is formative for the person's ethical constitution. This encounter isolates the person from the objective spirit of the fallen community, leading the person to decide in ways that may be unprecedented. While not every moment of encounter arises in this manner, nevertheless such a moment could arise, which is analogous to the type of moment that Kierkegaard describes in *Fear and Trembling*. This dynamic continues in Bonhoeffer's thought when he reflects on the transformation of history and human action in light of disruptive divine revelation.

The Undoing of History and Ethics in Revelation

The connection between fallen accounts of history and ethics is that both originate in sin and center on human action and judgment. People create history through their deeds, and people decide upon and are judged for their acts on ethical grounds, and this often leads to history being narrated through a moral lens. In his early academic writings, Bonhoeffer echoes "the theology of crisis" by upsetting this paradigm and declaring it judged by God.[41] The center event of history is the self-revelation of God in Christ within which "all human order and ranking is subverted, for God's new order has been established, which is contrary and beyond all human understanding."[42] As Bonhoeffer suggests in his essay, "Concerning the Christian Concept of God," the event of justification casts all historical events in its light, refusing judgment on moral grounds or explanation within the nexus of historical cause and effect. The event bears its meaning and origins in itself, evoking a new understanding of all other historical events and reality a posteriori. While one can only encounter God in history, this encounter disrupts human interpretive structures for comprehending history, calling principally for decision:

---

40. DBWE 1:57, FN 12. Bonhoeffer's critique of Kierkegaard's self-establishing I may stem from his reading of *Works of Love* and its interpretation of the command to love the neighbor as oneself, since this is the only other work of Kierkegaard listed in the bibliography of *Sanctorum Communio*. Søren Kierkegaard, *Works of Love*, ed. and trans. Howard V. Hong and Edna H. Hong (Princeton: Princeton University Press, 1995). For a reading *Works of Love* in a register closer to Bonhoeffer, see Koert Verhagen, "God, the Middle Term: Bonhoeffer, Kierkegaard, and Christ's Mediation in *Works of Love*," *Religions* 11, no. 78 (2020), https://doi.org/10.3390/rel11020078.
41. DBWE 10:462–76.
42. DBWE 10:464.

"The true attitude of man toward history is not interpretive, but that of refusing or acknowledging, that is to say, deciding. Decision in its most inward sense is possible only as a decision for or against God."[43]

These claims are simply indicative of the nature of God's revelation in history. It is a divine decision that transcends models of intelligibility, enacting a new reality hidden from the wisdom of the world.[44] The hiddenness of revelation affirms the indirect character of divine action that eludes human evaluation but nevertheless reconstitutes reality, including history and ethics: "justification is pure self-revelation, pure way of God to man. No religion, no ethics, no metaphysical knowledge may serve man to approach God. They are all under the judgment of God. They are works of man."[45] The implications for accounts of ethics are notable. Just as history is determined by divine action rather than human action, so, too, is human action determined by divine action and grace, and this contextualizes all ethical judgments of human action and history. As Bonhoeffer argues in his essay, "The Religious Experience of Grace," the absoluteness of grace undermines all human action and ethical thought before God. "Grace destroys all these attempts, destroys religion and ethics and experiences of grace and it declares the man in all his ways as a sinner, who offends the sole glory of God. Grace is the absolute opposite to all human endeavor, otherwise it would not be entirely grace."[46] While Bonhoeffer does not condemn ethical thought wholesale in the essay—he maintains that grace becomes the only "genuine foundation" for ethical life—it raises questions about how to narrate human action in light of God's superabundant activity. Grace threatens to immobilize human action, rendering ethical thought redundant.

Bonhoeffer reflects on this charge in his paper, "The Character and Ethical Consequences of Religious Determinism." The paper addresses the concern raised by "Erasmus, the later Scotists, and all liberal theology" that the concept of determinism threatens free action and ethics.[47] While Bonhoeffer affirms that certain accounts of determinism threaten free action, Bonhoeffer argues that "Christian determinism" avoids this conclusion. This is because Christian determinism begins with God's justifying act that liberates human action. It begins with a divine pronouncement that reveals and reconciles simultaneously: "This is God's free and sole act; human beings remain completely in God's omnipotence."[48] Such a reading, Bonhoeffer recognizes, is consistent with Luther's *The Bondage of the Will*, and thus narrates all free action within God's overarching and

---

43. DBWE 10:457. On this point in twentieth-century theology and philosophy, see Judith Wolfe, "The Eschatological Turn in German Philosophy," *Modern Theology* 35, no. 1 (2019): 55–70.

44. DBWE 10:457; DBWE 12:325–6.

45. DBWE 10:461.

46. DBWE 10:449.

47. DBWE 10:441.

48. DBWE 10:443.

3. Bonhoeffer on History and the Moment

determinative activity. The "ethical consequences" of this account are twofold. First, it does not demolish or equivocate good and evil, but it defines both in direct relation to God—good and evil are only revealed in divine decision and revelation; they are not mediating realities in creation. Second, the good act is only the act that participates indirectly in God's good activity, since finite human activity is always visibly mired in sin and impotent:

> Good is good before God. Human beings know they are incapable of accomplishing this good. They recognize their own sin and struggle against it, yet it is as if they were in a moving train running in the opposite direction from the train itself. Yet precisely by recognizing their own lack of freedom before God and their exclusive determination by God, they begin to perceive God's sole power; their faith in this determinism through God, rather than becoming a means of interpreting the world, reveals itself as power within them. This recognition of faith, recognition bestowed by God, is creative power that makes human beings free—free from the world and for God. Where human beings see they are weak, God is strong, bringing about the good, but God alone does this.[49]

While Bonhoeffer is cognizant that questions remain about the "speculative" question of divine determination of evil as well as the question of what civic righteousness entails, he affirms the primacy of the justifying event that frames divine judgment (ethics) and divine guidance (history).[50]

What is striking is how Bonhoeffer revisits these themes ten years later, speaking in the same idiom on the relationship between good human action and God's action in history. Bonhoeffer affirms that good action is only God's action and that human historical action is only deemed good indirectly. In the 1942 manuscript, "History and Good [1]," Bonhoeffer again suggests that the good action of history is solely God's justifying action and that the freest human action is passivity: "What is good is God's action alone; human historical action is good only insofar as God draws it into God's own action and as the human agent completely surrenders all to God's action without claiming any other justification."[51] No one can claim to participate directly in God's history forming activity "which cuts across human good and evil."[52] Even Judas' betrayal, Bonhoeffer continues, participates in God's good. This does not negate "the distinction between good and evil" as much as it entails that these are only divine judgments that affirm how "human beings" depend "on God's grace."[53] Bonhoeffer continues that God's action does not diminish human historical action as much as it affirms that the good act is only a surrendering of one's action to God as revealed in the Christ-event, the

---

49. DBWE 10:444.
50. DBWE 10:444.
51. DBWE 6:227.
52. DBWE 6:227
53. DBWE 6:227

center of history. The result is that the Christ-event reorients one's account of history and human historical action around divine action, and this, further, shifts all ethical thought as proceeding from God's sole justifying act that undoes any noncompetitive account of the relationship between the human and divine will.

The emphases on the disjunction between divine action and human action as well as the rupture between revelation and the structures of this world contribute to a suspicion that the moment is utterly destructive. The sheer negating power of God's revelation in history threatens the destruction of creation and meaningful human action. It is thus necessary to reflect on these dangers in a sustained manner. The next section performs this task by reflecting on Bonhoeffer's voluntaristic doctrine of God.

Divine Voluntarism and Creation in the Exception

Whatever promise the exception may hold, one nevertheless loses the world in the process. This is a common critique of the exception, centering on the nature of divine action in history and how it impinges upon every dimension of reality. According to critics, any divine incursion that supersedes the laws of reason or nature could also unravel them, destroying the conditions for meaningful and intelligible human life and action.[54] In this frame, divine action becomes arbitrary, displaying that God can act not only for the world in freedom but against it by disregarding the orders of creation. God can unravel what was established in creation through divine decision.

There is a wariness about a voluntarist doctrine of God in this criticism, since the emphasis on God's will over God's rationality generates a gap between the Creator and creation. In a doctrine of God that prioritizes divine rationality, the intrinsic intelligibility of creation is preserved in that creation reflects the source of its existence. The effect (creation) reflects something about its cause (the Creator), and this testifies that God's action works in accordance with the creation order established in the beginning. With voluntarism, which is often subsumed under nominalism, the link that secured the intelligibility of creation to its Creator is severed, and thus meaning is no longer embedded within creation.[55] Louis Dupré

---

54. Oliver O'Donovan offers a paradigmatic account of this criticism. O'Donovan, *Finding & Seeking*, 220–30. Within *Sanctorum Communio*, Bonhoeffer appears to affirm this conclusion in relation to human identity. In contrasting the Christian view to the idealist view of time, Bonhoeffer asserts that what follows from it is that "the person is re-created again and again in the perpetual flux of life" through the encounter that elicits "ethical responsibility" (DBWE 1:48).

55. Nominalism, as related by William Courtenay, is frequently narrated as being defined by five elements: "(1) atomism, particularism, or individualism; (2) excessive stress on the omnipotence of God; (3) voluntarism; (4) skepticism; and (5) fideism." William Courtenay, "Nominalism and Late Medieval Religion," in *The Pursuit of Holiness in Late*

narrates this gap in voluntarism between creation and Creator as the place where exceptions become expected and even normal occurrences in history. For the inscrutable will of God entails the ever-present possibility of God suspending and even acting against the invariable laws of nature established in creation.[56] Such "contemporary" exceptions reflect the very origins of creation insofar as the act of creation is inexplicable on the basis of law.[57] This fear extends to a political idiom when the sovereign represents God and the juristic order represents creation.[58] If God can act beyond law even to the point of destroying creation, then the sovereign can act beyond all law to the point of dismantling the juristic order. This connection contributes to O'Donovan's description of voluntarism as reflecting the spirit of the antichrist.[59]

The question is whether Bonhoeffer actually affirms such a destructive voluntarism. In *Sanctorum Communio*, Bonhoeffer explicitly espouses a voluntarist doctrine of God, though in passing with little description.[60] It is not until *Creation and Fall* that Bonhoeffer gives sustained attention to God's *voluntas* in creation. In these lectures on Genesis, Bonhoeffer describes God's activity in a voluntarist manner, delineating the character of God's action in relation to the world, which leaves open the possibility of divine exceptions.

Bonhoeffer describes creation as absolutely contingent in *Creation and Fall* with God's freedom standing at the origin of creation, remaining inscrutable and beyond any necessity or compulsion. This entails that creation does not have an intrinsic intelligibility within it that reflects the rationality of God: "creation is not

---

Medieval and Renaissance Religion, ed. Charles Trinkaus and Heiko A. Oberman (Leiden: Brill, 1974), 43. Bonhoeffer describes nominalism as rooted in Anglo-Saxon rather than German-Continental thinking in DBWE 15:443.

56. Dupré, *The Enlightenment*, 18–19.

57. Kahn, *Political Theology*, 31–61.

58. The connection strengthens given Duns Scotus' employment of the juridical analogy in developing his account of *potentia absoluta* and *potentia ordinata* in *Ordinatio* I, dist. 44. John Duns Scotus, *Duns Scotus on the Will and Morality*, ed. William A. Frank, trans. Alan B. Wolter, O.F.M. (Washington, DC: Catholic University of America Press, 1997), 191–4.

59. Oliver O'Donovan, *The Desire of the Nations* (Cambridge: Cambridge University Press, 1996), 273–84.

60. Bonhoeffer criticizes idealism for lacking a "voluntaristic doctrine of God" (DBWE 1:48) and he rejects an Aristotelian concept of God that is "intellectualist-monotheistic," lacking any substantive voluntarism within it (DBWE 1:35). In Bonhoeffer's seminar paper, "The Holy Spirit According to Luther," Bonhoeffer refers to the "voluntary form of the concept of the Spirit" as well as Luther's "voluntaristic concept of God's will" (DBWE 9:344). Bonhoeffer certainly learned of Luther's voluntarism through Karl Holl, who led this seminar. As a doctoral student of Reinhold Seeberg, Bonhoeffer would likewise reflect on voluntarism at length. Bonhoeffer later reflects on Seeberg's voluntarism in *Act and Being* (DBWE 2:55–6, 101–2). In *Ethics*, Bonhoeffer rejects ethical voluntarism outright as an abdication of reality (DBWE 6:184).

an 'effect' of the Creator from which one could read off a necessary connection with the cause (the Creator); instead it is a work created in freedom in the word."[61] Even the regularities of creation—such as mathematics or the invariable laws of nature—are contingent, emerging only with creation. These are "nothing other than the command of the word of God itself."[62] If God willed, these, too, would fall into oblivion like the rest of creation.[63] Bonhoeffer further emphasizes the creatureliness of these regularities in how they are affected by sin; they are estranged from their Creator and thus tempt humanity to trust in them rather than the Word that upholds them.[64] These achieve a certain independence that marks an asymmetry between God's command that preserves their being and their continuing opposition to God in sin. There is nothing in creation that is identical to God's Word and will outright: "For this reason we no longer see the Creator in the world of what is fixed, but instead we believe in the Creator. We see law, numbers, but in their godlessness, and we believe in God beyond this created world."[65] In this passage, the gap between creation and Creator is maintained by Bonhoeffer, which leaves open the potential for a divine incursion which disrupts and undoes the invariable laws of creation.

Nevertheless, Bonhoeffer also speaks of God's fidelity to creation in *Creation and Fall*, which diminishes the destructive qualities of God's action in the world. This emerges in his rejection of *creatio continua* because it fails to regard the "unique" and once-for-all character of God's original creation, which God preserves and directs to God's good purposes.[66] There is a fidelity to what God has decided once-for-all in the beginning, and this is reflected in how "creation and preservation are two sides of the same activity of God."[67] Bonhoeffer argues that God's will affirms that God not only preserves the world from "complete destruction" (*Vernichtung*) but also directs the fallen world to God's purposes. The lecture notes of Erich

---

61. DBWE 3:43.
62. DBWE 3:51.
63. DBWE 3:58.

64. When Bonhoeffer speaks of the Word of God, it has a specifically Lutheran understanding. The Word of God is the creative, providential, and revelatory activity of God in the world. Human life is likewise a product of God's Word, and God's sustaining and forming activity is performed through the Word in history. The Word is spoken in Christ by the Spirit throughout the world but paradigmatically heard as law and Gospel in political life. On this view in Luther, see Robert Kolb, *Martin Luther and the Enduring Word of God: The Wittenberg School and its Scripture-Centered Proclamation* (Grand Rapids: Baker Academic, 2016), 35–74.

65. DBWE 3:54.

66. Within common narrations of medieval nominalist theology, Bonhoeffer thus reflects a reading of *potentia ordinata* instead of *potentia absoluta*. For a summary of this debate, see Francis Oakley, "Voluntarist Theology and Early-Modern Science: The Matter of the Divine Power, Absolute and Ordained," *History of Science* 56, no. 1 (2018): 72–96.

67. DBWE 3:45.

Klapproth thus record Bonhoeffer saying: "The world is upheld not as inherently valuable but as something that has been given direction and receives its value only from being directed in this way."[68] God thus upholds creation because of God's fidelity to creation and God's redemptive work therein, and this remains true after the fall as well. One could say that for Bonhoeffer, God remains faithful not so much to a divine order instituted in the invariable laws of creation but to the divine promise which culminates in God's redemptive work in Christ for the sake of the world.

Bonhoeffer makes an important distinction at the end of this discussion of *creatio continua*, which clarifies the freedom of God's activity in the world for exceptions. Bonhoeffer argues that "upholding the original creation and upholding the fallen creation are different things."[69] While upholding original creation affirms the being of creation before the incursion of sin, upholding fallen creation preserves the world for God's redemptive purposes and activities therein. The latter is epitomized in Bonhoeffer's notion of "orders of preservation."[70] It is within and for the upholding of fallen creation that exceptions occur. If God acts in a "miraculous" manner that suspends or disrupts the invariable laws of fallen creation, it is not in order to destroy them and start anew, but, rather, to reaffirm and uphold them for divine service—it is to liberate these entities from the determinations of sin that close them off from God's coming redemption. Such renewal is entirely possible precisely because even the regularities of creation, as Bonhoeffer observes, can turn against their Creator; God's miraculous incursion can thus be a form of revealing their dependence on God's Word, putting them back into a proper relationship to their Creator. The exception demolishes any illusions of the sufficiency of any aspect of creation and thus continues God's upholding activity.[71]

This is true for God's disruptive encounter in the moment of decision when God sets the individual apart from all that she knows, but only in order to set the individual back into a proper relation to the world she inhabited before. Bonhoeffer narrates this in his reading of the *Akedah* in *Discipleship*, which importantly echoes Kierkegaard's reading in *Fear and Trembling*, since what God destroys is any illusion of immediacy of Abraham to Isaac, his riches, or any aspect of the world. God makes Abraham a single individual only for a moment, subsequently setting Abraham back into the world but now through Christ. In Bonhoeffer's words:

> Abraham remains completely alone. He is again completely the single individual. . . . He receives the call as it is given. He does not try to interpret it, nor does he spiritualize it. He takes God at God's word and is prepared to obey. Against every natural immediacy, against every ethical immediacy, against every

---

68. DBWE 3:47, FN, 13.
69. DBWE 3:46.
70. See DBWE 11:267–8.
71. DBWE 3:53–4.

religious immediacy, he obeys God's word. He brings his son to be sacrificed. He is prepared to make the secret break visible, for the sake of the mediator. At the same time, everything that he had given up is restored to him . . . Abraham received Isaac back, but he has him in a different way than before. He has him through the mediator and for the sake of the mediator . . . Abraham comes down from the mountain with Isaac, just as he went up, but everything has changed. Christ came between the father and the son. Abraham had left everything and had followed Christ and while he was following Christ, he was permitted to go back to live in the same world he had lived in before.[72]

The moment is never disruptive arbitrarily, but it is for the sake of the regular, remaining true to what God purposes from the beginning. It is for the sake of Abraham's life in relation to God and the world.

Through this narration of God's once-for-all action in creation, it emerges more clearly how Bonhoeffer's account of divine voluntarism can avoid the dangers of the destructive exception. A further strength of Bonhoeffer's account is that it affirms God's fidelity to creation while also recognizing how the determinations of sin distort and fragment reality, allowing for a narration of the moment that attends to both the free and faithful activity of God for creation as well as the powers and principalities that act against God's creation and reconciling activity. Bonhoeffer performs a narration of a concrete historical moment that manifests this dynamic in his "Bible Study on Temptation."

The Moment of Temptation

Dietrich Bonhoeffer wrote his "Bible Study on Temptation" during what Bethge calls "the darkest moment of the Church Struggle."[73] Paradigmatic of this dark moment were the calls by Dr. Werner for all pastors in Pomerania to give an oath to Hitler.[74] Ministers in the Confessing Church had to decide whether to give the oath or to refuse and subsequently lose their ministries and livelihoods. Bonhoeffer meditates at length on the theme of temptation in the face of these events; the theme is found frequently in his circular letters to the Finkenwalde brothers where he links the current struggles to concrete temptation,[75] and it is likewise found in

---

72. DBWE 4:97.
73. DB-ER, 501.
74. DB-ER, 503–8.
75. In the circular letter from January 1938, Bonhoeffer wrote: "In recent weeks, I have received letters and personal messages that make it clear that our church and our young theologians, particularly in Pomerania, are encountering an hour of severe temptation" (DBWE 15:29). And in a letter from August 23, 1938, Bonhoeffer further writes on the theme of temptation, enclosing at the end of the letter a segment from August Friedrich Christian Vilmar on a Christian account of oath-taking (DBWE 15:60–3).

sermons and public devotions from the season.[76] The most concentrated reflection on temptation is the "Bible Study on Temptation" delivered in June 1938 at a retreat in Zingst.[77]

Bonhoeffer describes temptation in terms analogous to the moment in *Sanctorum Communio*. Temptation arises not in the cause and effect of natural history but emerges unexpectedly, surprising the Christian with its demands. It occurs within history but is not the product of history: "Temptation is a concrete event, a sudden deviation from the normal course of life" (388). The difference from the moment of decision is its dark and isolating character; it is not an encounter with the neighbor but an ambush of the isolated Christian by the devil who sows doubt in the heart, brings an overwhelming weariness to life, and tempts the Christian to waver and sin. The Christian is unexpectedly left alone and disoriented like Abraham on Mt. Moriah. The temptation saps the Christian of all strength, revealing their utter ineptitude to respond adequately to the moment. This is because temptation quickens lust, which inflames all human strengths for evil: "Indeed, truly all my strengths, even my good and pious strengths have fallen into the hands of the enemy power and are now enlisted in the fight against me" (387). And this, for Bonhoeffer, reveals that "the powers of the body, of thinking, and of willing—which were once kept in obedience under the discipline of the word which I believed I had control—make it clear to me that I in no way had power over them" (404). The Christian is confronted and defenseless, revealed to be weak and insufficient before an imposing accuser, and yet still having to respond.

The combination of the indeterminacy of the moment and the insufficiency of persons to respond leads Bonhoeffer to posit that temptation is not an ethical struggle, since this would assume that the human can overcome the challenge through their own insight and virtue. Temptation in an ethical register would be the testing of human strength, whereas Bonhoeffer emphasizes how the moment completely disarms the Christian. If Christians have the ability to overcome the tempter by their abilities, then there is no reason for Christians to pray: "lead us not into temptation." Temptation would rather be a welcomed incursion for the ethical person, creating heroes in the process of the "challenge," thus negating temptation's ability to vanquish the person absolutely (388).

Moreover, Bonhoeffer emphasizes that the moment of temptation is incomprehensible to ethical thought, since it supersedes the postlapsarian division of good and evil (387). Temptation occurs beyond good and evil in accordance

---

76. In a confirmation sermon given on Mark 9:24 delivered on April 9, 1938, for instance, Bonhoeffer speaks at length on how the confirmands as Christians will "be led into difficult temptations" as Christ was tempted "more than all" (DBWE 15:479). These temptations elicit "fear and trembling" and is overcome through the faith of the Christian that clings to God (DBWE 15:480).

77. DBWE 15:386–415. In this section, all references to Bonhoeffer's "Bible Study on Temptation" are inline.

with the primordial temptation of Adam that precedes such divisions: it is the temptation to forsake God's Word and to live on another basis, trusting in one's own insights or strengths.[78] When Adam is tempted, he could either cling to God's Word or enter into the pious questioning of God's Word wherein he gives himself over to other logics and modes of discourse that depersonalize God, establishing oneself as an arbiter of truth and source of life. This is why one's strengths, insights, and possibilities are insufficient to overcome temptation, since any engagement with the tempter through one's abilities is already an attempt to overcome the tempter on a basis other than the Word of God. To engage in ethical discourse is implicitly to agree with the tempter that there is some other origin behind God's Word whereby one can engage and overcome the temptation (391).[79] Ethical discourse eschews the demands of the moment.

There is a certain counterintuitiveness to Bonhoeffer's account of temptation given that the experience of temptation is common to all, but rarely do persons consider it a cosmic disruption of history that plunders their strengths. Further, when considering Bonhoeffer's biographical context, an inconsistency emerges between how Bonhoeffer describes temptation and the specific character of the imposing oath to Hitler. It seems patently obvious that one can reason about how to respond to this oath, and Bonhoeffer, in fact, reasons about this through his circular letters.[80] Bonhoeffer's account of temptation, however, is derived less from experience or biography as it is a theological narration drawn from the well-springs of Scripture.[81] The biographical situation is the context of Bonhoeffer's reflections, but it does not determine his reflections. Put differently, Bonhoeffer's account of temptation cannot be comprehended from "below," that is, from historical or biographical context (important as that is), but rather it can only be understood from above, from the unique vantage point gifted in Christ. Bonhoeffer thus reasons that one only understands the character of temptation through the two biblical accounts of temptation: the temptation of the first Adam in the Garden and the temptation of the Second Adam in the wilderness. The latter account makes the former account intelligible: "we can understand what temptation means for us only in the temptation of Jesus" (390).

When Bonhoeffer considers temptation from the "perspective of the living God" (388), there are two angles to this perspective that are integral to his account. First, there is the perspective of the God who stands over and above history as its providential author. God appoints all times and seasons, including the hour of

---

78. Bonhoeffer is notably influenced by Nietzsche by asserting the finitude of morality. See Friedrich Nietzsche, *Beyond Good and Evil*, ed. Rolf-Peter Horstmann, trans. Judith Norman (Cambridge: Cambridge University Press, 2012).

79. See also DBWE 3:106–10.

80. DBWE 15:90–3.

81. In agreement with this reading is Philip G. Ziegler, "'Tempted for Our Sake'—Bonhoeffer on Christ's Temptation," in *Polyphonie der Theologie: Verantwortung und Widerstand in Kirche und Politik*, ed. Matthias Grebe (Stuttgart: Kohlhammer, 2019), 259–60.

temptation, with the Christian continually living from and in response to God's "appointed times and not from his own notion of life" (388–9). To respond to temptation is to recognize such a moment as proceeding from a divine movement of permission and purpose. Temptation is, therefore, a unique moment arising within the divine outworking of grace in history. It is, after all, the Spirit who drives Jesus into the wilderness (392). While God is an author of temptation, Bonhoeffer also insists that God is not the only author. If God is the origin of temptation, Bonhoeffer reasons, then the will of God is set against the believer and God's Word is internally divided. Bonhoeffer thus argues that temptation has two other authors: the devil and human desire. The former is the objective author of temptation, who acts in opposition to God's will in tempting the Christian to forsake God. The latter is the subjective author of temptation, arising from one's sinful desire.[82] Nevertheless, the confession that God is the author of temptation accentuates how temptation ultimately serves God's purposes over against all that stands opposed to God. Temptation is a revelatory and reconciling event in spite of its dark and destructive character. When the devil rages against the Christian, God turns what was meant for evil to good; and when the devil torments the believer through their lustful desire and suffering, God reveals that "the tempted person is held only by God's grace, which is no longer felt and experienced, but is nonetheless firm" (401). In the moment of temptation, one encounters the grace of God against all appearances.[83]

Second, there is the perspective of Jesus Christ, who suffers temptation alone in the weakness of the flesh. For Bonhoeffer, the temptation of Jesus is not only the paradigmatic account of all temptations but is likewise the representative temptation for all. All present and future temptations are only temptations in Christ and are only understood and overcome in Christ (396). When Bonhoeffer looks at Christ in his temptation, he does not see Christ warding off Satan by his inner strength or through ethical discourse; rather, he sees Christ alone in the wilderness in weakness and defenselessness. Yet Bonhoeffer also sees Christ clinging to the Word, which likewise delivers Christ in the dark hour (395). Bonhoeffer posits that if the Word is the sole deliverer and aid for Christ, it can be no different for Christians. By clinging to the Word in Christ, one overcomes temptation and thereby receives the kingdom and God's victory (415). The end of temptation is the renewal of one's life on earth and the conferral of the kingdom in

---

82. "While the objectivity of the temptation becomes evident in its origin in the devil, here we are stressing the full subjectivity of temptation" (DBWE 15:399).

83. It is the recognition of the devil and God's activity that requires the Christian to distinguish between the authorship of God and the devil in temptation, between responding in submission or resistance: "The *concrete temptation of the Christian* always requires making the distinction between the hand of the devil and the hand of God. In other words, it is a matter of *resistance* (*Widerstand*) and of *submission* (*Unterwerfung*) at the right moment; resistance to the devil is possible precisely in complete submission under God's hand" (402). This formulation echoes Bonhoeffer's famous letter in *Letters and Papers from Prison*, which speaks of *Widerstand und Ergebung* (DBWE 8:565).

and through Christ. The separation from the world through sinful desire and the devil is overcome in Christ by clinging to the Word, revealing that Christ alone is the mediator of reality.

The benefit of Bonhoeffer's account of temptation is threefold. First, Bonhoeffer's narration of temptation highlights how the individual undergoing temptation is isolated and defenseless, unable to respond through ethical discourse or human cunning. The limits of ethics and the sufficiency of God's Word are revealed in the moment of temptation through how the Christian can only be upheld and delivered by God's intervening Word. The temptation echoes Kierkegaard's *Fear and Trembling* in this emphasis but stands apart by its singular emphasis on the determinations of sin that separate rather than a teleological suspension of the ethical. Second, Bonhoeffer's narration of temptation reflects how God's providential activity is nevertheless within fallen history, which means that Christians are not only encountered by God through the neighbor but also through the disarmed rulers of this age: sin, death, and the devil. Temptation becomes a paradigmatic example of how the present is not defined by its relation to past and future; it is, rather, defined by God's schedule even in the darkest of moments. Third, the moment of temptation becomes an example of a moment that distances a person from the world (with its ethical and rational resources) without becoming an abdicating of responsibility; it is a surrender of oneself to God, who alone is able to set the individual back into the world which has been re-oriented to God's purposes and presence. The "irrational" activity of the Christian in temptation is nothing short of a simple clinging to God who alone can deliver and redeem the world and the Christian. While the moment of temptation is not equivalent to the moment of exception, explicating Bonhoeffer's reflections on temptation is helpful in demonstrating how his reflections on fallen history and the moment were not an idiosyncratic feature of his early theology but has a continuing role in his Finkenwalde writings and, as I argue in Chapter 4, in his later reflections in "History and Good [2]."

Coda: The Relation of History to Political Orders in Bonhoeffer

The present discussion on history and the moment has focused primarily on its relation to ethics. The danger in this emphasis is that it subdues the political dimensions of Bonhoeffer's reflections on history and the moment which figure more prominently in the following chapters. The purpose of this coda is to survey the relation between history and politics for Bonhoeffer, particularly in his developing account of the orders of creation, orders of preservation, and the mandates.

Bonhoeffer's reflections on the character and interrelationship of political orders develop throughout his corpus. While there is a noted consistency that extends across the various writings, there is also a recognized transformation of his political thought, culminating in his ever-developing account of the mandates. Akin to his description of personhood and community in *Sanctorum Communio*, Bonhoeffer's developing reflections on political orders are determined by which events he emphasizes in the dialectic of history. Broadly construed, Bonhoeffer begins by emphasizing creation in his early theology, shifts to emphasize the effects of the fall and Christ's coming reconciliation in the middle period, and ends with an emphasis on the reconciling presence and eschatological origin of the mandates.

Bonhoeffer's earliest theology is the most optimistic about the ability of Christians to discern the orders of creation. In a student paper for Seeberg, Bonhoeffer argues that "[the church] will know how to differentiate between creation and human disorder."[84] The belief that one can identify and respond according to the orders of creation in distinction from the distortions of sin contributes to Bonhoeffer's early political vision insofar as the division of peoples [*Volk*] is grounded in creation. This aspect most closely resembles the *völkisch* theology of Paul Althaus, since the division of peoples justifies the defense of one's homeland in war.[85] In his lecture, "Basic Questions of a Christian Ethic," Bonhoeffer describes how the "divine orders" compel Christians to defend one's people [*Volk*] from the enemy, since the divine orders include the separation of peoples and the imperative to prioritize and defend one's own in the event of war.[86] The articulation of divine orders weighted toward creation, then, contributes to an account of warfare that prioritizes national self-defense and self-interest as rights grounded in creation.

In the following years, Bonhoeffer drops the concept in preference of orders of preservation, arguing that the orders of preservation avoid this nationalist conclusion, since the separation of and conflicts between nations derive from the fall and not from creation.[87] Indeed, the shift to orders of preservation specifies the lack of direct access to the orders of creation through the incursion of sin in history. There is no direct identification between historical orders and the orders of creation since the former "do not possess ontological validity in an absolute sense but are only preserved by God for the sake of their openness to the gospel, for the hope of new creation."[88] All worldly orders, then, are orders of preservation that remain valid only in remaining open and oriented to God's reconciling work in history. When the orders close themselves off to Christian proclamation, they "can" and "must be" broken.[89] In the orders of preservation, Bonhoeffer now emphasizes the irrevocable

---

84. DBWE 9:321.

85. Matthew Puffer, "Creation," in *Oxford Handbook on Dietrich Bonhoeffer*, ed. Michael Mawson and Philip G. Ziegler (Oxford: Oxford University Press, 2019), 193–4. This discussion on Bonhoeffer's account of the orders of creation, orders of preservation, and the mandates is informed by Puffer.

86. DBWE 10:370–1.

87. DBWE 11:267–8, 351–2; DBWE 12:387–91.

88. DBWE 11:267–8. In narrating the Two Kingdoms in 1933, Bonhoeffer thus argues that their origin is the Christ-event in history (DBWE 12:325–6) and their terminus is at the eschaton when they are transformed and sublated in the singular reign of Christ in the Kingdom of God (DBWE 12:296).

89. DBWE 11:364.

distortions of sin and the orientation of the orders to reconciliation rather than the discernment of creation. One of the under-observed emphases for Bonhoeffer's political theology that emerges in this account is an exaggerated emphasis on the government's task of preserving law and order in the formation of political life. The emphasis on preserving the openness of political life for divine activity in the proclamation of the Gospel entails a primary emphasis on the exercise of the sword in restraining the power of evil and protecting the task of the church in its midst.

With the turn to the language of mandates in his late theology, Bonhoeffer drops the language of "orders" due to their potential for misunderstanding.[90] What continues in Bonhoeffer's account is the primacy of the dialectic of history in narrating political life. While Bonhoeffer shifts from the language of orders to mandates, his initial attempts at developing the concept revolve prominently around creation and preservation. In "State and Church" and "Christ, Reality, and the Good," for instance, Bonhoeffer indexes the mandates primarily to creation.[91] Even the preservative function of government is indexed to creation insofar as Christ exercises his authority through government as a mediator of creation.[92] Only the mandate of the church originates explicitly in reconciliation, proclaiming the reality of Christ that reveals and sanctifies the other mandates. A year later in "'Personal' and 'Objective' Ethics," Bonhoeffer indexes all of the mandates principally to the eschaton, finding each mandate's "prototype in the heavenly world."[93] Marriage reflects Christ and the church community, family reflects the relation of Father to Son and Christ as brother to human beings, work reflects the service of God to the world and humans to God, and government reflects Christ's eternal dominion in the city of God. Bonhoeffer intensifies this claim in the *Ethics* manuscript, "The Concrete Commandment and the Divine Mandates," arguing that the mandates are "implanted in the world from above" and are "in no way an outgrowth of history."[94] In "The 'Christian' and the 'Ethical' as a Topic," Bonhoeffer specifies in a similar idiom that God's commandment (which encompasses and comes through the mandates) "does not arise out of the created world, but rather comes from above to below."[95] In these later writings, Bonhoeffer grounds the mandates more explicitly in revelation that enters history from the end of history. While the God of the eschaton is the self-same God of creation, preservation, and reconciliation, the emphasis on their eschatological character maintains their openness to transformation and disruption within the economy of grace. As argued in Chapter 6, one of the implications for Bonhoeffer's political theology is a shift of emphasis from the government's preservation of law and order through violence to the miraculous renewal of politics in a divine *adventus*. The limits of political technique and violence emerge in this eschatological frame.

90. DBWE 6:389.
91. DBWE 16:511, 518–19; DBWE 6:70–1.
92. DBWE 16:511; DBWE 6:72.
93. DBWE 16:550.
94. DBWE 6:390.
95. DBWE 6:380.

Chapter 4

READING THE EXCEPTION IN "HISTORY AND GOOD [2]"

Readings of Bonhoeffer's resistance rationale almost always center on his unfinished manuscript "History and Good [2]." Even when commentators avoid direct reference to the manuscript, they often employ its unique vocabulary to summarize Bonhoeffer's resistance activity and thought. The reason this manuscript is central in narrations is unsurprising. Biographically, Bonhoeffer appears to articulate a rationale for participating in the conspiracy plot. While Bonhoeffer was never able to write directly on the topic in case his writings fell into the hands of the authorities, this manuscript appears to speak more directly and perspicuously than others.[1] But this so-called perspicuity is quickly tempered when one recounts the varied and mutually contradicting readings of Bonhoeffer's resistance rationale forwarded in Chapter 1, which remains true of readings of this unfinished manuscript.

The manuscript is lengthy and complex, forwarding varying lines of argumentation that do not directly center on the exception. Indeed, the passage that is most often quoted in relation to the exception occurs midway through the manuscript. Bonhoeffer there references Machiavelli's *necessitá*, *ultima ratio*, and the extraordinary situation of necessity:

> There are occasions when, in the course of historical life, the strict observance of the explicit law of a state, a corporation, a family, but also of a scientific discovery, entails a clash with the basic necessities of human life. In such cases, appropriate responsible action departs from the domain governed by laws and principles, from the normal and regular, and instead is confronted with the extraordinary situation of ultimate necessities (*außerordentliche Situation letzter Notwendigkeiten*) that are beyond any possible regulation by law (*Gesetz*). In his political theory Machiavelli coined the term *necessitá* for such a situation. For politics this means that the craft of political governance (*Staatskunst*) becomes political necessity (*Staatsnotwendigkeit*). There can be no doubt that such necessities actually exist. To deny them would mean ceasing to act in accord with reality. It is equally certain, however, that these necessities, as primordial facts (*Urtatsachen*) of life itself, cannot be captured by any law and can never

---

1. Dramm, *Dietrich Bonhoeffer and the Resistance*, 61.

become laws themselves. They appeal directly to the free responsibility of the one who acts, a responsibility not bound by any law. They create an extraordinary situation, and are in essence borderline cases (*Grenzfälle*). They no longer permit human reasoning (*ratio*) to come up with a variety of exit strategies, but pose the question of *ultima ratio*. In politics this *ultima ratio* is war, but it can also be deception or breaking a treaty for the sake of one's own life necessities. In economic life it means the destruction of people's livelihoods for the sake of business necessities. The *ultima ratio* lies beyond the laws of reason; it is irrational action (272–3).[2]

Even those readings of "History and Good [2]" that emphasize differing passages in the manuscript tend to circle back to this passage to solidify their conclusions. The "success" of a given reading is often measured by its ability to account for the above passage.

This chapter performs a reading of "History and Good [2]" that engages debates directly about this passage. The reading of the exception presented in this chapter moves from this central passage outward before returning to it at the end. In the first section, I identify the tensions and difficulties in balancing the boundedness and freedom of responsible action in the exception. Next, I suggest that in order to avoid imbalanced readings in this manuscript, one should de-emphasize Bonhoeffer's employment of Machiavelli's logic of *necessitá*, since it introduces a subtle account of self-justification to responsible action, it skews and encourages the manipulation of reality to defend one's action, and it denies the unity of the Christ-reality by asserting conflict, division, and the necessity of violence into responsible action . I then argue that it is preferable to emphasize Bonhoeffer's employment of history in the manuscript, which follows the Lutheran distinction between law and promise. Following from this prioritization of Bonhoeffer's account of history, I forward a reading of the exception as a moment in history characterized by divine action which opens human action to participate in the emergence of new political and moral formations within the activity of God, who overcomes all the conflicts and dichotomies of this age.[3]

---

2. The key section pertaining to the exception continues through DBWE 6:275. All inline page citations in this chapter are from "History and Good [2]" (DBWE 6:246–98).

3. Before proceeding a caveat is in order. As argued in Chapter 2, Bonhoeffer's thought is fragmentary in character and he develops multiple lines of argumentation on the exception. This remains true in this manuscript. Thus, I cannot claim that my reading is the only defensible reading or that it accounts for every facet of this manuscript. For instance, by de-emphasizing an account of *necessitá* it will become clear that I likewise de-emphasize and resituate Bonhoeffer's discussion of taking on guilt. This diminishment is not necessarily violent to the text, since it emphasizes what is silently diminished by many readings of this manuscript: Bonhoeffer's account of history. The point is not that the reading I am proposing is airtight as much as it rightly accentuates and emphasizes what is primary to Bonhoeffer's theo-logic, thus recovering currently overlooked aspects of the manuscript.

Responsible Action in the Exception

Bonhoeffer discusses the borderline case in the section, "The Structure of Responsible Life" (257–88). Bonhoeffer argues in this section that responsibility is answering God's call in concrete action and that such action has various dimensions which are summarized as the structure of responsible life. These dimensions are classified under the headings of boundedness and freedom (254–7). Under boundedness falls vicarious representative action (*Stellvertretung*) and action in accordance with reality. Vicarious representative action acts on behalf of and is bound to other people (259). Action in accordance with reality is responsive to and bound by reality and the situation at hand. One acts in contexts and spheres that form as well as limit one's action (261–75). That *Stellvertretung* and action in accordance with reality fall under boundedness remains consistent throughout the section.

What falls under the heading of freedom varies in the course of the section. Initially, "my accountability (*Selbstzurechnung*) for my living and acting" and the venture (*Wagnis*) of concrete decision fall under freedom (257). After this initial listing, Bonhoeffer replaces accountability with taking on guilt (*Schuldübernahme*), discussing it at length later in the manuscript.[4] Taking on guilt expresses how responsible persons refuse the fiction of moral purity by willingly incurring guilt on behalf of other people.[5] Lastly, responsible action is free through the venture of concrete decision. The venture is free by not depending on or appealing to circumstance, law, or principle to defend one's action. One acts in defenselessness, vulnerable to the judgment of others (283).

Bonhoeffer suggests that responsible action is bound and free with every act reflecting all four dimensions of the structure of responsible life: vicarious representative action, action in accordance with reality, taking on guilt, and the free venture. This remains true in the free venture of *ultima ratio*. But striking the balance between these dimensions in narrating the responsible act is difficult, since a real tension exists between one's bond and freedom. As Bonhoeffer writes: "In responsibility both obedience and freedom become real. Responsibility has this inner tension. Any attempt to make one independent of the other would be the end of responsibility. Responsible action is bound and yet creative" (288). The tension intensifies in the passage on *ultima ratio* through Bonhoeffer's account of action in accordance with the state (bond) and his appeals to the defenseless venture (freedom).

---

4. The preparatory notes for the manuscript list *Schuldübernahme* as a dimension of responsible action instead of *Selbstzurechnung*. Under *Schuldübernahme*, however, Bonhoeffer includes a cognate of accountability (*Sichzurechnen*). See ZN, 105–6.

5. On guilt in Bonhoeffer's theology, see Christine Schliesser, *Everyone Who Acts Responsibly Becomes Guilty: Bonhoeffer's Concept of Accepting Guilt* (London: Westminster John Knox Press, 2008).

Bound Action in Accordance with the State

In his reflections on action appropriate to its subject matter (*Sachgemäßigkeit*), Bonhoeffer argues that every entity has an intrinsic law (*Wesensgesetz*) that one will recognize and act in accordance with in responsible action. Human life is tied to these intrinsic laws, since everything has its "origin, essence, and goal" in being "related to God and human beings" (270). How one acts in relation to these intrinsic laws has direct implications for human life. When one neglects the intrinsic law in action, human life suffers and the entity is distorted; when one heeds the intrinsic law in action, human life and the entity flourish (271).

Bonhoeffer suggests that acting in accordance with the intrinsic law of an entity is particularly difficult for entities "inextricably" related to human life. This is because the more intimately an entity is connected to human life, the more difficult it is to discern and act in accordance with an entity's intrinsic law. This is particularly true in the case of the state. While the state necessarily pertains to the art of statecraft (*Staatskunst*) and the formulation of codified law, the intrinsic law of the state nevertheless exceeds such technique and legal definition "precisely because the state is inextricably linked to human existence" (272). Bonhoeffer asserts that action in accordance with the intrinsic law of the state may not cohere with "the explicit law" of the state, which is precisely what happens in the borderline case (272–3). Such action is paradoxically both against and in accordance with the law. The act is against the explicit law of the state but is nevertheless performed for the state and human life by being in accordance with the state's intrinsic law. The act is on the basis of human and political necessities, resisting codification. Bonhoeffer employs Machiavelli's *necessitá* in this context to capture how there are moments when "the craft of political governance (*Staatskunst*) becomes political necessity (*Staatsnotwendigkeit*)" (273).

Bonhoeffer suggests that the one most capable of acting against the explicit law is the politician or prominent citizen with political authority. In the list of examples Bonhoeffer later gives of political necessity, each example assumes a figure of authority who can enact it: "In politics this *ultima ratio* is war, but it can also be deception or breaking a treaty for the sake of one's own life necessities. In economic life it means the destruction of people's livelihoods for the sake of business necessities" (273). The emphasis on authority in the *ultima ratio* closely connects to Bonhoeffer's account of vocation (*Beruf*), which determines how to act in one's context (292). One's vocation, Bonhoeffer suggests, may entail acting on behalf of others (*Stellvertretung*) who cannot perform the necessary act themselves.[6] While Bonhoeffer argues later that responsibility extends to all humans (285–7) and that responsibility "bursts" the bounds of one's vocational limits (290–3), the borderline case centers on authorities who act for human life and the intrinsic law of the state in moments of political necessity.

---

6. Gerald McKenny, "Freedom, Responsibility, and Moral Agency," in *The Oxford Handbook on Dietrich Bonhoeffer*, 310.

4. Reading the Exception in "History and Good [2]"

The Freedom of the Defenseless Venture

In contrast to action in accordance with the intrinsic law of the state, Bonhoeffer likewise argues that the free action of *ultima ratio* is "not bound by any law." Those who act freely are defenseless and unable to "turn to" any law for "cover" (273–4). While Bonhoeffer is primarily arguing in this passage that necessary action cannot rely on positive law or moral principles to bolster it, he suggests at the end of the manuscript that action in the *ultima ratio*[7] also contradicts the mandates, which includes the state and its intrinsic law:

> But now is it not the case that the law of God as revealed in the Decalogue, and the divine mandates of marriage, work, and government, establish an inviolable boundary for any responsible action in one's vocation? Would any transgressing of this boundary not amount to insubordination against the revealed will of God? Here the recurring problem of law and freedom presents itself with ultimate urgency. It now threatens to introduce a contradiction into the will of God itself. Certainly no responsible activity is possible that does not consider with ultimate seriousness the boundary that God established in the law. Nevertheless, precisely as responsible action it will not separate this law from its giver (296–7).

Bonhoeffer further argues in this passage that free action is responsible to God alone, leaving the person defenseless before the tribunal of law in particular situations. There is no authority behind which one can take cover and "be exonerated and acquitted" (283). And by implication, this includes the intrinsic law, the mandates, and one's vocation. The disciple is free "from the entire divine law" in being responsible to Jesus Christ alone "as the ultimate reality" (297). In considering the *ultima ratio*, the emphasis is that such action cannot employ reason to valorize the act. It is "irrational action" that "lies beyond the laws of reason" (273). This is further emphasized when Bonhoeffer asserts that one cannot determine the good action in advance, since the good is ambiguous and concealed within the relativity of history. The good only emerges in the act itself: "[The ethical] thus misses the genuine decision in which the whole person, with both understanding and will, seeks and finds what is good only in the very risk of the action itself, within the ambiguity of the historical situation" (248). Only in concrete action is "the world's nature and character" revealed "ever anew" (267). Discernment crystallizes in the venture itself and not beforehand.

---

7. What evidences the return to the theme of *ultima ratio* most clearly is how Bonhoeffer echoes the examples of "lawless" action in the spheres of war, breaking of treaties, and economics: "killing, lying, and seizing of property . . . to reinstate the validity of life, truth and property" (DBWE 6:297). The two passages also have overlapping themes such as accepting guilt in breaking the law freely to sanctify the law (DBWE 6:296–7).

Tensions and Polarities in Responsible Action

A number of polarities emerge between the bound act according to the intrinsic law and the free act that transgresses all law, which further captures the tensions of responsible action in narrations of the exception. First, there is the polarity between whether one discerns or decides the arrival of the exception.[8] The emphasis on discernment emerges in Bonhoeffer's discussion of the necessary act in accordance with reality and the intrinsic law of the state. The emphasis on decision emerges in Bonhoeffer's discussion of the venture that attends to the circumstances of a situation without defending the action on that basis (283). A second polarity is whether the act obeys or breaks God's commandments. In discussing the necessity of action, Bonhoeffer emphasizes the obedient and responsive character of the act in a given situation. Bonhoeffer epitomizes this when he says: "[Responsible persons] seek to understand and do what is necessary or 'commanded' in a given situation" (261). And yet, Bonhoeffer also emphasizes that one breaks God's commandments in the extraordinary situation: "the commandment is broken out of dire necessity" (274). Much depends on how one explicates these different senses of command in relation to necessity.[9] Third, there is the polarity between whether the act is justifiable on the basis of necessity and thus intelligible to others or whether the act is irrational and defenseless in freedom. The emphasis on justifiability stems from the necessity of the act in accordance with the situation, which is open to public scrutiny. One can appeal to vocation, the mitigating circumstances, and political necessity to bolster one's decision. The emphasis on defenselessness and utter irrationality stems from the freedom of the venture unconstrained by law in all its senses.

The Logic and Tension of Necessitá

The tensions in responsible action capture different aspects of the readings forwarded by Robin Lovin and Petra Brown identified in Chapter 1. Lovin's reading emphasizes the boundedness of responsible action in accordance with the intrinsic laws of the mandates in emergency situations. There is a reasonableness to Bonhoeffer's action even as it transgresses law and the typical means of defending action. Brown's reading emphasizes the defenseless and irrational freedom of responsible action, which exceeds narration on the basis of law, reason, or moral principles. Fanaticism runs through Bonhoeffer's action by refusing to give a defense of one's action, opening itself up to endless violence. Each reading prioritizes one aspect of responsible action in the exception, which influences their diverging descriptions of Bonhoeffer's argument in the manuscript.

---

8. See Chapter 1 on this point.
9. A reading of God's commandment in the exception is forwarded in Chapter 6.

The point of agreement between both readings is their recognition that Bonhoeffer's appeal to the Machiavellian concept of *necessitá* is central to a reading of this key passage.[10] The theme of necessity permeates the two main paragraphs on the exception in "History and Good [2]." Bonhoeffer speaks of necessity (*Notwendigkeit*) and need (*Not*) eleven times not including the reference to Machiavelli's *necessitá*.[11] The connection between *necessitá*, necessity, and need is intentional with Bonhoeffer prioritizing the Machiavellian concept, indicated in the preparatory note where he writes: "*necessitá* – Notwendigkeit, Not."[12] Indeed, Bonhoeffer not only engaged Machiavelli's work when writing *Ethics* but also employed secondary works on Machiavelli's political thought when writing this manuscript, particularly the works of Gerhard Ritter and Friedrich Meinecke, who both asserted that Machiavelli understood there to be an irreducible dualism between politics and ethics revealed in moments of necessity whereby one must forsake ethical principles for the sake of political realities.[13] As Machiavelli suggests in *The Prince*, necessity requires the prince to know not only when to do good, but when to do evil: "he should not depart from the good if it is possible to do so, but he should know how to enter into evil when forced by necessity."[14] Necessity requires action beyond the law characterized by force.[15] Indeed, there is a

---

10. Brown, *God's Conspirator*, 58–73; Lovin, "Becoming Responsible," 395.

11. Bonhoeffer primarily uses the term *Notwendigkeit* and variations of it (e.g., *Lebensnotwendigkeit* and *Staatsnotwendigkeit*) to speak of necessity in the manuscript. Bonhoeffer also uses *Not*, which the critical edition translates "dire necessity."

12. ZN, 90.

13. Bonhoeffer engaged the following works of Meinecke and Ritter in writing "History and Good [2]:" Friedrich Meinecke, *Der Idee der Staatsräson in der Neueren Geschichte* (München und Berlin: Druck und Verlag von R. Oldenbourg, 1925); Gerhard Ritter, *Machtstaat und Utopie: vom Streit um die Dämonie der Macht seit Machiavelli und Morus* (München: Oldenbourg, 1940). It is noteworthy that Schmitt viewed his reading as a clear alternative to Meinecke's (and by extension Ritter's) by probing beyond the dualism to the question of political authority: "Das Problem liegt nämlich gar nicht in der inhaltlichen Normativität eines Moral-oder Rechtsgebotes, sondern in der Frage: Wer entscheidet? Die große staatsphilosophische Literatur des 17. Jahrhunderts, insbesondere Hobbes und Pufendorff haben dieses *quis judicabt?* immer betont. . . . Natürlich wollen alle nur Recht, Moral, Ethik, und Frieden; keiner will Unrecht tun; aber die *in concreto* allein interessant Frage ist immer, wer im konkreten Fall darüber entscheidet, was rechtens ist: worin der Friede besteht; was eine Störung oder Gefährdung des Friedens ist, mit welchen Mitteln sie beseitigt wird, wann eine Situation normal und 'befriedet' ist usw." Carl Schmitt, "Zu Friedrich Meineckes 'Idee der Staatsräson,'" in *Archiv für Sozialwissenschaft und Sozialpolitik* (Tübingen: Verlag Von J. C. B. Mohr, 1926), 231.

14. Machiavelli, *The Prince*, ch. 18. See also Niccolò Machiavelli, *The Livy Discourses*, trans. Harvey C. Mansfield and Nathan Tarcov (Chicago: The University of Chicago Press, 1996), I. 26–7.

15. Ibid., ch. 18.

Machiavellian logic that runs through these paragraphs that reverberates through the manuscript, shaping readings of Bonhoeffer's account of the exception.

The Logic of Necessitá

The logic of Machiavelli's *necessitá* draws together a number of elements into mutually inflective relationships. It draws together the concepts of history and politics insofar as necessity is a historical occurrence constraining political action to political ends. And while it is doubtful that Machiavelli held to what modern intellectual thought calls "ethics" in any substantive way, the logic of *necessitá*, at a minimum, lends itself to a reading that suggests that political action exceeds ethical norms by acting beyond them when necessity demands. Within this logic, there is a constellation of corresponding concepts that mutually implicate each other: history, politics, and ethics. Bonhoeffer's employment of *necessitá* also brings these elements into mutually inflective relationships.

History: Machiavelli describes necessity broadly in two registers in *The Prince*. He describes it as a historical event and as an action. The two are closely intertwined with the event constraining and directing the action of the prince. Necessity describes a suprahuman force that overwhelms humans and political life, coercing and limiting human action.[16] Necessity is a forceful event with Machiavelli closely pairing *necessitá* with the verb "to force" (*forzare*).[17] The prince does well not to battle necessity, which would only lead to defeat, but to manage it and anticipate its emergence through forceful action. Necessity, however, is not a force set against human life. Machiavelli describes necessity as a teacher, directing and forming political action to good political ends. Neither is necessity merely an instrumental force; it is also a revelatory event that unveils the current state of affairs, providing a principle of intelligibility for action in the historicopolitical field.[18] Machiavelli's contention that history is cyclical undergirds this principle of intelligibility, since the prince looks to previous political events for instruction in the situation of necessity.[19]

Bonhoeffer follows Machiavelli in describing necessity as both a historical event and an action. He introduces *necessitá* as a situation requiring responsive action irreducible to law or political technique. There are no "exit strategies" available (273). While Bonhoeffer does not describe history as cyclical, he follows

---

16. Necessity is a political concept; force is a natural suprahuman occurrence and power. See Yves Winter, "Necessity and Fortune: Machiavelli's Politics of Nature," in *Second Nature: Rethinking the Natural through Politics*, ed. Crina Archer, Laura Ephraim, and Lida Maxwell (New York: Fordham University Press, 2013), 26–45.

17. Yves Winter, *Machiavelli and the Orders of Violence* (Cambridge: Cambridge University Press, 2018), 78–9.

18. Ibid., 80–1.

19. Friedrich Meinecke, *Machiavellism: The Doctrine of Raison D'état and Its Place in Modern History*, trans. Douglas Scott (London: Routledge and Kegan Paul, 1957), 36–8.

Machiavelli by describing it as a repeatable phenomenon, characterized as *ultima ratio* and *Grenzfall*. The former characterizes the types of appropriate responses political authorities make, such as declaring war, breaking treaties, and destroying livelihoods beyond the confines of law. The latter describes how the statesman learns about this situation from previous political actors and understands how the situation has a delimited time and tolerates certain actions. The historical force of necessity becomes unwieldly and chaotic in the hands of what Bonhoeffer calls "the dreamer." Contrastingly, "the statesman" learns and comprehends the contours and possibilities of the moment at hand (274).

Politics: Necessity describes a political event in its orientation and context. It emerges within a given polity and directs political life and law. Necessity constrains action to the "primordial facts of life" while being against moral law—it is realistic political action that breaks the law in service to the law (273). Advocates of political realism suggest that the accounts of Machiavelli and Bonhoeffer unveil the antipathy between the realities of political life and the ideals of ethical law. Michael Walzer famously argues that the dilemma of dirty hands is "a central feature of political life," where the good politician acts against the law and moral guidelines for the sake of political life.[20] According to Walzer, Machiavelli is the founder of this tradition of thought and the best representative of it. Machiavelli never described the act of necessity as justified but only as excused through its success. It is an exceptional act that nevertheless remains at the heart of political life.[21] Jean Bethke Elshtain reads Bonhoeffer in a similar vein, arguing that his employment of Machiavelli's *necessitá* does not justify the conspirators, it only gestures to their willingness to incur moral guilt in pursuing good political ends.[22] The act only reveals the moral ambiguity of reality, resisting personal moral apologetics. As political realists emphasize in their readings of Bonhoeffer, there is always a gap between the ideal and the real, the ethical and the political, which emphasizes the dependence of the responsible individual on divine grace in performing political action against the ethical.[23] One thus narrates violence never as justified or legal action but as realistic and effective political action ventured in extreme scenarios for laudable ends. As Bonhoeffer notes, violence resists codification or becoming a technique: "there is only one evil greater than force (*Gewalt*), namely, force as a principle, a law, a norm" (273).

---

20. Michael Walzer, "The Problem of Dirty Hands," *Philosophy and Public Affairs* 2, no. 2 (1973): 164, 168.

21. For a reading that puts Bonhoeffer in conversation with Walzer, see Dallas Gingle, "Justification and Judgments: Walzer, Bonhoeffer, and the Problem of Dirty Hands," *Journal of the Society of Christian Ethics* 37, no. 1 (2017): 83–99. See also Leslie Griffin, "The Problem of Dirty Hands," *The Journal of Religious Ethics* 31 (1989): 31–61.

22. Jean Bethke Elshtain, "Reflection on the Problem of 'Dirty Hands,'" in *Torture: A Collection*, ed. Sanford Levinson (Oxford: Oxford University Press, 2006), 84.

23. Lovin, *Christian Realism*, 199.

Two aspects of this emphasis on the priority of political necessity over law and moral norms ironically result in violence becoming depoliticized action. First, there is the emphasis on the extremity of violence as a last resort. By moving it to the margins of political life, the implicit premise is that violence is tantamount to a mechanism of enforcement; it is beyond political reason and law and remains irreducible to both. Violence forms law and establishes the political but is not subsumable thereunder.[24] This leads to the second aspect that lends itself to this depoliticization: the antithesis of violence/force versus law/right.[25] Throughout the paragraph, Bonhoeffer emphasizes that the *ultima ratio* involves *Gewalt*, which interchangeably means force and violence, that cannot become law, technique, or norm.[26] The force of violence thus exceeds political rationality and technique, becoming "irrational" action that sanctifies law and political life. The violence of *necessità* becomes commensurate with the historical force of *necessità* that occurs within but emerges from beyond political life. While Bonhoeffer never held that humans exist in a prepolitical state of nature, he nevertheless follows Kant's lead by emphasizing that violence stands in contrast to political right and justice and that the former becomes a means of establishing the latter.[27] Violence becomes necessary for political life as a founding activity.[28]

Ethics: While the demands of *necessità* exceed the ethical, this does not entail its discarding. The force of law and ethics remains operative in these moments, providing intelligibility for the act insofar as it categorizes and condemns the act on its own terms. In the idiom of "History and Good [2]," responsible action never discards the witness to the conscience by the "law of life," which includes the Decalogue, the Sermon on the Mount, and the apostolic parenesis (282).[29]

---

24. Winter, *Machiavelli*, 5, 120-1.

25. Kant reflects on the difficulty of achieving "supreme power (*Gewalt*) for public right that is itself just." See "Idea for a Universal History with a Cosmopolitan Aim," in *Immanuel Kant: Anthropology, History, and Education*, ed. Günter Zöller and Robert B. Louden, trans. Allen W. Wood (Cambridge: Cambridge University Press, 2007), 8:23.

26. On the dichotomy of *Gewalt* and *Recht*, see Walter Benjamin, "The Critique of Violence (1921)," in *Walter Benjamin: Selected Writings, Volume 1: 1913-1926*, ed. Marcus Bollock and Michael W. Jennings, trans. Edmund Jephcott (London: Harvard University Press, 1996), 236-52. In "The Church and the Jewish Question," Bonhoeffer employs this double sense of *Gewalt* when he argues that the character of the state (*Staatlichkeit*) is " its function of creating law and order by force (*Gewalt*)" (DBWE 12:352).

27. Immanuel Kant, *The Metaphysics of Morals*, in *Practical Philosophy: The Cambridge Edition of the Works of Immanuel Kant*, ed. and trans. Mary J. Gregor (Cambridge: Cambridge University Press, 1996), 456.

28. For further discussion on the function of violence in these narrations of Bonhoeffer, see Chapter 6.

29. See also "A Theological Position Paper on the *Primus Usus Legis*" (DBWE 16:584-600). Bonhoeffer there describes the law of life that speaks through reason "for the establishment of the *iusitia civilis* or the *rationis, carnis*" (DBWE 16:590).

According to Friedrich Meinecke, the emphasis on the authority of the ethical over against the political is essential to resisting totalitarianism, since totalitarianism becomes effective by subsuming morality totally under political life. The subsistence of the ethical maintains the freedom of the individual conscience against mindless obedience. In reflecting on National Socialism, Meinecke argues that the inability to resist totalitarianism emerged in the transition from Machiavellian thought to *Massenmachiavellismus*, which made political goals the only good of reality, becoming the responsibility of all citizens to fulfill.[30] As Bonhoeffer notes, the inverse to the claim of Jesus Christ as one's conscience is that Hitler is one's conscience (277). Without the ability of an individual to be impervious to the claims of a totalizing political logic, the potential of free responsible action becomes near impossible.[31]

In "History and Good [2]," the emphasis instead falls primarily on how the law stands over one's responsible action, declaring it under judgment regardless of the extenuating circumstances. The primary sense of law in this instance is Kantian in character. The demands of the law do not mutate based on circumstance but necessitate principled obedience and thus condemn those who breach its terms. The moment of necessity requires action that breaks the ethical law, which emphasizes the risked, finite, and judged character of the act (280). It also emphasizes how the ethical becomes unreal when it rules over human action even to the detriment of one's neighbor. The mark of real love and responsibility is not letting one's personal purity outweigh the good and benefit of another. Hence Bonhoeffer upholds Christ as the one who breaks the Sabbath law for the sake of fallen humanity in responsible love, and Bonhoeffer laments how Kant allows the principle of truthfulness to lead to "the grotesque conclusion" that one must tell the truth at the peril of a friend's safety (278–9). The former displays selfless love for the other in breaching the law and the latter allows the law to obscure the demands of reality. One hears echoes of Meinecke's claim that while *necessitá* is against moral norms and commandments, it paradoxically becomes the sole ethical element of Machiavelli's thought: by acting for others in political life against ethical law, the individual allows the conscience to justify their action.[32] While Bonhoeffer may not say that the conscience justifies the act, he certainly notes that the conscience acquits the individual (282–3). This bolsters the individual's free transgression as long as it does not lead to their destruction.

In summary, this is the logic of *necessitá* that Bonhoeffer employs in the manuscript: *necessitá* is a historical force that constrains the political actor to act in a particular manner for good political ends. This moment reveals the priority of political reality over against moral purity. One acts for the sanctification of political

---

30. Friedrich Meinecke, "Der Massenmachiavellismus," in *Die Deutsche Katastrophe: Betrachtungen und Erinnergungen* (Wiesbaden: Eberhard Brockhaus Verlag, 1946), 79–81.

31. On this point, see Hannah Arendt, *Eichmann in Jerusalem: A Report on the Banality of Evil* (Middlesex: Penguin Books, 1964), 295–8.

32. Meinecke, *Machiavellism*, 45.

life and law even when transgressing these boundaries through violence. The demands of the ethical remain in force, providing an authority that supersedes the political and resists totalizing impulses. Even so, the ethical can distort responsible action if one acts slavishly in obedience to it—sometimes the most "moral" action is the one that breaks moral laws on behalf of the other.

Distancing from Necessitá

Bonhoeffer intentionally employs Machiavelli's logic of *necessitá* in "History and Good [2]." This logic extends throughout the manuscript, inflecting upon crucial themes like responsible action and taking on guilt, and it contributes to the tensions between the boundedness and freedom of responsible action identified in the first section. Nevertheless, while the employment of Machiavelli by Bonhoeffer is important, it does not determine all readings of the manuscript. Exegetical judgments are unavoidable in these passages, demanding that readers prioritize some elements and diminish others when developing a theology of the exception in Bonhoeffer.

Both the provisional character of the manuscript and the fragmentary character of Bonhoeffer's late reflections on the borderline case provide reason to treat the employment of *necessitá* with caution.[33] What strengthens this contention is how the employment of *necessitá* is akin to the employment of *Schuldübernahme*: both remain unique to this manuscript. There is no other reference to Machiavelli's *necessitá* in the Bonhoeffer corpus, and it is the only positive reference to Machiavelli in his writings.[34] The unique turn to Machiavelli in this exploratory text thus warrants critical scrutiny. In this section, I critique this employment of *necessitá* by reading Bonhoeffer against Bonhoeffer. I argue that the logic of *necessitá* mutates Bonhoeffer's narration of responsibility from a responsiveness to God and neighbor to the "modern" logic of responsibility, which has three effects that one should resist: it introduces a subtle account of self-justification, it skews and encourages the manipulation of reality in seeking to defend one's necessary action, and it denies the unity of the Christ-reality by asserting conflict, division, and the necessity of violence into responsible action. These effects reverse crucial theological impulses in Bonhoeffer's theology, which one should resist by de-emphasizing Bonhoeffer's employment of Machiavelli's *necessitá*.

When Bonhoeffer introduces the concept of responsibility in "History and Good [2]," he emphasizes its responsivity to God's Word encountered in history. "We live by responding to the word of God addressed to us in Jesus Christ. . . . This life, lived in answer to the life of Jesus Christ (as the Yes and No to our life),

---

33. On this point, see Chapter 2.

34. Bonhoeffer speaks of necessitas and necessity elsewhere in his corpus, but these usages are not tied to Machiavelli and they likewise have a different logic tied more closely to providence. See DBWE 8:268–9, 301, 426–7.

we call *'responsibility'"* (254). Paradigmatic of such responsiveness is a radical turning away from the self in attending to the other and God's concrete command. This is epitomized in Bonhoeffer's account of simplicity.[35] Simplicity describes the naiveté of the disciple who responds wholly, and without questioning, to the divine command. There is a single-minded orientation to God that suspends self-judgment by depending upon God's judgment already spoken in Christ. This utterly outward orientation entails that a person is totally ignorant of the merits of their action by confessing that the only Good action belongs to God.[36]

The logic of *necessitá* reverses this impulse by turning attention back toward the self and one's narration for their action. This often goes under observed due to Bonhoeffer's emphasis on the defenselessness of action in the exception. Readers often assert that this emphasis in "History and Good [2]" entails a blanket refusal to narrate the justifiability of one's action, but this is not quite true. More precisely, the logic of *necessitá* refuses narrations forwarded on solely ethical grounds while still prioritizing the interpretation and narration of necessary violence enacted in the borderline case. The act is ethically indefensible, but there is a defense forwarded for why such violence remains reasonably responsible and necessary for the sake of political life.

Bonhoeffer's emphasis on the appearance of responsible action in giving an account to others is indicative of this reversal, particularly in the narration of responsibility in extreme moments: responsibility displays itself to others through the extenuating circumstances, the laudable character of the act, and the anticipatable consequences of the action (268); the circumstances display the lack of available options, leaving the person with little choice (282); how the person incurs guilt in real love for others displays the laudable character of the act (279-81); the intention to sanctify the law and political order becomes apparent through the open confession of lawbreaking and incurring guilt (297); and the lack of defensive appeal proves freedom in action (283).

The employment of *necessitá* subsequently changes Bonhoeffer's logic of responsibility from a responsive turning away from the self in simplicity to what Esther Reed terms the "modern" account of responsibility. As Reed persuasively describes, responsibility in this frame is a possession of the sovereign self, which emphasizes the continual demand of accountability looming over the agent, their act, and the consequences of their action. One can trace a consequence to an act attributed to an agent, thus holding the agent accountable for the act and its consequence. Responsibility becomes personal and traceable. The chain of

---

35. The most notable text explicating this theme is *Discipleship* (DBWE 4). It remains a key theme in *Ethics*, particularly in "Ethics as Formation" (DBWE 6:76-102) and "God's Love and the Disintegration of the World" (DBWE 6:299-388). I offer a reading of simplicity in Chapter 5.

36. For more on this theme, see Bernd Wannenwetsch, "'Responsible Living' or 'Responsible Self'? Bonhoefferian Reflections on a Vexed Moral Notion," *Studies in Christian Ethics* 18, no. 3 (2005): 125-40.

cause and effect is open to public perception, emphasizing its externality as an essential aspect of holding a person to account. Responsibility thus entails that a person must always be ready to give an account for what they do and what sort of effects stem from their action.[37] One effect of this "modern" logic of responsibility is that it inverts the perception of individuals from the neighbor to themselves by turning accountability into a moral demand. Responsibility no longer rests in the judgment already declared in Christ; it rather anticipates an unknown future judgment in moral deliberation. Frequently, the notion of the "responsible self" paradoxically responds not to the claim of the other but to one's interpretation of the other's claim, forming one's action by anticipating how the other will respond to it. As Niebuhr argues in *The Responsible Self*: "Our actions are responsible only insofar as they are reactions to interpreted action upon us, but also insofar as they are made in anticipation of answers to our actions."[38]

There are three problems with this reversal of responsibility. First, a subtle form of moral self-justification emerges in this account, since it turns the responsible self into the main arbiter and interpreter of one's own action in anticipation of another's judgment.[39] Importantly, this is an impulse that Bonhoeffer resists explicitly earlier in the manuscript. In the paragraph immediately preceding the section "The Structure of Responsible Life," Bonhoeffer unpacks the various senses of *Verantwortung*, which the critical edition of *Ethics* translates in three senses: "my answering," "being accountable," and "taking responsibility." And for the final use of *Verantwortung* in the paragraph, the critical edition employs all three senses, reflecting Bonhoeffer's own broad usage of the term.[40] But it is noteworthy that whereas "my answering" and "taking responsibility" have moral connotations, Bonhoeffer resists this impulse for "being accountable." In the one sentence that employs an explicit term for a person's being called to account (*Zur Rechenschaft gezogen*), Bonhoeffer asserts unequivocally that one can only respond through the testimony of Jesus Christ: "Called to account by human beings and before God, I can only answer for myself by witnessing to Jesus Christ who was the advocate of God before human beings, and of human beings before God" (256). When an account is requested by one party, Bonhoeffer points to the judgment already made in Christ. Accountability is thus deflected from one's own activity to the

---

37. Reed, *The Limit of Responsibility*. On the genealogy of responsibility, see also Paul Ricoeur, "The Concept of Responsibility: An Essay in Semantic Analysis," in *The Just*, trans. David Pellauer (Chicago: The University of Chicago Press, 1995), 11–35; Georg Picht and Winston Davis, trans., "The Concept of Responsibility: Introduction and Translation," *Religion* 28, no. 2 (1998): 190–203.

38. H. R. Niebuhr, *The Responsible Self: An Essay in Christian Moral Philosophy* (Louisville: Westminster John Knox Press, 1999), 64.

39. Wannenwetsch, "Bonhoefferian Reflections," 136–7.

40. "Responsibility, answering, and being accountable exist only in confessing Jesus Christ in word and life" (DBWE 6:256); "Verantwortung gibt es nur im Bekenntnis zu Jesus Christus mit Wort und Leben" (DBW 6:256).

prior and pervasive activity of Christ. This becomes the basis for the simplicity and self-forgetfulness that marks responsible action.

Second, the focus on appearances in narrating responsibility ironically skews attentiveness to reality. This is because appearances are easy to manipulate in seeking a favorable judgment. This is a common critique levied against modern narrations of responsibility, since these often provide nothing more than a legitimizing function.[41] One narrates the act as responsible, though it may really be an exploitation or self-deception. Declaring responsibility can become nothing more than a spectacle that obfuscates reality.[42] Machiavelli understood well the manipulation of appearances for political leverage, and it is here that the modern logic of responsibility converges with *necessità* most acutely. In outlining an account of necessary action, Machiavelli argues that what matters is not whether an act is actually good but only that it appears good and necessary to others and that it achieves a favorable result: "For ordinary people are always taken in by appearances and by the outcome of an event."[43] This is not to declare Bonhoeffer malicious in his own account of necessity. He resists the cynicism of Machiavellian politics. Nevertheless, self-deception remains a great danger in the turn to *necessità*, since the emphasis on appearances can likewise deceive the self. Such self-deception often bolsters the "necessary" actions of fanatics, a danger observed well in Brown's reading of Bonhoeffer.[44] The line between decision and discernment in a narration of responsible action becomes blurred and difficult to negotiate in this light. When the emphasis on necessity as a perceivable phenomenon rises to the forefront of narrations, the obvious question becomes whether necessity actually exists or is only claimed to exist in order to pursue a desired political end.

Third, the turn to *necessità* in responsibility divides human action, narrating it in terms of division and conflict. This emerges most evidently in the logic of *necessità* with the political and the ethical remaining in an irreducible dualism revealed in the moment demanding necessary violence. This division is epitomized in Bonhoeffer's development of *Schuldübernahme*, which narrates the responsible action as guilty before the divine law and yet sinless in its self-giving for the neighbor.[45] To act in accordance with necessity may mean killing, thus breaking the fifth commandment, or participating in a coup d'état, thus violating the authority of those in government. Responsible action is marked

---

41. Wolfgang Schoebert, "The Concept of Responsibility: Dilemma and Necessity," *Studies in Christian Ethics* 22, no. 4 (2009): 426.

42. Reed, *The Limit of Responsibility*, 40–5.

43. Machiavelli, *The Prince*, ch. 18. "For the generality of men feed on what appears as much as on what is; indeed, many times they are moved more by things that appear than by things that are" (Machiavelli, *Livy Discourses*, I. 25).

44. See Brown, *God's Conspirator*.

45. For a criticism of this logic, see McKenny, "Freedom, Responsibility, and Moral Agency." The argument of this chapter distances from *Schuldübernahme*, seeing its development in tandem with the Machiavellian logic.

simultaneously by its guilt as well as by its virtue. It is marked by its freedom against and judgment under the law in the moment of necessity.

Yet this counteracts Bonhoeffer's assertion throughout *Ethics* (particularly in the earlier manuscript "Christ, Reality, and the Good" and the later manuscript "God's Love and the Disintegration of the World") that Christ has reconciled all things to himself, affirming there is no conflict or division at the center of reality or free human action.[46] The adventitious work of God in Christ reconciles opposites and divisions in his very self—the complete intercourse of divine and human, eternity and history, necessity and freedom, and so on. The disintegration of the fall and the fragmentation of human action is thereby overcome in Christ, who grants unity to Christian action within the reconciled Christ-reality.[47] There is no longer a division between "ought and is" or "idea and realization."[48] Responsible action bypasses "insoluble conflicts" or "the inevitability of becoming guilty," since Christ unites all seeming oppositions in himself at the center of history (264–5). As Bonhoeffer states in a Lutheran idiom:

> What must ultimately be taken seriously in the view of the Bible and in Luther's view is not the conflict between the gods as expressed in their laws, but the unity of God and the reconciliation of the world with God in Jesus Christ; not the inevitability of becoming guilty, but the plain and simple life that flows from reconciliation; not fate, but the gospel as the ultimate reality of life; not the cruel triumph of the gods over the perishing human being, but the election of human beings as children of God in the midst of the world reconciled by grace (266).

This impulse is quickly forfeited by readers of Bonhoeffer who are drawn to his conspicuous and short-lived development of *Schuldübernahme* isolated to this manuscript.[49] While this criticism does not entail the necessary abandonment of necessity or *Schuldübernahme*, it at least opens the possibility that the terms can be read within a different logic closer to Bonhoeffer's consistent assertion that Christian action springs from reconciliation, not the inevitability of becoming guilty.

Emphasizing History in "History and Good [2]"

A particular strength in de-emphasizing Machiavelli's *necessitá* and emphasizing the concept of history in narrating the exception is that the latter holds a thematic

---

46. DBWE 6:47–75, 299–338.
47. Philip G. Ziegler, "'Completely Within God's Doing': Soteriology as Meta-Ethics in the Theology of Dietrich Bonhoeffer," in *Christ, Church, and World: New Studies in Bonhoeffer's Theology and Ethics*, ed. Michael Mawson and Philip G. Ziegler (London: T&T Clark, 2016), 109–12.
48. DBWE 6:49.
49. See Chapter 2.

prominence to the manuscript that the former does not. Unlike the reference to *necessitá*, which only features in one paragraph (though, admittedly, a very key paragraph), history permeates the manuscript and finds prominent reference in the section on the structure of responsible life, with Bonhoeffer intimately connecting the concept to sociality, the divine command, and the good.[50] It is not incidental that Bonhoeffer titles both manuscript attempts "History and Good." While Bonhoeffer made many changes between the two manuscript attempts, the title of the manuscript and the prominence of history nevertheless remain consistent between them.[51] As Bonhoeffer writes at the end of the first paragraph of "History and Good [2]:" "The question about the good can no longer be separated from the question of life, of history" (247). To read the manuscript well requires attending to Bonhoeffer's prioritization of the concept of history, which aids any narration of the "extraordinary situation of ultimate necessities" (273).

Nevertheless, Bonhoeffer's references to history are not uniform, possessing different senses in their employment. One way to organize Bonhoeffer's disparate reflections on history is to read them as following the Lutheran distinction between law and promise. Where the law tells humankind what to do, restraining human iniquity and putting humankind under judgment, the promise declares what God is going to do apart from both the law and human action while transforming them in its fulfillment. In this schema, law and promise are not de-historicized entities that stand over above history, since both are given and ultimately fulfilled in history. Nevertheless, the narration of history is determined by God's twofold action best summarized as law and Gospel/promise, which comes through in this manuscript.[52]

Bonhoeffer first describes history akin to the second use of the law. It is the source of unrelenting demands on human action that are simultaneously ambiguous and conflicted. While the responsible person is responsive to its pressure, doing "what is necessary or 'commanded' in a given situation" (261), the necessary response is neither straightforward nor perspicuous, and the moment even exceeds the ability of the person undergoing the "humanly impossible situation" (288). This is, in part, because history is fallen and therefore obscure. The result is that the ambiguity of history discredits any attempt to identify human action directly with the absolute good (247). The "Good" always supersedes human "good," and God's judgment rests in a higher plane than human judgment. It is also because there is not only a single demand that presses upon the person in the moment, but multiple demands with conflicting moral aspects that refuse clear arbitration. This is what emerges in the logic of *Schuldübernahme*: sometimes guilt is unavoidable because

---

50. DBWE 6:247–8, 263–4, 267–8, 273, 284–5, 288.

51. The following sections center on history and historical action in the manuscripts: DBWE 6:220–2, 225–9, 233–7, 247–8, 263–4, 272–5, 284–5.

52. On the primacy of law and Gospel in a reading of Bonhoeffer, see DeJonge, *Bonhoeffer's Reception of Luther*. It will become clear, however, that the Lutheran logic of this reading diverges from DeJonge's reading in many important respects.

the historical moment always leaves one implicated in its guilt, and the options for action are always condemned on the basis of some moral precept. An abstract ethical ideology proves unreal in such moments, since the conflicting demands of moral precepts reveal themselves as insufficient to guide human action (247). Thus Bonhoeffer states:

> Responsible action takes place in the sphere of relativity, completely shrouded in the twilight that the historical situation casts upon good and evil. It takes place in the midst of the countless perspectives from which every phenomenon is seen. Responsible action must decide not simply between right and wrong, good and evil, but between right and right, wrong and wrong (284).

The ambiguity of history does not produce responsible action in love of neighbor, it instead produces uncertainty and conflict.[53]

Second, Bonhoeffer describes history as the domain of God's sovereign and reconciling activity, culminating in the Christ-event where history and promise find fulfillment:

> Jesus Christ does not encounter reality as someone who is foreign to it. Instead, it is he who alone bore and experienced in his own body the essence of the real, and who spoke out of knowledge of the real like no other human being on earth. He alone did not lapse into any ideology but is the Real One as such, who in himself has borne and fulfilled the essence of history, and in whom the inner law (*Lebensgesetz*) of history itself is embodied. As the Real One he is the origin, essence, and goal of all reality. That is why he himself is the lord and the law of the real. The sayings of Jesus Christ are therefore the interpretation of his existence, and thus the interpretation of that reality in which history finds its fulfillment. They are the divine commandment for responsible action in history insofar as they are the reality of history that has been fulfilled in Christ, that is, insofar as they are the responsibility for human beings that has been fulfilled in Christ alone. Therefore they are valid not [within] an abstract ethic—indeed, there they are completely incomprehensible and lead to insoluble conflicts. Rather, they are valid within the reality of history, because this is their source. Any attempt to disconnect them from this origin distorts them into a weak ideology. Only when rooted in their origin do they possess the power to gain control of reality (263-4).

The center of reality is the fulfillment of the promise in Christ, which transforms both history and law. In a Pauline idiom: the Christ-event is the fulfillment of a promise given in history that both precedes and exceeds the law. Because the promise precedes the giving of the law, the promise ultimately finds fulfillment apart from the

---

53. Steven D. Paulson, *Doing Lutheran Theology* (New York: T&T Clark, 2011), 41. For more on this theme, see Chapter 5.

law. Because the promise exceeds the law, this means that the law is ultimately not the means of receiving the promise. Only a divine act beyond determination by law fulfills the law and even history, transforming them in light of the Christ-event.

It is within this frame that Bonhoeffer's emphasis on history as the domain of God's present and sovereign activity comes to the fore. If the Good comes apart from the law and human action, this entails that the Good comes on its own accord in its own time. Indeed, God accomplishes the Good in the most unlikely of places. In "History and Good [1]," Bonhoeffer even points to the betrayal of Jesus by Judas as a prime example of how God's Good comes both through and despite human action thereby concluding: "Free action, as it determines history, recognizes itself ultimately as being God's action, the purest activity as passivity. Only in this perspective is it possible to speak now of good in history."[54]

While the stress on passivity contextualizes human action, revealing its insufficiency before God's sovereign action, this does not negate intentional human action in history, making it arbitrary or beyond intelligible discourse. Instead, the emphasis on God's sovereign fulfillment of the promise and enactment of the Good empowers a positive mode of perception that informs responsible action even though it remains outside of the logic of law. It narrates faithful human action principally as trust in God's promises rather than law-keeping.[55] Put differently, such action is marked by confession rather than obedience to the law. In Chapter 3, this emphasis came through in the moment of temptation whereby one clings to God's Word while recognizing the insufficiency of human resources to respond adequately. And it is should be no surprise that this account of free action continues in Bonhoeffer's resistance activity.

The personal dimension to this confession comes through most clearly in Bonhoeffer's 1942 letter concerning the resistance, "After Ten Years," which is often read in conjunction to "History and Good [2]."[56] Bonhoeffer there gives prominence to his confession of faith in God's providential action that empowers responsible action. As Kai-Ole Eberhardt argues, the section "Some Statements of Faith on God's Action in History" becomes the theological center of the letter, unique in being the only section where Bonhoeffer speaks in the mode of confession.[57] This is indicated by being the only section where Bonhoeffer employs the confessional refrain, "I believe," using it four times.

> I believe that God can and will let good come out of everything, even the greatest evil. For that to happen, God needs human beings who let everything work out

---

54. DBWE 6:226.
55. The act can still be narrated as obedience, but it is an obedience undetermined by the law and thus outside of the category of law-keeping. For more on this point, see Chapter 5.
56. DBWE 8:37–52.
57. Kai-Ole Eberhardt, "Das Geheimnis des Waltens Gottes in der Geschichte: Providenz und Ethik in Dietrich Bonhoeffers Glaubenssätzen von 1942," *Kirchliche Zeitgeschichte* 31, no. 1 (2018): 221–44.

for the best. I believe that in every moment of distress God will give us as much strength to resist as we need. But it is not given to us in advance, lest we rely on ourselves and not on God alone. In such faith all fear of the future should be overcome. I believe that even our mistakes and shortcomings are not in vain and that it is no more difficult for God to deal with them than with our supposedly good deeds. I believe that God is no timeless fate but waits for and responds to sincere prayer and responsible actions.[58]

Eberhardt subsequently argues that these confessions inform Bonhoeffer's resistance activity, offering an approach to historical moments that does not capitulate to fear but proceeds with sacrificial faith that God's Good will overcome the temporary and passing phenomenon of evil.[59] One of Eberhardt's astute observations is that Bonhoeffer's emphasis on free action as derivative of God's providential activity in and for the world is a particularly Lutheran confession.[60] If the good work depends on God's gratuitous activity, epitomized in justification, then all good works confess fully and single-mindedly their own continual dependence on God's providential activity and presence. Faith looks away from itself and its own merits in love of God and neighbor, and in looking away one perceives and engages the world anew ever trusting in God's continual guidance.[61] This is a frequent theme in Bonhoeffer's prison writings, forming his perception of his time in prison,[62] and it becomes an under observed, but equally essential confession that shapes his perception of the difficult years of resistance.[63]

The themes that Eberhardt identifies in Bonhoeffer's account of free action before God's action capture well the theological themes identified in the last section: responsible action is not characterized by accountability but genuine responsiveness to the neighbor in history, responsible action surrenders self-judgment and attempts for self-justification, and responsible action is not characterized by division or conflict but the overarching action of God that reconciles all things in the Christ-reality. As Bonhoeffer summarizes in describing free action in the ambiguity of the historical moment:

> This very fact defines responsible action as a free venture (*Wagnis*), not justified by any law; rather, those who act responsibly relinquish any effectual self-

---

58. DBWE 8:46.
59. Eberhardt, "Das Geheimnis des Waltens Gottes in der Geschichte," 229.
60. Ibid., 241.
61. See Martin Luther, "The Freedom of a Christian," LW 31: 333–77.
62. On this point, see Wolf Krötke, "'Gottes Hand und Führung:' Zu einem unübersehbaren Merkmall der Rede Dietrich Bonhoeffers von Gott in der Zeit des Widerstandes," in *Barmen—Barth—Bonhoeffer: Beiträge zu einer zeitgemäßen christozentrischen Theologie* (Luther-Verlage; Auflage, 2009), 381–402; Heinrich Ott, *Reality and Faith: The Theological Legacy of Dietrich Bonhoeffer*, trans. Alex A. Morrison (Philadelphia: Fortress Press, 1971), 287–311.
63. Ott, *Reality and Faith*, 297–8.

justification; indeed, in so doing they relinquish an ultimately dependable knowledge of good and evil. As responsible action, the good takes place without knowing, by surrendering to God the deed that has become necessary and is nevertheless (or because of it!) free, surrendering it to God, who looks upon the heart, weighs the deeds, and guides history. Thus a profound mystery of history as such is disclosed to us. Precisely those who act in the freedom of their very own responsibility see their activity as flowing into God's guidance. Free action recognizes itself ultimately as being God's action, decision as God's guidance, the venture as divine necessity. In freely surrendering the knowledge of our own goodness, the good of God occurs. Only in this ultimate perspective can we speak about good in historical action (284–5).

The Lutheran logic of this passage diverges sharply from the Machiavellian logic of *necessità*. Where the Machiavellian logic keeps the narration within the determinations of law and historical necessity, the Lutheran logic escapes the determinations of law by confessing the only necessity being divine action beyond all determination that liberates free human action: "extraordinary necessity appeals to the freedom of those who act responsibly" (274).[64] Where the Machiavellian logic ultimately depends on the instrumental character of violence to renew political life, the Lutheran logic depends on a divine act in history beyond instrumentality or anticipation.[65] Where the Machiavellian logic maintains an essential dualism or contradiction to responsible action, the Lutheran logic affirms that all dualisms are reconciled in the Christ-event where human passivity and divine activity are not sharp oppositions, but have complete intercourse in the Christ-reality.[66] Bonhoeffer's theology of history, ultimately, has a distinctive Lutheran logic that reframes free action and the historical moment in light of a divine *adventus*.

---

64. One can hear in Bonhoeffer echoes of Luther's distinction in *The Bondage of the Will* between the necessity of compulsion and immutability. The good act is never a "free choice" and neither does it emerge through the compulsion of threat or circumstance, since the choices and compulsions of this age are determined by sin and Satan. The good act derives necessarily from the vivifying activity of God that liberates and transforms the will for free responsivity. Where experience teaches the impossibility of willing and doing the good by compulsion, one is directed to the immutable God that liberates the will for joyful responsivity in freedom. LW 33:64–5. For more on this reading of Luther, see Simeon Zahl, "Non-Competitive Agency and Luther's Experiential Argument Against Virtue," *Modern Theology* 35, no. 2 (2019): 199–222.

65. As argued in Chapter 6, Bonhoeffer's employment of violence is important as a restraining force within the political rather than being a founding activity for the political.

66. As Bonhoeffer argues in the manuscript: free action cannot fall under an account of indeterminism or determinism (283, FN 6) as this is a false opposition.

Narrating the Exception in "History and Good [2]"

With Bonhoeffer's reflections on history in view, a narration of the exception emerges in reading the key paragraphs in the manuscript (273–4). The first thing to observe in the main paragraphs is how appeals to history bookend the passage, highlighting the centrality of history for reading them. The section begins with the assertion that there are moments "in the course of historical life" (273) when the explicit law clashes with human necessities, and the section concludes with the assertion that when the individual refuses any appeal to law to defend their action, there is "finally a surrender of one's own decision and action to the divine guidance of history" (274). The section begins with history reflecting the demands of the law on human action and it ends with the surrender of action before God's providential guidance in history. The historicity of this section suggests that before discussing the exception as an action, one should discuss it as a moment in history that is set apart, distinct in its demands and the resulting human action that results.

Bonhoeffer describes this moment five times as "extraordinary" in these paragraphs.[67] The moment is extraordinary in two senses. First, it is extraordinary by how it eludes human control and disrupts the hegemony of technique, law, and rationality to direct human action therein (273). Bonhoeffer does not describe immediately in this passage what makes the situation so elusive of human control, but his description of the ambiguity and relativity of the moment certainly factor in (268, 284). There is no clear path forward insofar as every possible action is mired in the relativities and disjunctions of the present, displaying how the available ethical and political resources have been distorted by the determinations of sin. The law subsequently is revealed to be insufficient to direct action in this moment, requiring an act beyond its arbitration. This is the impulse behind Bonhoeffer's rejection of Kant's exceptionless law. Obedience to the letter of the law is an insufficient response to the exception, since the demands of the law distort the character of responsible action in this instance (279–80). While the law maintains its "legitimacy" (274), it loses its preeminence to guide all action. The demands of the moment are "beyond any possible regulation by law" (273).

Second, it is extraordinary by how God liberates free action apart from the law in the moment. Another form of action is needed to respond faithfully, which appears "irrational" (273) and transgressive to observers. Contrary to what one might expect, Bonhoeffer reasons not that the necessities of the moment appeal to one's bond, vocation, or civil responsibilities to bolster one's action, but that "extraordinary necessity appeals to the freedom of those who act responsibly" (274). The necessity of the exception paradoxically liberates one to act without defense, directing one's attention away from oneself to the neighbor in freedom.

---

67. Observing Bonhoeffer's emphasis on the "extraordinary" originates with Petra Brown, and I am indebted to her for this interpretive insight. See Brown, *God's Conspirator*, 57–78. Unlike Brown, I do not think the concept lends itself to arbitrariness and boundless violence.

The exception is a borderline case (*Grenzfall*) as one encounters the boundary (*Grenze*) of moral and legal judgments to direct one's decision, requiring a surrender of the venture to God (274). This does not make human action hopeless, since the revelation that persons are "without ground under their feet" to direct action definitively is simultaneously the revelation that God's Word and action is the only sure foundation for good action; it is when one is defenseless and exposed that God frees a person for action ventured apart from the law but in hope that God will still have mercy on *this* act, making it fruitful.[68] What is "extraordinary" in the exception is the activity of God that transcends the determinations of moral and political life, guiding history and liberating human activity in the most perilous of moments.

In this frame, the exception is defined principally by divine action rather than human action. It is a moment when God judges the distortions of law in its various, historicized forms (mandates, the natural, the ethical), and liberates generative human action for a new beginning apart from the law.[69] The result, however, is not the destruction of law or reason, but their re-establishment and sanctification for everyday life. The exception affirms that it is only "through Christ that the world of things and values is given back its orientation toward human beings, as was originally intended in their creation" (260). God sanctifies law, political life, and human action in the exception while revealing their dependence on God's activity and presence—God is the ultimate and they remain penultimate. The exception is a founding event that ultimately subverts the totalitarian drives of the moment, revealing that the ethical and the political are gifts of grace, which are affirmed anew by the God who graciously responds to responsible action and prayer.[70]

Narrating the Structure of Responsible Life in the Exception

The exception bears directly on a narration of the structure of responsible life insofar as the moment not only clarifies and shapes one's action but also discloses the nature of reality, which includes the structure of responsible life. In light of this reading of the exception, I forward the following narration for the structure of responsible life that differs from common readings of these dimensions. Identifying these differences is important, since they foreshadow the reading of responsible action in the exception forwarded in Chapters 5 and 6.

Freedom: The extraordinary situation demands the free venture undetermined by the law. It is "irrational" and defenseless, appealing to God's guidance and judgment in its execution. Bonhoeffer further characterizes freedom as the refusal to appeal to any authority "to exonerate and acquit" one's activity—it surrenders

---

68. DBWE 8:38.
69. On the theme of new beginnings in Bonhoeffer, see Andrew D. DeCort, *Bonhoeffer's New Beginning: Ethics after Desolation* (Minneapolis: Fortress Press, 2018), 83–120.
70. "I believe that God is no timeless fate, but waits and responses to sincere prayer and responsible actions" (DBWE 8:46).

itself entirely to God's judgment (283). Many commentators attempt to soften this account by arguing that Bonhoeffer is more rational than these statements suggest, which balances out the picture presented.[71] Contrary to this impulse, this "radical" account of freedom should remain unobstructed in a narration of the exception. The danger of minimizing this account too quickly is that it misses what is so extraordinary in it: an utter refusal to judge the merits of one's activity by remaining totally oriented to the activity of God.

Bonhoeffer suggests that God's reconciling activity liberates persons from the knowledge of good and evil, gifting them an ignorance of the merits of their activity, since "in freely surrendering the knowledge of our own goodness, the good of God occurs" (284–5). To begin with freedom in narrating the structure of responsible life is to refuse to domesticate freedom through law, foreclosing avenues of free action through self-doubt and conflicted moral conscience. As Bonhoeffer suggests later in the manuscript, responsibility does not undergird freedom, but freedom undergirds responsible action as its substantive presupposition (283).

This account of freedom is not radical and private as detractors fear, but politically generative since it affirms the potency of any given moment to elicit a free act beyond political determination. When Bonhoeffer later discusses whether those who are "below" can exercise free responsibility, he suggests that even in the most structured of societies, all persons remain open to free responsible action in encounter (286). This liberation for action, however, is not intrinsic to a political organization or through a capacity for freedom in the individual but remains a gift that befalls the person in the encounter mediated by Christ: "Those who act responsibly do so while bound to God and neighbor as they encounter me in Jesus Christ, the only bond that is liberating, totally liberating" (284). In this light, the question regarding whether the free venture is best characterized by discernment or decision becomes secondary insofar as the narration centers primarily not on the "I" who surveys the moment, then acting into it, but the "I" who encounters and is encountered by the neighbor in the moment, eliciting a free response. The question of decision versus discernment in a narration of responsible action needs further articulation, but it remains secondary to the radical encounter that spurs free response before God and neighbor.

Taking on Guilt: Bonhoeffer's account of freedom raises the question of whether a person can judge the good of their action in any meaningful sense in the exception. Answering this question often centers on Bonhoeffer's account of taking on guilt, since its logic closely connects to questions of how a person adjudges their own activity. Nevertheless, this does not seem to be the primary dynamic Bonhoeffer wrestled with in developing the concept. Bonhoeffer was not attempting to develop a language to judge the goodness of one's conduct in morally complicated situations. He was instead developing an ethical orientation to the neighbor that refuses the pursuit of personal innocence at the expense of real love for the neighbor (275). For Bonhoeffer, some moments prove that the love

---

71. A discussion and rebuttal of these accounts is offered in Chapter 5.

of neighbor cannot be mediated through an exceptionless law. If the law opposes self-giving love, then one must break the law in the process.

To be sure, there is good reason to critique the deployment of taking on guilt in the manuscript, which is what I argued in the third section. Nevertheless, Wannenwetsch's suggestion that the concept be read not as conflicted moral judgment but as a confession holds promise for repurposing the concept. In this frame, taking on guilt is a "negative theology of ethics" that "does not promote proactive complicity with the transgressors of the law; its actual purpose is rather to ward off that most subtle form of self-justification which is born from the desire to sustain one's purity of conscience above all things."[72] The benefit of this account is that as a confession, taking on guilt is able to contradict the fiction of personal innocence that discourages involvement with others while also contradicting accounts that turn one's moral judgment inward. The confession informs the self's turning away from anticipatory moral judgments in the exception by being wholly immersed in and dependent upon God's reality. As Bonhoeffer states: "Ultimate ignorance of one's goodness or evil, together with a dependence on grace, is an essential characteristic of responsible action."[73] As a confession, taking on guilt continues to affirm the external orientation of human action that surrenders itself to the divine guidance of history epitomized in the exception.

Vicarious Representative Action: Bonhoeffer links responsibility directly to vicarious representative action in the manuscript: "As vicariously representative life and action, responsibility is essentially a relation from one human being to another" (259). Bonhoeffer grounds this dimension of responsible life Christologically, extending it to all humans insofar as it remains a possibility for all. Nevertheless, Bonhoeffer also argues that acting on behalf of another remains a more common reality for those in positions of authority (284), and he concretizes

---

72. Wannenwetsch, "Bonhoefferian Reflections," 135.

73. Admittedly, such a reading distances from elements of Bonhoeffer's account of the conscience in "History and Good [2]," but it is not a full rejection of his account. Rather, it extends what he argues a few months later in "God's Love and the Disintegration of the World." In "History and Good [2]," Bonhoeffer notes that the fallen conscience seeks unity with itself by judging good and evil. The act of salvation exposes this conscience "as the most godless self-justification," which has now been overcome in Christ, who "has become my conscience" (278). The redeemed conscience, however, continues to operate to limit and direct responsible action through moral judgment, culminating in Bonhoeffer's declaration that the conscience acquits oneself in accepting guilt (282–3). In "God's Love and the Disintegration of the World," the confession that "Jesus is my conscience" is radicalized to confess that moral judging "is itself the apostasy from God" (DBWE 6:315), since the conscience by definition operates by judging good and evil rather than by hearing and doing God's will. As Ziegler summarizes: "the redemption of the conscience now comprises its utter displacement and unmaking. The 'freed conscience' of which Bonhoeffer can speak no longer functions as a seat of moral judgment at all, but rather now simply names the total alignment of the human being with Christ" (Ziegler, "Within God's Doing," 110).

this account by giving two examples of figures who perform *Stellvertretung*: the father and the statesman, who respectively act on behalf of their children and their constituents. There is a Christological analogy in these examples with those in authority acting for others in a manner that those "below" cannot act. This is particularly true in common narrations of the exception: as Christ broke the law in real love for others, so, too, does the statesman break the law for the sake of political life in a way that the ordinary citizen cannot. Gerald McKenny argues that this account lends itself to a troublesome paternalism, since those in authority are liable for and act on behalf of others without ever being accountable to them in the exception. By turning vicarious representative action into an ethical concept in common political life, Bonhoeffer allows political authorities to break the law for others without ever being accountable to them for those transgressions.[74] In this frame, *Stellvertretung* could be translated as representation or substitution, since the act is analogous to Christ's action in its representative mode.[75]

In attempting to avoid this criticism, "History and Good [2]" also allows for a narration of vicarious representative action not as representation, but as self-giving in freedom. For starters, Bonhoeffer argues that Jesus exercised vicarious representative action without a vocation on behalf of humanity (258), thus acting in simplicity apart from institutional authorization. Likewise, Bonhoeffer argues that Christ's action is unique from fallen human action in its universality, sinlessness, and once-for-all character, and this is true even when one participates in Christ's overarching action (279). Vicarious representative action thus originates not in one's vocation or position, but in Christ's universal self-giving in freedom that exceeds vocation, and this elicits a different Christologically informed narration of free action in the exception. Where the logic of representation emphasizes the analogy of Christ breaking the law on behalf of others, the logic of free "vocationless" action emphasizes the analogy of Christ's forfeiture of position and rights in sacrificial love (Phil. 2:4-10).[76] To act vicariously for the other is to expose oneself freely in seeking the good of another when one is in the position to act,

---

74. McKenny, "Freedom, Responsibility, and Moral Agency," 314–15. Bonhoeffer was notably wary of the whims of the *demos* and any revolutionary *ethos* from below. This remains true in the borderline situation when the people become "stupid," requiring liberation (DBWE 8:43–4). In a letter to Paul Lehmann from September 20, 1941, Bonhoeffer evinces this judgment by insisting that Germany needed "an authoritarian *Rechtstaat*" and a re-education initiative post-totalitarianism if people were eventually to act well in political freedom (DBWE 16:220).

75. Jennifer Moberly, "'Felicity to the Original Text'? The Translation of Bonhoeffer's *Ethics*," *Studies in Christian Ethics* 22, no. 3 (2009): 350. On the jurisprudential origins of *Stellvertretung* in Bonhoeffer's theology and how it refuses the logic of representation, see Karola S. Radler, *"Decision" in the Thought of Dietrich Bonhoeffer and Carl Schmitt: A Comparative Study*, diss. (Stellenbosch University, 2019).

76. "Disciples live with not only renouncing their own rights, but even renouncing their own righteousness" (DBWE 4:106).

which is what Bonhoeffer ventured in the conspiracy.[77] Such an account affirms that one's position opens opportunities for responsible action. This avoids treating one's vocation or position as superfluous for action. But it likewise asserts that one's vocation becomes the occasion for self-surrendering vulnerability in freely giving up one's rights, which ultimately confesses that one is powerless and dependent on God's activity and renewal in such exposure.[78] *Stellvertretung* submits all activity to God for the benefit of others, which concretely displays the Christological character of free action in the exception.

Accordance with Reality: A common worry in readings of Bonhoeffer's theology is that the free venture becomes a private, enthusiastic affair divorced from the world. There is no doubt that Bonhoeffer's description of action in accordance with reality undercuts this danger. While the free venture is ignorant of its merits, it nevertheless attends to God's world, affirming the external orientation of the actor, and in this sense one's activity is always public and open for discursive engagement. The danger in emphasizing action in accordance with reality in narrating the exception, though, is that one narrates the definitive features of the moment as atemporally constituted, which assumes their stability and uniformity in encounter. It further assumes that one can anticipate and understand the character of the moment based on the preexisting possibilities of its context. Subsequently, the shortcoming with common narrations is that they abdicate Bonhoeffer's earlier emphasis that encounter with reality is always provisional and in flux insofar as entities are always temporally saturated: "The question about the good is asked and decided in the midst of a situation of our life that is both determined in a particular way and yet still incomplete, unique and yet already in transition" (247).

There is a sense that action in accordance with reality in the exception must first attend to the time insofar as the meaning and impetus of the moment is the interruptive activity of God that exceeds the moment's preexisting possibilities. Put differently, one cannot act in accordance with the moment without undergoing the liberating event that enables responsive action beyond anticipation. It is to affirm that one can act into a given context through one's pre-understanding of the world and the historical context, but these contextual and factual elements are insufficient to account for the character of the moment and one's action within it, since the moment exceeds and disrupts one's interpretive paradigms.[79] The moment always remains (at least in part) beyond the limit of the communicable and appearance, belonging only to God who judges in grace and mercy.

---

77. As Bonhoeffer argues earlier in *Discipleship*: "What is clear, however, is that those suffering in the power of the body of Christ suffer in a vicariously representative action 'for' the church community, 'for' the body of Christ. They are permitted to bear what others are spared" (DBWE 4:222).

78. DBWE 4:164.

79. Romano, *Event and World*, 60–5.

To act in accordance with reality thus requires a response that exceeds the possibilities of external inquiry or self-examination available in the moment. And this further entails that a coherent narration of responsible action in the exception is often not available in the moment, but only emerges after the dust has settled. Indeed, the reflection that emerges from the exception is characteristically retrospective, being open in principle to all who witness the event or hear testimonies concerning it. Post-eventual narrations of the exception reflect with Bonhoeffer on the character of responsible action in a moment that relativizes the ordinary modes of parsing reality, calling for a renewal of political and ethical language in light of the exception.

Conclusion

By situating Bonhoeffer's description of the exception within his theology of history rather than Machiavelli's problematic account of necessity, an alternative narration of the structure of responsible action emerged. By prioritizing an account of freedom resting on God's liberating activity in history, how one narrates responsible action in the exception is repositioned. A primary emphasis on self-reflective moral deliberation shifts to the confession of God's reconciling activity and guidance, highlighting the individual's single-minded attention to God and neighbor rather than the self. The disruptive activity of God in history liberates human action to respond in undetermined freedom for the good of political life, and it discloses and renews the character of law and political life in accordance with the divine commandment. The next two chapters substantiate this reading by showing how these themes had long been important to Bonhoeffer. In Chapter 5, Bonhoeffer's radical notion of free Christian action is further developed, narrating how this action remains political in orientation and effect. Contrary to common critiques of Bonhoeffer's account of simple obedience, the chapter argues that his radical account of extraordinary action is not arbitrary. In Chapter 6, Bonhoeffer's account of politics and ethics in the bond of responsible life are re-narrated in considering how the exception sanctifies and reorients them for the flourishing of human life. The exception and the responsible action that occurs therein unleashes theological resources for the subsequent reimagination of concrete political life and its tasks (i.e., the mandates). It accomplishes this by following a very different theological route than the one proposed in the Machiavellian picture, which remains common in many readings of Bonhoeffer today. The two chapters, ultimately, develop a single logic that describes the "extraordinary situation" as God's liberation in history (Chapter 4) that transforms and orients free political action (Chapter 5) and bound political life (Chapter 6).

Chapter 5

THE POLITICS OF EXTRAORDINARY FREEDOM

The Christian life begins with a liberating event that sets one free for a life of faith and service. The political begins with a founding event that initiates space for free political action and the pursuit of the common good. While there is a resemblance between the two events, the relationship between them is not self-evident or even necessary; a connection between them requires explication.[1] The purpose of this chapter is to develop an account of free individual action oriented to the formation of political life in a reading of Bonhoeffer's theology. In continuation with Chapter 4, the account of freedom developed is founded upon and responsive to God's liberating activity in history. It is a freedom undetermined by law and ethics without becoming arbitrary and utterly private. Such undetermined free action is epitomized by Bonhoeffer's concept of simple obedience which responds immediately to the call of God.

The chapter develops this argument in four steps. The first section follows Bonhoeffer's critique of insufficient modes of political freedom that contribute to the emergence and maturation of totalitarian politics. Through an engagement with Hannah Arendt and her analysis of totalitarianism, the section finishes by considering the question of how spontaneous freedom persists in a political context that actively works to demolish free action in toto. In the next section, I turn to Bonhoeffer's account of undetermined freedom founded by God's liberating activity in the event of Christ's call. Through a reading of *Discipleship*, the section argues that Bonhoeffer's impulse to describe extraordinary freedom as remaining free from material or ideological determination is essential for a liberating politics in a totalizing context. This impulse is exemplified in Bonhoeffer's account of the "extraordinary" command to love one's enemies. The final section anticipates and combats the objection that

---

1. Luther, for instance, maintained that spiritual liberation does not bolster political revolution. Spiritual liberation reorients and renews one's relationship to temporal authority and office but does not liberate one from temporal authority and office. "For baptism does not make men free in body and property, but in soul" (LW 46:51). As Luther notes in his 1935 Commentary on Galatians, civic righteousness and Christian righteousness are two different things that one should not mix together (LW 26:4–12, 249). See Marius Timmann Mjaaland, "Sovereignty and Submission: Luther's Political Theology and the Violence of Christian Metaphysics," *Studies in Christian Ethics* 31, no. 4 (2018): 435–51.

undetermined freedom necessarily becomes arbitrary and private. It insists that freedom undetermined by law nevertheless remains in relation to the law, affirming the intelligibility and public character of individual free action. It is responsive and oriented to God's action in history, maintaining space for discerning reflection in the Christian life. This "wise" discernment, however, is characterized by a post-eventual reflection that seeks not to hinder God's liberating and formative action moving forward. As Bonhoeffer argues in "God's Love and the Disintegration of the World," discernment does not necessarily precede action but often occurs through or follows after simple obedience. Bonhoeffer thus maintains the hermeneutic priority of action in the narration of simple obedience. The chapter concludes by describing Bonhoeffer's conspiracy activity as repentance. This characterization captures the simplicity of political action in responsiveness to God's movement and liberation in history.[2] The end result is a different narration of the conspiracy that affirms the adventitious character of political freedom that is undetermined by but stands in relation to law and ethics.

The Annihilation of Freedom in Totalitarianism

Bonhoeffer wrote much of his corpus in a context of totalitarianism.[3] He observed firsthand its emergence and development, culminating in its expansion into and domination of all realms of human life. One of Bonhoeffer's long-standing critiques of totalitarianism was that it eliminates human freedom and ultimately the human being. Bonhoeffer forwards this critique in his 1933 radio lecture, "The Führer and the Individual in the Younger Generation."[4] One of the principal strengths of this lecture is how Bonhoeffer captures the movement toward the ideology of the leader in the years following the Great War, culminating in the forfeiture of the free individual.[5]

---

2. It would be an egregious oversight not to recognize the influence of Bonhoeffer's theology on liberation theology, particularly in the theology of Gustavo Gutiérrez and James H. Cone. See Gustavo Gutiérrez, *The Power of the Poor in History*, trans. Robert McAfee (Mary Knoll: Orbis Books, 1983), 169–232; James H. Cone, *A Black Theology of Liberation: Fortieth Anniversary Edition* (Mary Knoll: Orbis Books, 2018). For the influence of Bonhoeffer on liberation theologies, see Geffrey B. Kelley and Matthew D. Kirkpatrick, "Dietrich Bonhoeffer and Liberation Theologies," in *Engaging Bonhoeffer*, 139–68. Bonhoeffer's resistance activity and theology contributed to liberation theology through its prioritization of "the perspective from below" as enunciated in "After Ten Years" (DBWE 8:52).

3. I follow O'Donovan in defining totalitarianism as an "order that, implicitly or explicitly, offers itself as the sufficient and necessary condition of human welfare." O'Donovan, *Desire of the Nations*, 274.

4. DBWE 12:268–82.

5. On the failures of the Weimar Republic in the postwar years and the emergence of National Socialism as the background to Bonhoeffer's developing political theology, see Radler, "Decision," 37–82.

Bonhoeffer describes three generations in the lecture, each separated from one another by five years. In normal times, they would constitute a single generation, but the Great War generated greater difference and hostility between them. The primary difference between them is when they reached maturity in relation to the war. The first generation matured during the war. Inundated by bloodshed and death, they scorned those who matured after the fighting had stopped, such as the second generation who reached maturity in the postwar period. This younger generation faced the rubble of the postwar world and attempted to find "a foothold that could help sustain their lives in this chaos." In the face of the meaninglessness and isolation of individual life (and the scorn of their older peers), they yearned for new authority and for "a new meaningful common life."[6] They were convinced of the impotence of liberalism, individualism, and other "ideologies" to provide these desires, and thus they cried out for and willed a new leader—a singular individual, unconstrained by bonds and office, who embodied the group's ideals and would liberate them. Bonhoeffer narrates repeatedly how the authorization of the leader was the free choice of the mass in pursuing liberation. The choice was "the movement's first creative act" with no rational basis.[7] But this leader failed them, falling short of their ideals thereby losing his authority.[8]

The third generation reached maturity with the collapse of the second generation's hopes. But instead of scorning the leader, they scorned their own futures in service to another. Bonhoeffer suggests that this generation totally surrenders the self to the leader, embracing as their duty unconditional obedience to political authority. "The individual is totally dissolved; he becomes a tool in the hands of the leader."[9] It is the total forfeiture of one's freedom and responsibility to the leader. Certainly, the existence of the leader reveals a latent freedom among the masses insofar as they continue to elect and authorize the leader. As Bonhoeffer emphasizes, the leader has authority from below, not above. Nevertheless, individual freedom recedes from view when the individual views their ultimate relation to the leader instead of God, willingly losing themselves in the process.[10] The free choice of the mass ultimately led to the dissolution of freedom that can only be received again from God.

Bonhoeffer again critiqued insufficient accounts of freedom a few years later in the *Ethics* manuscript "Heritage and Decay," reflecting there on the account of freedom developed in the French Revolution.[11] Bonhoeffer identifies various elements that propelled the French Revolution: the revolt of the masses, a newfound nationalism, and faith in historical and cultural progress. But the most central element was the rise of "liberated *ratio*" that makes an explicit break from

---

6. DBWE 12:272.
7. DBWE 12:273–4.
8. DBWE 12:276.
9. DBWE 12:277.
10. DBWE 12:281.
11. DBWE 6:103–32.

tradition and traditionally held orders, authorities, and institutions by stressing "the equality and freedom of all humans before law and one another." Liberated *ratio* ushered in a new era of "liberated humanity . . . liberated reason, liberated class, and a liberated people," but it also led to destructive technological progress and power.[12] Nature became wholly subject to the externalization of human *ratio* in a technological progress that subsumes all in its path.[13] The means of technology became an end in itself.[14] Bonhoeffer likewise identifies the French Revolution with the lionization of the masses and nationalism insofar as popular sovereignty fostered their development. The masses cry for their rights, including the right for national freedom and expansion. Bonhoeffer concludes that the West inherited technology, mass movements, and nationalism from this revolution.[15] In a similar manner to "The Individual and the Führer," Bonhoeffer concludes that the self-liberation of humanity via *ratio* leads ultimately to the destruction of human life.

> The French Revolution has created the new intellectual unity of the West. It consists in the liberation of humanity as *ratio*, as the mass, and as a people (*Volk*). In the struggle for liberation all three go together; after freedom is achieved they become deadly enemies. This new unity carries the seeds of its own destruction. It is further evident—and here a basic law of history becomes clear—that the desire for absolute freedom leads people into deepest servitude. The master of the machine becomes its slave; the machine becomes an enemy of the human being. What is created turns against its creator—a strange repetition of the biblical fall! The liberation of the masses ends in the horrible reign of the guillotine. Nationalism leads directly to war. Human liberation as an absolute ideal leads to the self-destruction of human beings. At the end of the road traveled by the French Revolution lies nihilism.[16]

This liberation ultimately led to utter servitude and the demolition of reason, human life, and freedom.[17]

---

12. DBWE 6:117.

13. DBWE 6:116–17. For more on Bonhoeffer's engagements with technology, see Stephan van den Heuvel, *Bonhoeffer's Christocentric Theology and Fundamental Debates in Environmental Ethics* (Eugene: Pickwick Publications, 2017), 164–206; Daniel J. Treier, "Modernity's Machine: Technology Coming of Age in Bonhoeffer's Apocalyptic Proverbs," in *Bonhoeffer, Christ, and Culture*, ed. Keith L. Johnson and Timothy Larson (Downers Grove: InterVarsity Press, 2013), 91–111.

14. On this point, see DBWE 11:246–57.

15. DBWE 6:119–21.

16. DBWE 6:122.

17. Robinson identifies the similarities between Bonhoeffer and Hegel's critiques of the French Revolution and its account of absolute freedom. Robinson, *Christ and Revelatory Community in Bonhoeffer's Reception of Hegel*, 163–9.

There are obvious differences between the two accounts of freedom depicted in "The Individual and the Führer" and "Heritage and Decay." The former epitomizes a priority on popular will and authority; the latter epitomizes a priority on reason and equality in law and human rights. But there is an obvious coalescence in how both conceive of freedom as immanently achieved and discontinuous with the structures and authorities that typify the eras that precede their emergence. In both cases it is a liberation birthed in crisis, seized by the people, and carried to the end of self-destruction. The coalescence extends to their shared histories as well. The two overlap and, while they are not identical, they emerge in the same context—the modern West—and they play off one another, particularly in the rise of totalitarianism. Turning back to "The Individual and the Führer," it is noteworthy that the crisis faced by the second generation stems from the destructive consequences of the liberated *ratio* of the French Revolution. Technology turned human lives into objects for destruction in the Great War, those in low positions faced economic peril and indignity, and the ideologies of old were thus revealed insufficient and cruel. And yet, the turn to the ideology of the leader reanimated the technological rationale, mass movement, and nationalism contained in the French Revolution. National Socialism drew these aspects together, intensifying them and setting them on a novel course in Germany. Immanent political liberation is seized again, but through sheer will that sacrifices itself to the leader. These modes of freedom beget totalitarianism.

In *The Origins of Totalitarianism*, Arendt similarly argues that the movement of totalitarianism culminates in the obliteration of freedom through technological organization and the ideology of the leader. The paradox is that the leader depends upon the masses electing favor for initial power but then initiates an ideological movement that extinguishes personal choice and judgment through political organization. The end goal is total control that safeguards total power from internal danger. "Total power can be achieved and safeguarded only in a world of conditioned reflexes, of marionettes without the slightest trace of spontaneity."[18] And this, Arendt observes, was largely successful with National Socialism. It transformed most of "civilized" society into cogs of the totalitarian machine.[19]

Yet, Arendt demurs, a few did not succumb to National Socialism. They exercised personal freedom and resisted totalitarianism. This leads Arendt to ask: How does an individual become free within a system that moves heaven and earth to destroy freedom?[20] And how does an individual distinguish between good and evil when all of respectable society proclaims evil as good?[21] Bonhoeffer asks the same question in the years of his resistance, reflecting on the origin and character of politically generative free action beyond determination. As articulated in the next section, Bonhoeffer argues that this freedom is utterly adventitious, originating

18. Arendt, *Origins of Totalitarianism* (London: Penguin Random House, 2017) 599.
19. Arendt, *Eichmann in Jerusalem*, 287–9.
20. Arendt, *Origins of Totalitarianism*, 601.
21. Arendt, *Eichmann in Jerusalem*, 295.

in a liberating event *extra nos* that generates a renewed politics in a world of domination. This comes through in Bonhoeffer's *Discipleship*—a text written in response to encroaching totalitarianism.[22] Bonhoeffer there describes an account of free individual action undetermined by law and politically generative, originating in the call to discipleship.

Adventitious Liberation and Undetermined Political Freedom

There is a tight interconnection between the call of Christ and the inauguration of a situation when discipleship commences. In the chapter, "The Call to Discipleship," Bonhoeffer describes how "a call to discipleship thus immediately creates a new situation" (62).[23] It is not a situation determined by preceding happenings, psychological states, or reason; it is instead based solely on the word of Jesus. Christ's Word calls the disciple to the situation of faith when one acts in direct and immediate responsiveness to the call. When Jesus called Peter onto the sea, the faithful response was to walk on water. There is a radicality to this account that is not lost on Bonhoeffer. For Jesus to call Peter onto the water is "completely impossible and ethically, simply irresponsible" (63), but nevertheless the sole path to faith. It is not a moment for reflection but action. There is no mediating reality and no creaturely category that explains the situation or empowers the response. A few pages earlier Bonhoeffer further expands upon this point in describing the call of Jesus to Levi. The call is abrupt and jarring, coming from nowhere in the flow of the Gospel narrative:

> It is quite offensive to natural reason. Reason is impelled to reject the abruptness of the response. It seeks something to mediate it; it seeks an explanation. No matter what, some sort of mediation has to be found, psychological or historical. . . . But the text is stubbornly silent on this point; in it, everything depends on call and deed directly facing each other. The text is not interested in psychological explanations for the faithful decisions of a person (57).

The situation and the response refuse reduction or immanent determination. They are thoroughly adventitious and singular.

When Bonhoeffer refuses to categorize the situation of Christ's call under determination, this repeats his consistent concern that God's freedom might be compromised. As interpreters of Bonhoeffer frequently observe, Christ's activity in revelation must remain under no dependency or determination to remain free. If Christ's call is necessarily mediated by some creaturely medium, then it becomes static and controllable, losing its freedom and authority. What is equally essential

---

22. Jennifer McBride, *The Church for the World: A Theology of Public Witness* (Oxford: Oxford University Press, 2014), 91–5.

23. All inline page citations in this chapter are from *Discipleship* (DBWE 4).

for Bonhoeffer is the contention that the immanent determination of the situation and the disciple's response would likewise undercut the freedom of the disciple. If the liberating act is determined by reason, one's circumstances, or psychology, then it becomes the victim of a reductive process that eludes liberation, since Christ's call alone remains undetermined by the totalizing reach of sin in the world. For liberation to remain total, it must remain a graced response to divine encounter that places one into freedom.[24] Like the call of Christ, liberation befalls the disciple. Grace is totally God's activity with even the response of the disciple being determined by the call.[25] Anything less is the denial of liberation.

Bonhoeffer suggests that one of the primary strategies to mitigate the call of Christ is to make the situation a topic of ethical discussion. This not only creates a distance between the one called and the situation of the call but also gives the inquirer a sense of control over the situation, turning the call into an object of ethical debate. By deliberating on the situation and its circumstances, the one called delays the response and decides on one's own schedule. Bonhoeffer repudiates this approach, perceiving that ethical discourse inevitably becomes ethical conflict. The unity and simplicity of God's call fragments in ethical conflict, and this undermines the responsiveness of obedient faith: "[Ethical conflict] tortures and subjugates people because it hinders their doing the liberating act of obedience. . . . Only the obedient deed is to be taken seriously. It ends and destroys the conflict and frees us to become children of God" (72). Ethical discourse does not terminate in faithful action but internal discord, revealing that God calls principally for immediate obedience that terminates in praise. Bonhoeffer contends that obedience alone places persons into a new liberating relation to God and world where their action remains undetermined and free. Their perspective, action, and thought enter a new relation that responds and ever looks to Christ's liberating presence without reducing it to any creaturely category or mode of knowledge (92–9). The adventitious response to the initial call thus becomes paradigmatic of free action after the call, extending into the daily life of the disciple. The danger for the liberated person is to subvert freedom back into the categories of law, determination, and the immanent nexus of cause and effect. It rationalizes the spontaneity of faith, making it normal.

There are typically two strategies to expunge freedom through determination. There is material determination and ideological determination. The former

---

24. Bonhoeffer echoes the Kierkegaard of *Philosophical Fragments* in this regard. The only possibility for the human to move from the untruth of sin to truth is through a liberating encounter with the God who became human, who sets the conditions for the reception and response to truth in the moment. See Søren Kierkegaard, *Philosophical Fragments*, ed. and trans. Howard V. Hong and Edna H. Hong (Princeton: Princeton University Press, 1985). On Bonhoeffer's employment of *Philosophical Fragments* in his Christology, see Rowan Williams, *Christ: The Heart of Creation* (London. Bloomsbury, 2018), 187–98.

25. "It is not *the works* which create faith. Instead, you are given a situation in which you can have faith" (DBWE 4:63).

explains free action on an empirical basis. What one does is determined by one's surroundings or past experiences. Its explanation, in other words, depends on a principle of natural causality.[26] When describing the original call to the disciples, Bonhoeffer describes material determination as "psychological or historical" (57). Material determination as psychological attempts to explain action on the basis of psychological states or dispositions.[27] One's action or thought reflects their own internal processing of their mental lives, formed through their personal histories and experiences. What one thinks or does is not a free response but the expression of one's psychology. Material determination as historical mirrors the psychological, since the thought and action are a response to one's external circumstances. They are reducible to and explainable within an immanent nexus of cause and effect.

Ideological determination works in the other direction; it attempts to describe the intelligibility and outworking of action on the basis of ideals. One mode of ideological determination is the suggestion that action becomes the material function of ideas. In a particularly Hegelian mode: ideas produce material effects with the individual or political act becoming the outworking of reason or norm.[28] In a less obvious way, a similar mode of ideological determination occurs when thinkers identify a group or figure as embodying a countercultural practice that witnesses to the ideals of the Kingdom of God. While these thinkers often emphasize the particularity of these communities or individuals as the starting point of their reflections, this declaration often obfuscates the constructive activity of the critic who narrates the ideals embodied by the historical group or figure. This occurs when commentators "find" in Bonhoeffer's life and resistance activity the realization of ideals that were already central to their ethical and political vision. There is a sleight of hand in this gesture as the narrator selectively maximizes the ideals and diminishes everything to the contrary in constructing the story. As Ted Smith argues: "The cultural elements attained authority through a tautological magic: ideals defined cultural practices that then embodied ideals."[29] Bonhoeffer's life is subsequently instrumentalized in service to the propagation of moral and political ideals. In a similar vein, when one suggests that Bonhoeffer's thought is paradigmatically and decisively formed by a tradition, the assumption is often that the outworking of that tradition determines Bonhoeffer's thought that forms action. There may be development, but it exists within the logic of a particular tradition. The thought does not disrupt the prevailing discourse; it rather proceeds in the direct development of it, participating in its own external outworking in the development of new texts and ethical programs. Thought and action become determined by prior discourse and explainable on its basis.

---

26. Kahn, *Political Theology*, 92.

27. On Bonhoeffer's resistance to psychological explanations of selfhood and action, see DBWE 2:142.

28. Kahn, *Political Theology*, 95.

29. Ted Smith, *The New Measures: A Theological History of Democratic Practice* (Cambridge: Cambridge University Press, 2007), 20.

When Bonhoeffer defends the free call to discipleship from both material and ideological determination, he perceives the roots of a totalitarian logic within them. When the disciple's response becomes determined by either, it misunderstands the adventitious origin and effect of the call that supersedes creaturely categories; it subsumes the liberating call once again under the tyranny of determination, losing its free responsiveness. This totalizing danger is not unique to National Socialism as much as National Socialism is the extreme outworking of this logic. The totalizing drive is implicit to reality where human *ratio* rebels against God's sovereign upholding of fallen creation, seeking mastery and sufficiency in itself.[30] Totalitarianism may be unique in its outworking, but its seed spreads through the daily determinations that overwhelm human action and thought. This danger extends to ethics. When Bonhoeffer writes about the ethicist a few years later, he resists any totalizing claim from the ethicist on human action. When ethics dominates, subsuming all of life thereunder, it impedes the free interplay of political life. Life thus consists in "the suspicious, watchful measuring of what is by what ought to be and in the anxious subordination of everything natural to the requirements of duty, of everything free to what is necessary, of everything concrete to the general, of everything without purpose to a purpose."[31] The freedom of the individual must remain true to its origin, remaining free of political and ethical determination (97).

Enemy Love and Friendship in the Political

The call of Christ liberates the disciple for a life of visible witness to and for the world. The call not only individuates but initiates a new political community into which the disciple is grafted. The immediate call of Christ "becomes the basis for entirely new community" (98).[32] Naturally, the community initiated in *Discipleship* is the church, who witnesses to the world concerning the presence of Christ and his reconciling activity in their communal life (218). Witness is the political task of the church in *Discipleship*, which continues to find articulation in Bonhoeffer's later emphasis on the church's mandate of proclamation.[33] Of course, there are obvious differences between the visible politics of *Discipleship*, *Ethics*,

---

30. DBWE 3:54.
31. DBWE 6:370.
32. Bonhoeffer is often criticized for having an insufficient pneumatology which is seemingly epitomized in Christ's immediate call to discipleship. At different points in *Discipleship*, Bonhoeffer diminishes this criticism by affirming that the Spirit witnesses to and makes Christ present in the church and history (DBWE 4:228), empowering responsive Christian action in history (DBWE 4:209–10). Bonhoeffer's ecclesiology exemplifies this pneumatological emphasis most prominently. For an argument on this point, see David Emerton, *God's Church-Community: The Ecclesiology of Dietrich Bonhoeffer* (London: Bloomsbury T&T Clark, 2020).
33. DBWE 6:73.

and Bonhoeffer's prison writings insofar as Bonhoeffer later extends the scope and nature of the church's relationship to the world, particularly in his late reflections on religionless Christianity. Commentators often exaggerate the differences between these writings by prioritizing one as constitutive of Bonhoeffer's mature political vision over the others. The result is that these contestations diminish what is continuous and important in the movement from *Discipleship* to the prison writings: the assertion that the renewal and formation of free political life originates in responsiveness to a liberating encounter, which is irreducible to the normal course of events or to postlapsarian politics. The purpose of this subsection is to demonstrate the importance of this assertion through Bonhoeffer's account of enemy love in *Discipleship* and his account of friendship in his letters from prison.

In *Discipleship*, Bonhoeffer describes obedience to the command to love one's enemy as the extraordinary deed of the church that simultaneously witnesses to and founds a politics characterized by reconciliation instead of division and violence. By subverting the logic and expectations of the world, Christian love of enemy becomes an "unbearable offense" to "the natural person" by undermining the very divisions that became foundational to their politics (138). It refuses the "common" understanding that one loves their own and that there are limits to human love and community justified on ethical, religious, or racial grounds (143).[34] Such love, Bonhoeffer insists, has no natural or normal basis as it emerges from Christ's historical action and command—enemy love encapsulates "the extraordinary, irregular, not self-evident" (144). The deed becomes revelatory, witnessing to a peaceable politics that transforms one's perception of the world beyond immanent possibilities. "What is distinctly Christian begins with *the extraordinary*, and that is what finally places what is natural in the proper light" (144). Through enemy love, one perceives how the visible politics and activity of the church occurs within the world and everyday political life, but its foundation and enactment have no natural basis.

In his January 23, 1944, letter to Bethge, Bonhoeffer speaks to the extraordinariness of friendship for political life by comparing it to the mandates. Bonhoeffer suggests that while the mandates are the God-given orders of human life that contribute to free political life, they are incomplete for "full" human life in themselves—they require something from outside for their sustenance and flourishing. Bonhoeffer suggests this something is friendship. While friendship emerges in the midst of the mandates, friendship is never reducible to one's earthly vocation within them: being a friend is not merely being a good citizen, mother, or

---

34. As the August draft of the Bethel Confession states: "We reject the false doctrine that struggle is the fundamental law of the original creation, and that an aggressive attitude is therefore God's commandment arising from the original creation. Struggle presupposes the condition of being friend or foe. This condition arises only from the existence of good and evil. The goal of this struggle, to annihilate one another, is a consequence of the fall, according to which good and evil are no longer separate in a human being" (DBWE 12:386).

5. The Politics of Extraordinary Freedom

worker.[35] This is because friendship originates not in the realm of command and obedience, but in the realm of freedom and contingency:

> Precisely because friendship belongs within the scope of this freedom ("of the Christian person"!?), we must defend it confidently against all "ethical" existences that may frown upon it—certainly without claiming for it the *"necessitas"* of a divine command, but by claiming the *"necessitas"* of *freedom*! I believe that, within this realm of freedom, friendship is by far the rarest—where is it still found in our world, which is defined by the *first three* mandates?—and the most precious good. It is beyond comparison with the benefits we have from the mandates; over against them it is sui generis, but belongs together with them like the cornflowers belong to the field of grain.[36]

Bonhoeffer captures how friendship occurs within political life and is essential for political life, but its origin nevertheless comes from elsewhere and refuses political instrumentalization. Guido de Graff thus describes friendship as parapolitical "insofar as it exists *alongside* politics in a significant sense." By this, de Graff suggests that friendship is "somehow parallel to political process. In contrast to the notion of analogy, parallelism suggests historical and/or social proximity in addition to mere resemblance. Thus, for example, friendship might be identified not only as resembling a political community in certain aspects, but also as functioning alongside it—or perhaps even as providing certain conditions for its very existence."[37] In the context of Bonhoeffer's letter, friendship enacts the freedom of full human life in the midst of political organization and determination. Friendship, in short, supports and even has the potential to renew political life without ever being reducible to political life or law. It witnesses to and enacts free and unified activity, even in conditions where political organization discourages free coordinated action.

Pairing Bonhoeffer's reflections on enemy love and friendship invokes the specter of Carl Schmitt, who argued that the political originates in the friend-enemy distinction.[38] To be sure, there are a number of prominent differences between Schmitt and Bonhoeffer. Where Schmitt argued that the political begins in the existential decision of a people between friend and enemy, Bonhoeffer identifies the

---

35. This point is emphasized in the first two stanzas of Bonhoeffer's poem, "The Friend" (DBWE 8:526-7). Bonhoeffer wrote the poem for Bethge, and his musings on friendship were prompted by their friendship.

36. DBWE 8:268-9. Emphasis original. On the development of Bonhoeffer's theology of friendship in the prison letters, see Eberhard Bethge, "Bonhoeffer's Theology of Friendship," in *Friendship and Resistance: Essays on Dietrich Bonhoeffer* (Grand Rapids: Eerdmans Publishing Co., 1995), 80-104.

37. Guido de Graff, *Politics in Friendship: A Theological Account* (London: Bloomsbury T&T Clark, 2014), 21.

38. Carl Schmitt, *The Concept of the Political*, trans. George Schwab (Chicago: The University of Chicago Press, 2007).

origin of a new peaceable politics in the love of God that overcomes such divisions in discipleship. Where Schmitt asserts that the political genuinely manifests only where the possibility of war and violence remains ever-present, Bonhoeffer asserts that the love of enemies breaks the cycle of violence and retaliation at the heart of the politics of this age—it overwhelms and refuses political division, calling such enemies friends (139).[39] Where Schmitt argues that love of enemy is a strictly private concept inapplicable to the political realm, Bonhoeffer suggests that "what is sinful for an individual person . . . can never be a virtue for a *nation*," thus the legitimacy of the command to love one's enemies between nations.[40]

But for all their obvious contrasts, Bonhoeffer affirms with Schmitt that the origin of the political emerges not through technical or political procedure but from a decision beyond determination or anticipation. The usual modes of political intervention, including the mandate of the government to restrain evil by bearing the sword, are insufficient to transform and renew politics—the impetus for political renewal exceeds the possibilities and means of the prevailing political orders. The renewal of the political originates in a free act that cannot be specified or guaranteed in advance, remaining in relation to but undetermined by the bonds of political necessity.[41] This is what Bonhoeffer's account of friendship captures in particular: the bonds that initiate political renewal are formed within but originate beyond political life through the spontaneity of friendship. In contrast to Schmitt, this friendship originates not in the preferential selection of friends that is simultaneously the rejection and exclusion of another (the enemy), thus proceeding on the basis of division, but it originates in the liberating call of Christ.[42] As Bonhoeffer notes in his letter to Bethge, friendship originates in "this freedom 'of the Christian person,'" thus echoing Luther's 1520 treatise. Just like the freedom of the Christian, such friendship emerges in the order of gift.[43] It embraces the other by a differing logic that does not form political bonds on the basis of similarity or preference, which easily and often shifts into enmity and violence, but on the basis of a Christologically mediated encounter in the experience of faith, witnessing to the coming Kingdom of God that supersedes the divisive politics of this age. Friendship derivative of Christ's call reorients political life, revealing that the mandates do not necessarily divide persons, but can flourish in a free political space—what Bonhoeffer calls a *Spielraum*—where the fullness of human life can arise over against divisive and othering politics in the reconciling activity of God.[44]

---

39. Ibid., 33–7.

40. Ibid., 28–9. DBWE 12:260. Emphasis original.

41. For more on this point, see Bonhoeffer's "Christ and Peace" (DBWE 12:258–562).

42. Following Jacob Taubes' reading of Romans 9–11, the political concept of enemy reflects the historical dialectic of election whereby "historical enemies of God" (51) are ultimately saved through election. Taubes suggested this to Schmitt, who responded: "Taubes, before you die, you must tell some people about this" (3). Jacob Taubes, *The Political Theology of Paul*, trans. Dana Hollander (Stanford: Stanford University Press, 2004).

43. Jacques Derrida, *Politics of Friendship*, trans. George Collins (London: Verso, 1997).

44. DBWE 8:268.

Undetermined Freedom Is Not Arbitrary

The frequent objection to an account of freedom undetermined by law and rationality is that free action subsequently becomes arbitrary. Critics argue that if free action exceeds law and rationality, it avoids the scrutiny of public judgment, thus becoming utterly private. Decision beyond law risks the demolition of all law and order. In the case of Bonhoeffer's account of the exception, Brown argues that such freedom threatens the enactment of pure violence that only begets more violence. Arbitrary violence deconstructs the necessary conditions for free political life, leading to the perpetuation of permanent revolution that unravels political order. Brown thus argues that freedom must be subsumed under law and rationality or else it threatens violence beyond reason. Law must bind the extraordinary or else freedom becomes unhinged.[45] The dynamics at play here draw back to the discussion of God's freedom in Chapter 3, particularly the worry that God's freedom becomes arbitrary if God's activity is undetermined by reason. The charge leveled is that if God's activity remains unconstrained by reason or law, then God is privy to demolish what God previously established. The same problematic holds for Brown when shifting to discuss free political action in an immediate relationship to God in the exception.

A primary shortcoming of critiques like Brown's is that they assume freedom undetermined by law has no relation to the law.[46] Inversely, they assume that freedom must proceed from law if freedom is to have a relation to the law. It echoes what Steven Paulson labels the legal scheme whereby one only lives commendably by exercising their free will in obedience to the law.[47] Bonhoeffer refuses the legal scheme by asserting that while freedom befalls a person apart from the law in Christ, this is not to live in lawlessness, which still lives within the world defined by law, it is to live in Christ who establishes and mediates a new law. In his exegesis of Matthew 5:17-20 in *Discipleship*, Bonhoeffer describes how Christ's fulfillment of the law does not release the Christian from the law, which is the error of Marcion (115–16), but rather places the Christian in a different relation to the law. Indeed, while the disciple remains "bound to the Old Testament law" (116), there is now a distinctiveness to the disciple's relation to it insofar as the binding proceeds from communion with Christ. The law does not mediate Christ but Christ mediates the law. To reverse this relationship is to switch "the gift and the giver," dissolving God into the law (117). The disciple thus remains bound to the law, but only because they are first bound to Christ in freedom.

Christ's mediation of the law thus maintains the relevance and demand of the law, but it nevertheless makes the law new—it is "the law of Christ" (120). It is new because Christ has fulfilled the law and its demands. Before the disciples

---

45. Brown, *God's Conspirator*, 101–21.
46. For an excellent discussion on this point, see Kahn, *Political Theology*, 46–61.
47. Paulson, *Doing Lutheran Theology*, 2–4, 170–92.

encounter the law, it is already fulfilled in the crucified Christ who sets them free. The law no longer awaits fulfillment in action since its fulfillment precedes and reconstitutes lawful action. Righteousness is gifted in the call of Christ, liberating Christian action for responsive discipleship in day-to-day life (120). This is "the better righteousness" of which Christ speaks (Mt. 5:20). The disciple's righteousness transforms their action and their very selves. A differing narration of individual free action emerges in this context, one that is in relation to the law without allowing the law to determine or mediate the action of the disciple.

Bonhoeffer calls this free action that proceeds from Christ's fulfillment of the law "simple obedience" (120). Bonhoeffer suggests that simple obedience mirrors the call of Christ by remaining undetermined by reason, law, or psychological factors. It responds immediately to Christ's call in simple faith. Bonhoeffer elaborates:

> The forces that wanted to get between the word of Jesus and obedience were just as great back then as they are today. Reason objected; conscience, responsibility, piety, even the law and principle of Scripture intervened to inhibit this most extreme, this lawless "enthusiasm." Jesus' call broke through all of this and mandated obedience. It was God's word. Simple obedience was required (77).

It is noteworthy that Bonhoeffer anticipates the charge of enthusiasm but thinks this charge does not apply. Simple obedience is not a context-less and private word, though Bonhoeffer thinks it must refuse ethical or rational determination.

The crucial element to understand this concept is the term "simple": *einfältig*. The word does not have the connotations of private immediacy, but naiveté. It is a trusting orientation to God that refuses to doubt or question God's Word in encounter. The concept has an existential orientation. Put simply, simple obedience is nothing other than a single-minded trust in God's Word and promise. Simple obedience denies that there is a gap between understanding and act, reflection and doing, and intention and response. It denies that the true act emerges from the self and one's reflective appropriation of their action.

Palpable hesitation emerges with this discussion of simple obedience because many assert that action undetermined by law can only be fanaticism or the transgression of law. It falls into the realm of the unintelligible. Commentators subsequently attempt to save Bonhoeffer by pointing to the various places where he provides space for common aspects of moral deliberation: reflection, discernment, self-examination, and so on. The juxtaposition of simplicity to discernment generates a "tension" or even a paradox within these renderings of Bonhoeffer.[48]

Commentators point, for instance, to Bonhoeffer's account of paradoxical obedience, which is when the disciple obeys Christ by responding to the law in a

---

48. For instance, Joshua Kaiser, *Becoming Simple and Wise: Moral Discernment in Dietrich Bonhoeffer's Vision of Christian Ethics* (Eugene: Pickwick Publications, 2015); Lisa E. Dahill, *Reading from the Underside of Selfhood: Bonhoeffer and Spiritual Formation* (Eugene: Pickwick Publications, 2008).

nonliteral and even "backward" manner. When Christ commands "Give away all that you possess," the paradoxical interpretation responds not by literally giving everything away but by being ready to divest oneself in the openness of faith. In this instance, the disciple does not obey the literal command of the Sermon on the Mount but responds in an unexpected manner that reflects upon Christ's "surprising" command in faith (79). Commentators suggest that paradoxical obedience chastens renditions of simple obedience.

But to leave Bonhoeffer's discussion here would be incomplete since it does not tell the whole story. For while Bonhoeffer affirms the place for paradoxical obedience, it does not become another "approach" to the command that chastens simple obedience. It rather takes the form of a concession, an admittance that Christ's freedom necessitates such a possibility. Paradoxical obedience is a confession that Christ's Word encounters the disciple in freedom, and this refuses a Scriptural legalism that determines God's will in advance. Paradoxical obedience does not prioritize reflection as much as it denies a literalistic hermeneutic that short-circuits attentive listening to God's command in the here and now. The suggestion that paradoxical obedience is a concession strengthens when considering Bonhoeffer's strong delimitation of it. Paradoxical obedience is riddled with danger, ever teetering toward the subduing of Christ's command. One can easily domesticate the command to avoid obedience through reflective deliberation. In seeking to avoid this temptation, Bonhoeffer suggests that paradoxical obedience is never an immanent possibility but is akin to the miracle. "In human terms it is an impossible possibility" (81). It is a concession to God's freedom rather than becoming the domestication of simplicity.

The character of simple obedience and discernment requires further explication, which will display more clearly how free action remains in relation to the law without becoming determined by the law. It is helpful at this point to turn again to Bonhoeffer's *Ethics* manuscript, "God's Love and the Disintegration of the World," as it continues to interact with these primary themes from *Discipleship*, but with explicit attention to the interrelation of simplicity and discernment. Whereas commentators tend to diminish the radicality of simple obedience in reading this manuscript, the reading I forward maintains the extraordinariness of simple obedience, narrating discernment in its light.

Discernment as a "Last Principle"

Bonhoeffer begins "God's Love and the Disintegration of the World" by asserting that ethics is a postlapsarian activity grounded in the knowledge of good and evil and that Christ's reconciliation is beyond good and evil and thus beyond ethics. Shame, conscience, ethical conflict, and ambiguity are all results of the fall with the Christian life proceeding on an entirely different basis: election.[49] God's

---

49. DBWE 6:299–302. As argued in Chapter 2, the theme of election emerges from Bonhoeffer's reading of CD II/2.

electing grace is the origin and sustenance of Christian life and action. Bonhoeffer presents the interactions of Christ and the Pharisees in the Gospel accounts as paradigmatic examples of action proceeding on entirely different bases. The Pharisees instantiate a fallen mode of action and reflection that attempts to sweep Christ into their ethical conflicts and debates.[50] What is striking is that Christ does not engage the Pharisees on their terms, he simply supersedes their discourse; he answers on another basis entirely. "Jesus," Bonhoeffer notes, "speaks out of a total freedom that is not even bound by the law of logical alternatives. This freedom with which Jesus rises above all laws must appear to the Pharisee as the destruction of all order, all piety, and all faith."[51] Bonhoeffer intensifies this comment later, specifying the simplicity of Jesus' freedom in greater detail:

> [Christ's] freedom gives him and those who belong to him something peculiarly certain, unquestioning, radiant, something beyond strife, something irresistible in their actions. The freedom of Jesus is not the arbitrary choice of one among countless possibilities. Instead, it consists precisely in the complete simplicity of his action, for which there are never several possibilities, conflicts, or alternatives, but always only one. Jesus calls this one option the will of God. . . . It is the source of freedom and simplicity in everything that is done.[52]

Bonhoeffer again maintains that simplicity and freedom are not arbitrary but nevertheless proceed on an entirely different basis unconstrained by the ethical conflict and logic of this age.

Nevertheless, Bonhoeffer eventually turns to discuss discernment (*prüfen*) in the Christian life. Akin to *Discipleship*, the concept of discernment emerges in his denial of simplicity as arbitrary intuition. In commenting on Rom. 12:2, Phil. 1:10, and Eph. 5:9, Bonhoeffer argues:

> These verses thoroughly correct the notion that a single-minded (*einfältig*) discerning of the will of God must occur in the form of intuition, by abandoning all reflection, by naively grasping the first thought or feeling that insinuates itself, that is, any psychologizing misunderstanding of the simplicity of the new life that has begun in Jesus. . . . The will of God may lie very deeply hidden among many competing possibilities. It is also not a system of rules that are fixed from the outset, but always new and different in each different life circumstance. This is why it is necessary to discern again and again what the will of God is. Heart, intellect, observation, and experience must work together in this discernment. This discernment of the will of God is such a serious matter precisely because it is no longer our own knowledge of good and evil that is at issue here, but the living will of God; because knowing the will of God is not at our human disposal,

---

50. DBWE 6:309–11.
51. DBWE 6:312.
52. DBWE 6:313.

5. The Politics of Extraordinary Freedom 127

but dependent entirely on God's grace; and, indeed, because this grace is and wants to be new every morning. The will of God can now no longer be confused with the voice of the heart, nor with any kind of inspiration, nor with any kind of absolute principle, since it reveals itself anew only to those discerning it in each particular case.[53]

The concession that discernment is necessary, here, has a different emphasis than *Discipleship* because the will of God now "may lie very deeply hidden among many competing possibilities." Since the will of God encounters Christians in fallen history, this entails an acknowledgment that Christians are not impervious to self-deception, claiming to receive the Word when they actually missed it. What is likewise distinctive is the shift to discernment in a more positive idiom. Only those who discern the will of God receive the will of God. Bonhoeffer raises discernment to new heights, allowing it a greater role in Christian life.

While Bonhoeffer gives an undeniable prominence to discernment in the manuscript, the danger that besets commentators is to give it an exaggerated prominence by where one positions it in a narration of simple free action. Discernment often takes a prominent position in narrations by preceding and directing action by its deliberative approach to the demands of the moment. The discernment of the will of God in history becomes the necessary prerequisite for responding to the will of God in simplicity. This constrains and contextualizes simplicity, taking priority in the narration of the free act.

Note, for instance, how discernment becomes prominent in Joshua Kaiser's study on discernment in Bonhoeffer's thought. In *Becoming Simple and Wise*, Kaiser is careful to emphasize that moral reflection cannot monopolize Christian action, since simplicity is not reducible to reflection. Simplicity remains an unreflective act. Nevertheless, simplicity stands in an irreducible relation to wisdom, which is a "rational, reflective approach" that seeks God's will in the muck and mire of one's circumstances.[54] Kaiser thus argues that simplicity and wisdom remain in "tension" in Christian action but one that Christ supersedes in his reconciling activity.[55] And yet, Kaiser subsumes both simplicity and wisdom into an account of discernment, which he defines as coming "to know [God's will] through a mental process of discriminating one option from another and determining the correct path amidst false alternatives and temptations."[56] The mental process becomes determinative since discernment becomes the overarching concept under which simplicity

---

53. DBWE 6:320–1.

54. Kaiser, *Becoming Simple and Wise*, 184.

55. Kaiser makes much of Bonhoeffer's use of *Aufheben* in "God's Love and the Disintegration of the World," suggesting that Bonhoeffer initially negates self-reflection, deliberation, and discernment but ultimately promotes a Christological mode of each activity. Ibid., 20–56, 74–5.

56. Ibid., 1. "Only through combining both simplicity and wisdom in the act of discernment can one accurately hear God's voice and respond accordingly" (Ibid., 82).

falls. Simplicity thus subtly falls under a narration of action that prioritizes reflective discernment as the controlling and stabilizing factor of action in a given situation. Simplicity characterizes the act itself and discernment characterizes the deliberative process that precedes the act.

In a similar vein, Jens Zimmermann elucidates the relationship between simplicity and discernment by narrating both within the preceding and overarching process of formation that a person undergoes in Christ.[57] In *Bonhoeffer's Christian*

---

57. Zimmermann, *Bonhoeffer's Christian Humanism*. See also Jens Zimmermann and Brian Gregor, eds., *Being Human, Becoming Human: Dietrich Bonhoeffer and Social Thought* (Cambridge: James Clarke & Co., 2010). In a similar vein, see Jennifer Moberly, *The Virtue of Bonhoeffer's Ethics: A Study of Dietrich Bonhoeffer's Ethics in Relation to Virtue Ethics* (Eugene: Pickwick Publications, 2013). Both Zimmermann and Moberly prioritize Bonhoeffer's manuscript, "Ethics as Formation" (DBWE 6:76–102). On the question of whether Bonhoeffer's "Ethics of Formation" is a separate ethical approach from commandment based ethics as articled in "God's Love and the Disintegration of the World," see Rasmussen, "A Question of Method," 103–40; Stephen Plant, *Dietrich Bonhoeffer* (Continuum: London, 2004), 111–26; Moberly, *The Virtue of Bonhoeffer's Ethics*, 163–218.

Leaving aside the question of whether Bonhoeffer's ethics are singular or twofold, it is notable that both manuscripts make reference to God's command and the necessity of formation for discernment, thus putting them in close correspondence. My argument does not require diminishing Bonhoeffer's emphasis on Christian formation, but it does situate it differently. It does not become a mode of virtue ethics, thus stressing habituation, practical reason, and character formation, since these are relativized in moments of danger and trial, which Bonhoeffer asserts at the very beginning of "Ethics as Formation" (DBWE 6:76–82). Indeed, formation in "Ethics as Formation" rather stresses the passivity of the self to Christ's formation necessitated by the character of Christ's hidden or incognito form. The result of its hiddenness is that it disrupts fallen modes of reasoning and displays the insufficiency of human reason and ethical programs for grasping Christ's form in the moment. These emphases come through in each iteration of Christ's threefold form (*Gestalt*) in the manuscript. The incarnate One disrupts all human attempts to categorize humanity on their own terms, since Christ assumed our fallen humanity that appalls "natural" human judgment (DBWE 6:83). Subsequently, action that conforms to Christ's incarnate form is thus marked by a suspension of judgment that makes space for Christ's claim and formative activity on humanity. The folly of the crucified Christ "disarms" all historical judgment forwarded on the basis of success or failure (DBWE 6:90). The form of Christ crucified calls for a surrender of all historical judgment to God, and conforming action responds by accepting Christ's judgment over themselves unto grace. They "let the justice of God prevail over them" (DBWE 6:94). Last, the risen One, whose form is hidden in the heavenlies (Col. 3:2), undoes any ideology that idolizes death in service to an eternal project. Action that conforms to the risen One refuses to promote oneself or to sacrifice one's own life needlessly; conforming action rather lifts up Christ to and for the sake of others (DBWE 6:91–5). In each instance, the emphasis is on receiving Christ's form through openness and deference to Christ's encountering form that renews and illuminates reality and human

Humanism, Zimmermann argues that Christians are habituated to the form of Christ, classifying Bonhoeffer's ethics as a mode of virtue ethics.[58] Both simplicity and discernment become virtues in this account, providing a habituated orientation that conforms a person to the narrative and practices of Christ's form. Nevertheless, this formation is not automatic; it proceeds from recognizing Christ's threefold form as the hermeneutic key to interpret the structures of reality. Zimmermann draws on the concept of Christ-reality, arguing that for Bonhoeffer Christ's form provides a "triadic structure of discernment (incarnation, cross, and resurrection)" that informs interpretive Christian action that culminates in "applicatory" obedience.[59] Christ's form thus mediates itself through practices and the structures of reality, becoming the basis for faithful action that transforms the Christian and inculcates virtue.[60] Simplicity once again becomes secondary to discerning action, which is crucial for the moral formation that prepares and precedes responsible action.

The account of discernment (*prüfen*) in "God's Love and the Disintegration of the World" has a different tenor that suggests that discernment does not necessarily precede action but often occurs through or follows after the act. In the idiom of Jean-Luc Marion, discernment is not a first principle that stands at the fount of action but a last principle that comes into play at the last moment, employed to ensure that one does not get in the way of the encountering phenomena.[61] Treating discernment in Bonhoeffer's narration as a last principle is a way for the will of God to retain primacy of determination, narrating discernment as a secondary activity that can even occur after the act. Indeed, Bonhoeffer argues that disciples must already know, respond to, and live in the will of God before being able to discern the will of God. "All of this discernment will be encompassed

---

life. This account coheres well with the account of discernment identified in this chapter through a reading of "God's Love and the Disintegration of the World."

58. Zimmerman, *Bonhoeffer's Christian Humanism*, 225–6.
59. Ibid., 165.
60. Ibid., 176.
61. Jean-Luc Marion, *Being Given: Toward a Phenomenology of Givenness*, trans. Jeffrey L. Kosky (Stanford: Stanford University Press, 2002), 19. "The principle set up by givenness is precisely that nothing precedes the phenomenon, except its own apparition on its own basis—which amounts to positing that the phenomenon comes forward without any other principle besides itself. In short, the principle, inasmuch as it is a principle of givenness, leaves primacy to the phenomenon—it is therefore not an issue of a first but rather a last principle. . . . *The fourth principle draws its privilege from the fact that it remains ultimate, comes into play only at the last moment, and judges a posteriori—that is to say, from the fact that it is no longer practiced as a principle that produces the phenomenon in advance, but as the rule decreeing that it is necessary to let the phenomenon come forward by itself*" (emphasis added, 19). The important theme of givenness in this manuscript lends itself well to a closer pairing between Marion and Bonhoeffer on this point.

and pervaded by the commandment."⁶² Bonhoeffer so diminishes discernment in his explication that he finds himself required to answer the question: "What room is left, then, for human discernment? Why is it necessary?"⁶³ Bonhoeffer corrects even the wording of this question, since it seems to imply that one can possess the will of God as if it is a "static possession," rendering discernment redundant. God's activity and presence is rather a "living reality" that is new every day, raising the better question of "how, today, here, in this situation, can I remain and be preserved within this new life with God, with Jesus Christ?" Bonhoeffer's answer to this question is telling. The prominence of the ever-active will of God leads to the negative delimitation of discernment: "And it is this very fact that daily gives rise to a new kind of genuine discernment, which must consist precisely in eliminating all other sources of knowledge about the will of God." Discernment eliminates what distracts from and impedes "the knowledge of being preserved, held, and guided by the will of God."⁶⁴ In the idiom of "Ultimate and Penultimate Things," discernment is a humble preparing of the way; it is an attentiveness to and a dismantling of the ways that human activity hinders Christ's coming, putting barriers in the way of Christ's clear and unambiguous Word.⁶⁵

Discernment as a last principle entails that it is not necessarily a preceding activity to human response. The verb Bonhoeffer's employs for this discerning activity (*prüfen*) expresses this insofar as it has more active connotations than the translation discernment suggests. *Prüfen* is not an epistemic act that necessarily precedes action, but a discernment that often occurs through or in light of action, reflected in the common translations of *prüfen* as "to prove" or "to test."⁶⁶ As Bonhoeffer argues: Christian knowledge is epitomized in doing, not reflection. "The knowledge of Jesus is translated entirely into doing, without any self-reflection whatsoever."⁶⁷ Discernment often proceeds from faithful action rather than preceding its enactment.

Many moments simply require discernment to follow after the event. Persons are not gifted eternity to adjudicate, and oftentimes the immediacy of response prioritizes simple obedience. An example helps to illustrate this point. Consider a moment of urgency when time is perilously short and one must act immediately to avoid injury. When a parent ushers the crucial command "Stop!" to a child about to walk into oncoming traffic, trusting obedience is the only appropriate response. The "immediate" response of the child reflects their awareness of the urgency and character of the command (even if this awareness is largely subconscious); it intuitively responds to the urgent cadence of the parent's voice, responding in an appropriate manner. Afterward, one can untangle what occurred, discerning in

---

62. DBWE 6:323–4.
63. DBWE 6:323.
64. DBWE 6:323.
65. DBWE 6:157–63.
66. I am grateful to Brian Brock for this insight.
67. DBWE 6:318.

retrospect the character of the parent's command, the peril of the situation, and the reflexive obedience of the child's response. The initial response is immediate, refusing to bifurcate hearing from doing,[68] whereas the post-eventual discernment lingers and abstracts the moment, learning in the process of reflection. The example is certainly imperfect, but it captures the urgency that is often lacking from narrations that place discernment at the forefront, since it can give the impression that discernment has the time necessary to reach a reasonable resolution when sometimes the only faithful response is to act. Such simple action is necessarily uncertain in moments of moral and political urgency. It is risky. There is the risk that one has misjudged the situation absolutely, and there is the risk that one's action will make things worse rather than better. The venture of immediate action in such moments, however, avoids two greater risks that lay at hand by prolonging discernment and discourse.

First, there is the moral risk that discourse will not terminate in action but inaction. The perpetuation of debate and moral deliberation can refuse the risk of the moment, culminating in tangled and loose threads of moral reasoning that never reach harmonization. Rationality, Bonhoeffer asserts, is fallen and conflicted, which means that moral reasoning can perpetuate conflict instead of leading to resolution.[69] Contrastingly, the risk of action simultaneously terminates the process of deliberation while also becoming a means of discernment. Such free action is both simple and wise, since discernment extends through and beyond the act.[70]

Second, there is the political risk that one curbs free action by remaining bound to the corrosive terms of conventional political discourse and action which are often beholden to the powers and principalities of this age. This is because deliberation on its terms assents to its claim to total sufficiency to direct discourse and action. It is in this vein that Kierkegaard asserts the necessary silence of the knight of faith in *Fear and Trembling*, since to defend oneself from judgment on the basis of the Ethical is to assume the terms of the Ethical, falling under its judgment and direction.[71] The shortcoming of this Kierkegaardian silence is that it can become anti-political, foreclosing opportunities to reflect on the witness and form of generative political action by refusing discourse. In this manuscript, Bonhoeffer notably avoids this shortcoming by asserting not the necessary silence of free action, but only the refusal of forms of discourse that hinder or foreclose free action. Christ, Bonhoeffer narrates, refused the debates and conflicts of the Pharisees, speaking from the reconciliation of God that sidesteps and thus refuses the monopoly of the law to determine speech and action. For Bonhoeffer, simple

---

68. "Now, doing of course presupposes hearing the law. But even this way of putting it is already problematic, because it gives the impression that hearing and doing can be distinguished and separated as presupposition and consequence" (DBWE 6:328).
69. DBWE 6:174–8. For more on this point, see Chapter 6.
70. DBWE 6:78.
71. Kierkegaard, *Fear and Trembling*.

obedience is not the refusal of discourse per se but only the refusal of discourse that remains bound to the machinations of totalizing moral and political thought. One can extend Bonhoeffer's argument to assert that some modes of moral and political speech must be refused rather than engaged, since they can suppress generative political action by demanding reflexive and unquestioning submission, which hinders free action that prepares the way of the Lord.[72]

Bonhoeffer recognized that undetermined free action will seem irrational and dangerous to most people. Many will vilify and even execute those who risk such free action, since they seem to threaten the intelligibility and viability of human action. Yet the risk of this venture holds promise for Bonhoeffer, since it depends not on its own merits but on divine guidance that exceeds human expectations by what it accomplishes.[73] The risked action may, for instance, prompt an unexpected discourse that elicits new forms of ethical and political speech that are responsive to the moment at hand. The post-eventual discernment elicits insights and forms of speech previously unarticulated. Likewise, the risked action may lead to encounters where former enemies become friends who join together in preparing the way of the Lord.[74] Stepping out without defense may lead to new collaborations with fellow wayfarers on a path of discipleship. In short, the gifts received through such action are beyond projection, since their emergence is apart from the narrow scope of totalizing political life which seeks to divide and reduce human life. They originate instead in the reconciling activity of God that makes all things new.

The Conspiracy as Repentance

Formative political action is not merely negative; it likewise affirms generative political action that participates in Christ's preceding and coming form. It emphasizes that Christ not only tears down but builds up political community through responsive action. It reorients and shapes the employment of reason, ethical categories, and wise perception in action. This emphasis features in Chapter 6, particularly when one considers that the mandates are tasks gifted to communities that participate in the sustenance and formation of political life in Christ. The emphasis on passivity, however, rightly situates activity for Bonhoeffer insofar as political action does not center on human programs that form the world. Whenever Bonhoeffer discusses political activity, he narrates it within God's overabundant activity, confessing its dependence upon the direction and sustenance of another. The confession emphasizes that free human action follows after the one who has liberated them to walk on a path of discipleship, participating

---

72. I am thankful to Ted Smith for prompting this line of argumentation through conversation.
73. DBWE 6:327.
74. Bonhoeffer describes this experience in "Church and World I" (DBWE 6:339–50).

in the formative activity of the Transcendent One in history.[75] Such an account of political action that follows after God should be paradigmatic of a narration of the *ethos* of the conspiracy circle.

In his notes on the Sigtuna meetings in May 1942, Bishop George Bell records Bonhoeffer suggesting that the conspiracy is best understood as an "act of repentance," and that the resistance circle does not "want to escape repentance, or chaos if God wills to bring it on us. We must take this judgment as Christians."[76] The theme of repentance is recurrent in Bonhoeffer's later works, finding life in unfinished *Ethics* manuscripts[77] as well as his letters from prison.[78] The account of repentance developed in these places coheres well with the vision of free action developed in this chapter, and it is telling that Bonhoeffer speaks of the conspiracy in this idiom, settings its details in its light.

The most essential aspect to an account of repentance is that it is not a mode of judgment, but a responsiveness to and acceptance in deed of a judgment already made. "Repentance demands deeds."[79] It suspends and counteracts attempts at self-justification or personal innocence, which is precisely what Bonhoeffer resisted in Schönfeld's account of the resistance at Sigtuna.[80] Repentance accepts one's complicity in the historical destiny and sins of the polity, and it suspends the "noble" option of representative judgment on behalf of the polity, opting instead for the representative act that seeks the welfare of the other by exposing oneself to risk and judgment.[81] It repents *from* self-justification and immanent judgment and it repents *for* the welfare of the polity on the basis of a judgment already made and encountered in the person of Christ. As de Graff suggests in narrating repentance in the Sigtuna episode:

> Such abstention from judicial practice also means *freedom* from it. This freedom is not apolitical, however, as if the church chose to live in a judicial vacuum. It is rather freedom following and resulting from a judgment already pronounced, like the freedom experienced in political society whenever a moderately satisfactory and conclusive judgment has been pronounced. This freedom from

---

75. As Bonhoeffer suggested in his "Outline for a Book," God is transcendent in and not beyond history (DBWE 8:501).

76. DBWE 16:300.

77. In *Ethics*, see "Ultimate and Penultimate Things" (DBWE 6:146–70) and "Guilt, Justification, Renewal" (DBWE 6:134–45).

78. In particular, see Bonhoeffer's July 16, 1944, letter to Bethge where he discusses *metanoia* (DBWE 8:480).

79. DBWE 6:164.

80. DBWE 16:300.

81. In "State and Church," Bonhoeffer speaks similarly: "Because in all decisions of the state the historical entanglement in the guilt of the past is incalculably large, it is for the most part not possible to judge the legitimacy of a single decision. Here the venture of responsibility must be risked" (DBWE 15:517–18).

judgment is freedom *for* something else, namely what judgment vindicates and restores and enables, namely participation in social life.[82]

Like the excess of friendship to political order (characterized even here by Bell and Bonhoeffer), such activity emerges from beyond the order while pursuing its proper foundation and sustenance.[83] In Bonhoeffer's idiom, repentance is a preparing of the way: it is concrete political activity that emerges from and depends upon something beyond the order itself that nevertheless participates in the formation of political order and life.[84] Ultimately, the conspiracy becomes an intensified account of this activity and thus resists narrations that place it once again within an account of law or treat it as wholly arbitrary. It instead operates within a different grammar, originating in Christ's justifying act in history that elicits the repentant deed that refuses the logic of law/application, but instead instantiates itself with the free response that refuses self-judgment in seeking the good of another. This, ultimately, allows a differing account of political judgment, ethics, and law that emerges in this light. Hans Ulrich's narration of the conspiracy as free action for the other captures these elements well:

> This was the logic behind Bonhoeffer's involvement in the plot against Hitler. In his eyes, this involvement was a stepping in for the other—not a kind of *ultima ratio* or even a justifiable way of revolution. It was no longer possible for "right" to be done, for this action to manifest both responsibility for the other and the experience of freedom, to begin something new. . . . Someone had to kill the tyrant. This was "the end of your action . . ." handing everything over to God, remaining powerless, casting aside the "powerful deed," and, in this case, embracing the ethically "wrong." The point was never to use violence in order to achieve power. Rather, the plot was the admission of powerlessness, submission to God, and suffering whatever the consequences might be.[85]

---

82. de Graff, *Politics in Friendship*, 150. Emphasis original.
83. On how Bonhoeffer and Bell's friendship is parapolitical, see de Graff, *Politics in Friendship*, 123–52.
84. DBWE 6:164–5.
85. Ulrich, "'Stations on the Way to Freedom,'" 163.

Chapter 6

THE DISMANTLING, RECONCILIATION, AND FUTURE OF THE LAW

This chapter reflects on how the exception sheds light on the boundedness and continuity of politics and ethics. The picture presented thus far would be decidedly incomplete without engaging this theme. Bonhoeffer presumes there is a persistent continuity to political and ethical forms of life, which continues in his later writings. The challenge is to affirm the continuity of ethics and politics for Bonhoeffer in the exception without losing his earlier emphasis on fragmentation, discontinuity, and rupture.

The chapter proceeds in three stages. First, I engage Bonhoeffer's unfinished commentary on Psalm 119, exploring the ways that Bonhoeffer's account of the law reflects upon the exception as well as the character of ethics and politics. I suggest that Bonhoeffer's account of the exception results not in the destruction (*Zerstörung*) of the law but in the dismantling of false receptions of the law that obscure God's present command and contribute to the disintegration of political life. Second, I engage a series of relationships in Bonhoeffer's theology that are prominent in narrations of the borderline case—the relationship between church and world, the relationship between the mandates, and the relationship between politics and ethics. Whereas common narrations of Bonhoeffer's theology read these relationships as necessarily conflicting in the borderline case, I propose that these relationships appear in a different light when framed by the reality of reconciliation as Bonhoeffer understands it, affirming their unity and coordination before God in the borderline case. Lastly, I reflect upon Bonhoeffer's attempts to imagine politics after the extraordinary moment, considering what it means to grasp after the future in a moment that disrupts "ordinary" attempts to anticipate the future in action. I argue that while Bonhoeffer could not reasonably plan for the future, his action still had an important though unintended effect on the younger generations, and this reflects the nonlinear and emergent causality of political action.

The Beginning, the Law, and the Moment of Exception

Some might find it counterintuitive to introduce Bonhoeffer's account of law and ethics by way of his unfinished commentary on Psalm 119. Why not begin with one of the more explicitly political works in his corpus? And does not such an opening immediately merge the various senses of law (positive law, Decalogue, natural law) to generate a tertium quid foreign to Bonhoeffer's own idiom? These are undoubtedly real dangers, and they require an answer for beginning here.

Perhaps the most direct route to an answer is biographical. Bonhoeffer was working on this commentary in tandem with his initial writings for *Ethics*, and the two works were not merely parallel in time of composition but mutually illuminating.[1] While a case can be made for the commentary exerting a stronger influence on *Ethics* than vice versa, a more modest claim is that Bonhoeffer developed a language in the commentary that became central to his theological ethics. As Bethge observes, Bonhoeffer considered the commentary "the climax of his theological life" evidenced by how often Bonhoeffer quoted the Psalm as well as by his frequent description of ethics as a way in his late writings—one of the central themes of the Psalm.[2] Indeed, Krötke has even suggested that the Psalm was "a personal guide" for Bonhoeffer that became decisive in his decision to return to Germany in 1939.[3]

The prioritization of the Psalm is also appropriate in a more theological sense. It reflects Bonhoeffer's conviction that it is through direct and continued exposition that one hears and articulates a Christian ethics for today.[4] Just as the text demands continual reading and meditation, so, too, do ethical and political schemas require constant testing and reformulation in the light of Scripture. This explains in part why the reading of Psalm 119 becomes helpful to have at the forefront of this chapter, since it frames the discussion to come. A final reason will suggest itself in my engagement with the commentary insofar as I directly tie its themes to the relation of God's law to the exception. In particular, I reflect on three aspects of the Psalm, connecting each theme to the exception: the primacy of the beginning and the event-character of the law in the Christian life, the political character of meditation on God's law, and the law as the path of the Christian life in the form of the Decalogue and creation.

The Beginning, the Timefullness of the Law, and the Exception

There is no getting behind the beginning. The beginning is the singular and unrepeatable redemptive act of God as the *adventus* and limit of human life. The beginning is an event in history but resists causal explication. The Christian does

---

1. Brian Brock, "Bonhoeffer and the Bible in Christian Ethics: Psalm 119, The Mandates, and Ethics as a 'Way,'" *Studies in Christian Ethics* 18, no. 3 (2005): 7.

2. DB-ER, 571.

3. Wolf Krötke, "Dietrich Bonhoeffer's Exegesis of the Psalms," in *Karl Barth and Dietrich Bonhoeffer: Theologians for a Post-Christian World*, trans. John Burgess (Grand Rapids: Baker Academic, 2019), 177–8.

4. See John Webster, *Word and Church: Essays in Church Dogmatics* (London: T&T Clark, 2016), 87–112.

6. The Dismantling, Reconciliation, and Future of the Law

not attempt to go behind the beginning but proceeds from it on a path walked within God's law.[5] This is the central claim of Bonhoeffer's exposition of Ps. 119:1: "Happy are those whose way is blameless, who walk in the law of the Lord." Bonhoeffer defends and expands this claim in his exposition, vigorously asserting its necessity for Christian action and thought. It is decisive for any exposition of the law and commandments of God.[6] The framing of the law through the singular and unrepeatable beginning of God's action is decisive and nonnegotiable, since this is the condition which decides whether or not the believer encounters the law within the economy of grace as a source of life. To stray from God's beginning is no longer to walk *within* the path of the law but to find oneself *under* the law in condemnation (498).[7] The law is no longer a demand requiring fulfillment for those who accept God's beginning, but a gift received in light of God's redemptive works (498). The beginning as well as the law befalls the disciple as divine acts, putting the disciple in a passive relation to both, and calling for the disciple's acceptance of both.

Bonhoeffer's exposition of the beginning highlights the temporal character of the law. By indexing the law to God's redemptive activity in history, Bonhoeffer disparages narrations of the law as transtemporal or ideal. "The question about the law of God is answered not by a moral doctrine (*Sittenlehre*), a norm, but by a historical event, not by an unfulfilled ideal but by an act completed by God" (499). Bonhoeffer emphasizes two aspects of the law's temporality throughout the commentary: its continuity and its event-character. The singularity of the beginning that initiates the path within God's law entails the permanence and continuity of God's commandments, thus undoing modern narrations of the divine commandment as punctiliar and occasional interventions in normal affairs.[8] "God's commandment is there not only for the moment but permanently" (505), offering decisive direction for every moment on the path (508). The event-character of the law emphasizes that the commandments of God are not static—as objectified commands—but are received daily in prayerful pursuit on the path. Bonhoeffer explicates this claim by probing the various senses of commandment in Hebrew, which "derives from the verb 'to seek,' 'to visit,' to attend.' Thus it refers to that which God pays heed, looks to, that by which he visits and besets human beings" (505).

---

5. There is an obvious resonance, here, to Bonhoeffer's commentary on Gen. 1:1-2 (DBWE 3:23–39).

6. Bonhoeffer switches between law (*Gesetz*) and commandment (*Gebot*) throughout the commentary. The two are interchangeable in this context, though in "The 'Christian' and the 'Ethical' as a Topic" Bonhoeffer indexes the law to the commandments of God (DBWE 6:385-7). This section will speak interchangeably between them in following Bonhoeffer's diction, emphasizing how God's commandments guide and transform human life, calling all to obedience in a form of life within the law.

7. All inline page citations in this section refer to Bonhoeffer's unfinished commentary on Psalm 119 (DBWE 15:496–528).

8. Brock, "Bonhoeffer and the Bible in Christian Ethics," 11.

The commandments are a gift received by those who seek, probe, and test God's commands, affirming the newness of the word for each portion of the path.

It is this dynamic of continuity and eventuality that animates Bonhoeffer's manuscript "Ultimate and Penultimate Things," which is usefully read alongside the commentary on Psalm 119. The two manuscripts were written within a year of each other, and articulate closely related themes.[9] While the emphasis in "Ultimate and Penultimate Things" is not on the irrevocable beginning but on the ultimate as an eschatological Word addressed to the penultimate, it likewise centers on the "event" (*Geschehnis*) of justification beyond historical causality that encompasses "the length and breadth of human life . . . in one moment, one point."[10] Utilizing the image of the path in Psalm 119, one could read "Ultimate and Penultimate Things" as centering on the end of the path, finding continuity with the beginning through the self-same God who addresses wayfarers on the path today. It is the Christ "who has come" in history and "is coming" from the end of history that addresses the penultimate in its finitude and historicity.[11] The ultimate shares the character of the law in its continuity and its event-character—it is the ultimate Word that prepares its own way within the penultimate (continuity), transforming the penultimate in expectation of its coming (event-character). The shared resonances between the two pieces are unsurprising given that Bonhoeffer's narration of ultimate and penultimate things is likewise steeped in the world of the Bible, though finding its central locus in the language of Pauline apocalyptic.[12] In this piece it is clear that Bonhoeffer remains within the orbit of the negating and annihilating power of the theology of crisis that characterized his early theology, and yet he is also narrating the ultimate as transforming and being present to the penultimate through its presence and history-altering visitation.

Bonhoeffer's exposition of the beginning and the ultimate discredits any notion that he ever imagined the exception as a "new" beginning that threatens to unravel political life and ethical thought absolutely. It would have made no sense to him to see the exception as unraveling the law that proceeds from God's beginning. The exception, rather, must be continuous with the beginning, affirming the law's continuity. As Bonhoeffer argues in his interpretation of Ps. 119:26, it is only haughtiness against God's law that culminates in "all rebellion, all tumult, and all destruction (*Zerstörung*)" (526). Or as Bonhoeffer suggests in "Ultimate and Penultimate Things," it is only radicalism that turns Christ into an arbitrary destroyer (*Zerstörer*) of the penultimate.[13]

What the event-character of the law rather emphasizes in a reflection on the exception is the danger attendant to disciples to forget and obscure God's law.

---

9. Bonhoeffer's commentary on Psalm 119 was composed in the winter of 1939–40, and "Ultimate and Penultimate Things" was composed a year later in the winter of 1940–1.

10. DBWE 6:144.

11. DBWE 6:151.

12. Philip G. Ziegler, "Dietrich Bonhoeffer—An Ethics of God's Apocalypse?," *Modern Theology* 23, no. 4 (2007): 590.

13. DBWE 6:153. "Arbitrary destruction of the penultimate seriously harms the ultimate" (DBWE 6:160).

Bonhoeffer identifies one danger in particular in this connection, the forgetting of the law as the event of the divine claim by attending instead to summaries of the law in the form of principles and moral maxims—the living word ossified into "the skeleton of my own principles" (523). According to Bonhoeffer, this seemingly innocuous danger can be devastating, as this substitution can so desensitize disciples to the law that they may "no longer even sense it were God one day to withdraw his living commandment" (523). In such a moment, God actively withdraws the gifting of the commandment in judgment, leading the disciple into the "deep night" when one cannot recognize or respond to God's obscured law, debilitating human action (520). Bonhoeffer shudders at this possibility, describing this obscuring as a "severe trial" (*schwere Anfechtung*) (523). This raises the troubling question: "what if God willed one day to hide his commandments from me?" (523). Bonhoeffer concludes that while God does not hide the commands, "it is within God's freedom and wisdom to deny us the grace of his commandment" (524). The command may be present but the grace to receive it is absent. The obscuration of the command bewilders the disciple, eliciting the desperate prayer: do not hide your commandments from me. The result of the prayer is that one receives the command again, having eyes to behold the inadequacy of one's principles and the sole sufficiency of God's command to guide one's action.

This description of the obscuring of God's law and its subsequent bestowal in prayer is instructive in highlighting the exception as God's dual work of illuminating or uncovering the law by first dismantling the sinful aberrations that have hidden it. In this sense, God does not dismantle the law in the exception but the insufficient and sinful history of the law's reception so that disciples can hear and respond again to God's law today.[14] Indeed, the law can always surprise us by exceeding all interpretive frameworks brought to it. This further entails that the exception not only discloses what became obscure or distorted in the law but includes what was always present but remained unsaid and beyond what human thought could anticipate. "The Torah," Bonhoeffer claims, "is God's casting over humankind, beyond all human expectations and thinking" (499).

---

14. This task is comparable to what Heidegger set out to do in *Being and Time*: "If the question of Being is to have its own history made transparent, then this hardened tradition must be loosened up, and the concealment which it has brought about must be dissolved." Martin Heidegger, *Being and Time*, trans. John Macquarrie and Edward S. Robinson (London: HarperCollins, 2008), 44. As Gadamer pointed out, this "destruction" (*Destruktion*) is not in the sense of utter annihilation for which the term *Zerstörung* would be used, but its dismantling (*Abbau*). Thus Gadamer states: "It has to do with making concepts and their expressions speak once more, with taking them out of the merely functional context in which they are employed as overdetermined terms, and bring them back to their original role within language. That was Heidegger's great service: the *Destruktion* of the academic language of metaphysics." Hans-Georg Gadamer, "Hermeneutics and Logocentrism," in *Dialogue and Deconstruction*, 121. While it is evident that Bonhoeffer is no Heideggerian, the notion of dismantling in order to liberate speech once again is inviting.

The exception can speak the singular command in the sense that it stands apart from what has otherwise been received. In this frame, the exception is not the destruction of the law, since the law remains firm from the beginning, but the exception is both the dismantling of the false reception of the law in moral and political life as well as the revealing of unforeseen or novel aspects to the law beyond anticipation in the event of God's command.

Meditation and Nonfoundational Ethics

In commenting on v. 15 ("I will meditate on your precepts, and fix my eyes on your ways"), Bonhoeffer explicates how the reception of God's command not only spurs "fast and immediate action" in the moment but also "silence and contemplation" in the prayerful pondering of the Scriptures. Bonhoeffer calls this prayerful reading meditation (517). Meditation, according to Bonhoeffer, is a daily and ongoing activity that pervades the whole of life and one's time. "God's word claims my time . . . To be a Christian is not the matter of a moment but takes time" (517). Meditation is repetitious in character and summons one to recall and repeat God's saving deeds continuously in sharpening one's understanding of what God demands today.

In contrast to Arendt's well-known criticism that Christian contemplation diminishes political action, Bonhoeffer integrates these two ideas and presents them as necessarily intertwining.[15] Meditation forms not only the activity of the individual but also the *ethos* and proclamation of the worshipping community.[16] Meditation is reflection upon the law that can never remain private but necessarily implicates a community and corresponding form of life that culminates in proclamation and mutual address (498).[17] The primary difference between contemplation and meditation is the object and source of reflection. Unlike ancient contemplation, meditation is not the wordless contemplation of eternal truths, but a response to the Word spoken in the congregation and the Scriptures, to the Word that proceeds not from an eternal foundation but from the initium of God's redemptive deeds in history.[18] Only by meditating upon God's beginning within the congregation can one comprehend, respond to, and declare God's law for today (514).

The relation of meditation to the law illuminates the nonfoundational character of law and moral proclamation in Bonhoeffer's theology, since the law is only actualized in the repetitious and prayerful activity of the congregation. In this it

---

15. Hannah Arendt, *The Human Condition* (Chicago: The University of Chicago Press, 1958), 14–17.

16. DBWE 14:387.

17. Philip G. Ziegler, "Witness to Christ's Dominion: The Political Service of the Church," *Theology* 116, no. 5 (2013): 324. See also Bonhoeffer's Finkenwalde lecture, "New Life in Paul" (DBWE 14:621).

18. Wannenwetsch, *Political Worship*, 18, 197–206.

is resistant to becoming a possession that is at the disposal of the individual or congregation. Bonhoeffer is dismissing two alternative narrations of the relation between law and action. He first denies that the law corresponds to an atemporal norm that needs application through particular acts. The law's cohesiveness and formation of a form of life in its daily giftedness counteracts this first narration. The second denial is that ethics springs from the essence of the church or from the already-possessed character of the community.[19] Bonhoeffer's emphasis on meditation within the church's ongoing, repetitious praxis denies this second more subtle foundationalism, on the grounds that "the fact that the practice is bound to repetition makes it impossible to identify a foundational claim that is somehow derived from its essence."[20] The church does not possess an ethic so much as it receives ethical knowledge through its daily activity. Even the law for Bonhoeffer is not a foundation since it is not something beyond or behind the life of the congregation. The law is the space within which believers walk with the law presenting the claim of God on their time. The law, in short, does not emerge from the congregation's activity, but it spurs and founds their activity while also being gifted anew through their activity each day. The law's temporal continuity is thus affirmed without positing an atemporal or essential basis on which it rests.

The emphasis on the nonfoundational character of law extends beyond the church, becoming an essential aspect of political life in its various dimensions. As Bonhoeffer suggests in his manuscript "The 'Christian' and the 'Ethical' as a Topic," every human being encounters, reflects upon, and engages God's concrete commandment as embedded in the spheres of daily life described by the mandates. God's commandment authorizes and liberates creative human life and discourse in their full historicity. It meets persons within relationships of authority and obedience, and it transforms political life through daily encounter and responsiveness to the command. There is a phenomenality to Bonhoeffer's reflections that extends to the borderline event (*Grenzereignis*) that threatens political life which Bonhoeffer describes as the Ethical. When community life disintegrates and persons question what was previously self-evident, the Ethical asserts itself in such times, making itself a topic of discussion as "the experience of the ought."[21] It raises its voice precisely when persons obscure and forget God's commandment by transgressing it, threatening the unity and continuity of political life. Bonhoeffer indicates that the Ethical is not the foundation of political life that needs renewed application in times of communal disarray, but the border of political life that asserts itself as persons wander toward the limit of formed political life.

---

19. Stefan Heuser, "Bonhoeffer and the Renewal of Political Practices," in *Bonhoeffer, Religion, and Politics: 4th International Bonhoeffer Colloquium*, ed. Christianne Tietz and Jens Zimmermann (Berlin, Peter Lang, 2012), 101–13. Contra Stephen Fowl and L. Gregory Jones' communitarian reading of Bonhoeffer in *Reading in Communion: Scripture and Ethics in the Christian Life* (Eugene: Wipf and Stock Publishers, 1991), 135–59.

20. Wannenwetsch, *Political Worship*, 3.

21. DBWE 6:366.

When considering the exception, it is the self-assertion of God's law that needs emphasizing. When political life disintegrates and reflection upon God's commandment becomes obscure and distorted, God's address can be trusted to undercut these aberrations, addressing and reforming human life in and through God's address as commandment and law. The exception is a *krisis* of human forgetfulness and the law's obscuration, necessitating a divine incursion that renews political life, bringing to life a community that speaks and reflects rightly upon God's commandment. In this manner, the exception does not suspend meditation on God's commandment and law, as if the moment was a lacuna in God's commandment, it is, rather, a time that generates renewed meditation on the character and form of life of the various mandates when they teeter toward dissolution.

The Path of the Law as Creation and Decalogue

Throughout his corpus, Bonhoeffer consistently emphasizes that one encounters God's commandments in the places where God promises them. Persons turn to these places in seeking after God's Word for today. Bonhoeffer's exposition of Psalm 119 continues this affirmation, attending to the particular content of the law that stands firm in God's redemptive activity. Commenting on v. 5, Bonhoeffer remarks:

> God's "statutes," this is what stands fast, what has been determined by God for all time. The course of heaven, earth, and humankind has been irrevocably prescribed by these statutes. God's covenant with his people is as unchanging as the change from day to night is . . . Creation and law are the two great inviolable statutes of God that belong indissolubly together, since the same God has given them (Ps. 19). God keeps his statutes; he is faithful (507).

Within the context of the Psalm, Bonhoeffer's affirmation of God's fidelity to creation and law undercuts Marcionite impulses to divorce the God of redemption from God's purposes in creation and God's covenant with Israel. Indeed, while the law in the foregoing passage may be a synonym for the broader category of commandment, there is precedent for reading it also as a reference to the Torah with a primary emphasis on the Decalogue. This subsection of the Torah is, like creation, a species of the commandment that demarcates the boundaries and contours of the path within which one walks in freedom.[22]

The strong parallels and similarities between creation and Decalogue in Bonhoeffer's broader thought reveal them to have an indissoluble connection in his theological imagination. First, both creation and Decalogue find their origin in and

---

22. Bonhoeffer refers to the Torah and Decalogue at various points in the manuscript. For instance: "God's law is inseparable from his redemptive deed. The God of the Ten Commandments is the God who led you out of the land of Egypt" (499).

orientation to God's redemptive activity; they always witness beyond themselves to God's saving deeds in Christ, becoming places of divine encounter and command. Second, God's command comes through the content of the Decalogue and creation. Unlike Barth who reads the Decalogue as the a posteriori grammar of God's saving command, Bonhoeffer affirms that the Decalogue is God's command, finding concretion in proclamation.²³ A similar pattern emerges with creation, which possesses orders and "intrinsic laws" that guide and shape human activity in accordance with reality.²⁴ It is no coincidence, Bonhoeffer observes, that the content of the Decalogue overlaps with the Natural since it is the same God who commands both.²⁵ Third, creation and Decalogue both structure and demarcate the boundaries of free social and political life. The Decalogue marks the negative limits of all worldly orders—the transgression of which leads to the disintegration of human life and authority.²⁶ While Bonhoeffer wavers between whether the mandates originate in creation or reconciliation, he speaks consistently of how human political and social life must attend to the concrete material conditions of the world and the embodiment of the neighbor, testified in the creation of Adam and Eve.²⁷ In light of these similarities, Bonhoeffer suggests it is not surprising that persons link the Decalogue to creation in the form of natural law.²⁸

Bonhoeffer is not, however, collapsing creation and Decalogue into one another, and he sees their differences paradigmatically elucidating key considerations in an articulation of the law illuminated by the exception. The primary difference between them is their relation to the fall and the disintegrating effects of sin. Creation has been unhinged by the fall now that its unity and perspicuity have been undone by the incursion of sin. Persons no longer have direct access to creation. The prelapsarian unity of creation can only be glimpsed through Christ's reconciling activity, which points forward to the redemption of all things in the new creation.²⁹ Hence Bonhoeffer's earlier preference for describing fallen creation as "orders of preservation" awaiting God's redemption.³⁰ Creation has taken the division of good and evil into itself, finding that its laws often culminate in irresolvable conflicts that require negotiation. This is particularly evident in

---

23. Philip G. Ziegler, "Graciously Commanded: Dietrich Bonhoeffer and Karl Barth on the Decalogue," *Scottish Journal of Theology* 71, no. 2 (2018): 127–41.

24. DBWE 6:272. Bonhoeffer also speaks of the "law innate to their created being (*eingeborenene eigene Gesetz*)" in "A Study on 'Personal' and 'Objective' Ethics" (DBWE 16:548).

25. DBWE 16:633–4.

26. DBWE 6:360.

27. DBWE 16:540–51.

28. DBWE 16:633–4.

29. DBWE 11:267–8. "Of course, the works of the second creation are different from those of the first—they are called the cross of Christ and resurrection" (DBWE 11:438).

30. As Bonhoeffer says in "Christ, Reality and the Good," the Kingdom of God and creation "are both equally far from us and yet near to us" (DBWE 6:53).

Bonhoeffer's later account of the Natural, which remains oriented to Christ but nevertheless has clear limits and conflicts stemming from its fallen character.[31] Thus Bonhoeffer's claim that the Natural requires positive law to judge between various human rights that conflict with one another.[32] The result is that any moral or political program that proceeds on its basis will maintain a relatively ordered social order, though its contradictions and injustices will multiply with every interjection leading to further unforeseen conflicts.[33]

The Decalogue, contrastingly, is a Word that pierces fallen creation in the fullness and unity of God's reconciling activity, standing apart as the only words written directly by God (Exod. 31:18).[34] Its transcendent origin, like the rest of the Torah, "is beyond all human expectations and thinking" (499), and thus beyond the divisions and conflicts that demarcate ethics and the Natural. The Decalogue persists and orders political and ethical life, presenting a unified "morality" that affirms, rather than contradicts, the Sermon on the Mount and the rest of Scripture.[35] The syntagma "law and gospel" encapsulates the unity of God's twofold Word with the law finding its fullest meaning and fulfillment in light of the Gospel. As Bonhoeffer says regarding the Decalogue: "In these 'ten words' God is speaking as truly of God's grace as of God's command. They are not an entity cut off from God that we could in some way designate as God's will; instead, the entire, living God is revealed in them as the one who God is."[36] While the Decalogue awaits God's visitation for its concretion in proclamation, its unity and origin in God's liberating presence emphasize its inexhaustibility for ordering and renewing human life. Its concretion eludes "application" since concretion is a gift and not a method. The upshot is that the Christian response to political and moral decay is positioned as a prayerful awaiting of God's daily bread.[37] Unlike the Natural, the Decalogue is not an assemblage of general laws negotiated by reason but God's very speech: "there reason speaks; here God speaks. . . . Human beings are confronted with this 'I,' not with some sort of general law—not with 'one should do this or that,' but with the living God."[38]

Two possibilities emerge for probing borderline cases (*Grenzfälle*) in considering the differences between fallen creation and the Decalogue. The first possibility is to elucidate the conflicts and irresolvable dilemmas posed by a particular situation in fallen creation. Such moments exacerbate the gap between "ideal" and "real,"

---

31. DBWE 6:173.

32. "The suum cuique as the paramount statement of rights does not take account of the conflict between rights within the natural itself. It is this actual conflict that requires positive law (*Recht*) that is set from outside nature, positive law both divine and civil (*weltlich*)" (DBWE 6:182).

33. DBWE 6:354.

34. DBWE 16:633.

35. DBWE 6:359.

36. DBWE 16:635.

37. DBWE 6:353–6.

38. DBWE 16:634.

eliciting the demand for imperfect and morally treacherous action that navigates the competing claims made on human action. The same formulation runs through accounts of political realism, which asserts that often human action can only achieve proximate goods through guilt-inducing means this side of the eschaton. Bonhoeffer describes borderline cases in this sense in "Natural Life" when he meditates on a situation where a plague breaks out on board a ship at sea where isolation is not possible. Whether the right to bodily life requires caring for the sick or saving "the healthy . . . by the death of the sick" is a decision that "would have to remain open."[39]

The second possibility is to elucidate the borderline case within the grammar of reconciliation, narrating it as a moment when one encounters the limits of human possibility and understanding, which subsequently suspends one's judgment in encountering God's commandment that overcomes and unites all things in Godself. It vigorously affirms the unity and completeness of God's address and action, expecting the overcoming of the seemingly irresolvable conflicts in God's *adventus*. The illumination of the limit (*Grenz*) through God's commandment simultaneously illuminates the limits and character of reality in a manner that frees persons for responsiveness before God. It is in this idiom that Bonhoeffer's comment on Ps. 119:18 should be understood:

> One whose eyes God has opened to his word will see into a world of wonders. What had appeared dead to me is full of life; contradictions resolve themselves into a higher unity; harsh demands become gracious commands. Within the human word I hear God's eternal word; in past history I recognize the present God and his working for my salvation. The merciful consolation becomes a new claim of God; the unbearable burden becomes an easy yoke. The great wonder in God's law is the revelation of the Lord Jesus Christ. Through him, the word receives life, contradictions receive unity, revealed things receive unfathomable depth. Lord, open my eyes (521).

The next section engages a series of polarities in following the second possibility for narrating the borderline case, affirming their unity before God's command rather than their disintegration and conflict due to the incursion of sin. Whereas common narrations of Bonhoeffer's theology read these polarities as conflicting in the borderline case, I propose that these polarities appear in a different light when framed by the reality of reconciliation as Bonhoeffer understands it, affirming their unity and coordination before God in the borderline case.

Reconciliation in the Borderline Case

There are numerous themes in Bonhoeffer's theology that feature in a narration of the borderline case. There is Bonhoeffer's account of the relationship between

---

39. DBWE 6:195.

church and world, the relationship between the mandates, and the moral authority of the Decalogue and Sermon on the Mount in political life. The task of this section is not to address each theme exhaustively in this space; it is, rather, to elucidate how the borderline case illuminates what is otherwise diminished or left unstated in common narrations of these themes, drawing out how they relate to God's reconciling activity therein, which extends into the character of "everyday" life that proceeds therefrom.

The Reconciliation of Church and World

Bonhoeffer's shift to the conspiracy is frequently narrated as a movement away from the church to the world. Hanfried Müller most famously developed this line, suggesting that Bonhoeffer discarded the clericalism of the Finkenwalde era in joining the conspiracy, eventually adopting the secularism and humanistic ethic of the prison letters.[40] A more nuanced version narrates Bonhoeffer broadening his ethical vision in the conspiracy from a narrow ecclesial ethic to a "Christo-universal" ethic accessible to the world; this more general ethic opens space for cooperative efforts with the world beyond the church, epitomized in Bonhoeffer's conspiracy participation.[41] The prevalence of this framework is remarkably consistent among its detractors. Those who affirm that Bonhoeffer maintained an ecclesial orientation throughout his life tend to diminish or deny the turn to the conspiracy, asserting that Bonhoeffer maintained the basic theological distinction between church and world.[42] In these narrations, Bonhoeffer either remained in the church over against the world or Bonhoeffer moved from the church to the world.[43] As Bethge attested: "Everything depends on whether [the resistance] is viewed from the framework of political resistance, or that of the church."[44]

Within these narrations there is a negotiation of Bonhoeffer's rejection of sphere thinking, which divides the world into discrete realms, and Bonhoeffer's affirmation of differentiation in the Christ-reality, which includes a space for the church in the world. The challenge, Bonhoeffer suggests, is to narrate the difference between church and world "without falling back into spatial categories." An articulation of the church and world relationship must maintain the integrity of each without solidifying their boundaries as "static oppositions."[45]

---

40. Hanfried Müller, *Von der Kirche zur Welt. Ein Beitrag zu der Beziehung des Wortes Gottes auf die societas in Dietrich Bonhoeffers theologischer Entwicklung* (Leipzig: Koehler & Amelang, 1961).

41. Rasmussen, *Reality and Resistance*; Kessler, "Bonhoeffer on Law Breaking."

42. Hauerwas, *Performing the Faith*; Nation et al., *Bonhoeffer the Assassin?*.

43. The most notable exception to this trend is McBride's excellent book, *The Church for the World*.

44. Bethge, *Exile and Martyr*, 127–36.

45. DBWE 6:68.

The issue with these prominent narrations is that they tend to function primarily through spatial categories. Bonhoeffer moved *from* the church to the world as a citizen, crossing the boundary that lay between them, or Bonhoeffer remained *within* the church in service to the world as a disciple, thus remaining "outside" the resistance in the church.[46] The flaw with spatial categories is that they necessitate a focus on boundaries, raising questions from the outset about who belongs and who is excluded from a community. Spatial categories serve to demarcate the nature of one community over against another. By focusing on the extension of church or world, the perception of boundaries from a bird's eye view becomes essential to its intelligibility and nature. The discernment of the shape of church or world depends on perceiving its outline by the way it runs up against its counterpart. The borderline case thus delineates the borders between church and world and between disciple and citizen. The perception of boundaries necessitates a decision to resist as a decision for church or world.

A frequent thread in Bonhoeffer's ecclesiology is that the boundaries between church and world are only encountered and are never defined on a "legal basis" or through "theoretical knowledge."[47] The boundaries, in short, are best explicated not through spatial categories but through temporal encounter. In fact, Bonhoeffer maintains that the church never seeks its boundaries but only seeks to encounter the faithful community of word and sacrament; it is content to encounter God's church, suspending judgment over its boundaries with the world or false churches. The question of the boundary only emerges when the church encounters unbelief and persecution. Only in the experience of suffering does the question of boundaries become valid.[48] What is ingredient to this claim is the affirmation that the church is a creature of the Word, entailing that the primary sense at play is not sight, which seeks an overview that captures the stable boundaries between two entities, but hearing, which remains oriented to the event of proclamation that is ever capable of surprise by overcoming seemingly impenetrable boundaries, including the division of church and world: "When one therefore wants to speak of the space of the church, one must be aware that this space has already been broken through, abolished, and overcome in every moment by the witness of the church of Jesus Christ."[49] Persons experience this reconciling Word in the most unexpected of encounters, testifying to the porousness between church and world.

This emphasis on the experience of reconciliation becomes primary in Bonhoeffer's 1943 manuscript "Church and World I."[50] Bonhoeffer claims throughout the manuscript that experience has necessitated and solidified a

---

46. Heuser, "Bonhoeffer and the Renewal of Political Practices," 49–69.
47. DBWE 14:660.
48. Paradigmatic of this approach is "Essay and Discussion on Church Communion" (DBWE 14:655–77); see also "Lecture on the Path of the Young Illegal Theologians of the Confessing Church" (DBWE 15:416–37).
49. DBWE 6.64.
50. DBWE 6:339–51.

renewed relationship between church and world.⁵¹ The experience of persecution by the National Socialists led proponents of "worldly values" (e.g., justice, truth, and tolerance) to migrate back to the church from which they were previously estranged, confessing Christ's name in the process.⁵² In the shared experience of oppression, Bonhoeffer experienced an unlikely alliance of the church with proponents of worldly values, undoing a hermeneutics of suspicion between church and world in establishing a hermeneutics of trust and mutual exchange, empowering shared political witness.⁵³ An essential aspect of this experience is the disclosure that the boundaries between church and world are not static, but porous and constantly discerned anew. While Bonhoeffer's formulation of this intersection through Mark 9:40 ("Whoever is not against us is for us") and Matthew 12:30 ("Whoever is not for me is against me") appears an "irreconcilable contradiction," it is "living experience" that necessitates their dual affirmation and exposition.⁵⁴ The Scriptural witness of these texts acts as a heuristic to frame Bonhoeffer's experience of surprising union in suffering witness and thus cannot be explicated within any logical positivism.

A porousness opens between church and world in this experience. The worldly values demonstrate their *ecclesial origin* through their confession of Christ before the world. Bonhoeffer witnessed the proponents of worldly values being faithful to Christ in confession rather than the Lutheran Church in the face of persecution. This experience affirms for Bonhoeffer that the church is a community defined primarily not by institutional form or doctrinal confessions but by its faithful witness to Christ. This emphasis foreshadows the developments of Bonhoeffer's letters from Tegel, which affirms the *worldly origin* of faithful witness, epitomized in his later reflections on a *mündige Welt* ("a world come of age")—with *mündig* literally meaning "having a mouth."⁵⁵ In this world come of age such witness

---

51. "We begin this section by calling attention to one of the most astounding experiences we have had during the years of trial for all that was Christian" (DBWE 6:339); "we experience in our own time. . . ." (DBWE 6:342); "once again we have the living experience on our side. . . ." (DBWE 6:343); "then the saying, 'whoever is not for me is against me,' became a concrete experience for the Christian community" (DBWE 6:343); "And thus it came to know the other saying of Jesus as a living experience" (DBWE 6:344); "and this experience caused the church-community. . . ." (DBWE 6:345); "this, too, is not a fictional construct but an experience we have had . . ." (DBWE 6:347); "our experience is that . . ." (DBWE 6:347); "we must not evade the question posed by our own experience and time" (DBWE 6:348).

52. On the historical background of this movement of humanist concepts becoming neutral, then anti-Christian, and then ecclesial, see Robinson, *Christ and Revelatory Community in Bonhoeffer's Reception of Hegel*, 189–91.

53. On this point, see the section "Trust" in "After Ten Years" (DBWE:46–7).

54. DBWE 6:343.

55. Stefan Heuser, "The Cost of Citizenship: Disciple and Citizen in Bonhoeffer's Political Ethics," *Studies in Christian Ethics* 18, no. 3 (2005): 62–3.

moves beyond religious division and interprets God's Word through nonreligious concepts that call all persons to suffer with God in and for the world.⁵⁶ Between the two texts, faithful witness intersects in both its *churchly and worldly* characteristics, emphasizing not their conflict but their intersection and promised unity in reconciliation.

If we follow Ziegler's suggestion that even the "political" conspiracy is *parrhesiastic* witness, then an intentional undecidability emerges regarding whether Bonhoeffer's resistance is churchly or worldly, particularly since the origin and character of his resistance activity is neither legal nor institutional.⁵⁷ In this undecidability there is no necessary opposition between church and world in the moment of exception, but a witness to their reconciliation in Christ, who renews, orders, and empowers political life in its various tasks (*Auftrages*) or mandates (*Mandaten*). As Bonhoeffer notes in "Christ, Reality, and the Good," the answer to the question "of how to think about this difference" between church and world "without falling back into spatial metaphors" is answered in the Bible through an account of the "*mandates of God* in the world."⁵⁸

The Reconciliation of the Mandates

Bonhoeffer frequently reflects on the divine mandates in his late writings. These "divinely imposed tasks" are the places where Christ's commandment forms and directs human life.⁵⁹ The list of mandates varies between Bonhoeffer's writings, but generally they maintain their fourfold character as church, government, work, and family. Interpreters tend to describe the mandates as "orders of preservation," suggesting that their primary function is to preserve the openness of human life to God's ultimate Word.⁶⁰ The mandates ordinarily coordinate well with one another in preserving space for God's Word therein.

A common aspect to narrations of the borderline case is to accentuate how in extreme moments the mandates fragment, becoming distorted and disjointed from one another. In the borderline case, the mandates no longer speak in unity; they instead make conflicting demands on human life that result in unavoidable guilt,

---

56. See DBWE 8:474. On the concept of religionless Christianity, see Wüstenberg, *A Theology of Life*.

57. Ziegler, "Witness to Christ's Dominion," 327. On the background of *parrhesia*: "The wider meaning of that term in antiquity to designate courageously frank and potentially dangerous public political speech is, in the earliest Christian writings, compressed to refer primarily to that courageous testimony to the lordship of Christ that is made possible and determined by the reality of the gospel itself" (Ziegler, "Witness to Christ's Dominion," 324).

58. DBWE 6:68. Emphasis original.

59. DBWE 6:68.

60. DeJonge, *Bonhoeffer on Resistance*, 34–44. See the Coda in Chapter 3 for Bonhoeffer's developing language from "orders of creation" to "orders of preservation" to "the mandates."

obscuring God's commandment.[61] The source of this fragmentation in Bonhoeffer's time is the absolutizing of the state over the other mandates, corrupting the other mandates by transgressing their mutually imposed limits. The result is that the mandates no longer preserve human life. The usual avenues to combat this distortion are ineffective in the borderline case, and the only option left is the violent overthrow of the tyrannical government in order to reestablish "normal" political life. The last resort paradoxically seeks peaceful politics through violent means. As Green remarks: "its purpose is healing and the peace of the human community."[62] Such violence appears to cohere with the government's mandate to restrain evil and promote *iustitia civilis* by bearing the sword.[63] The difference in the borderline case is that violence also becomes a constituting violence that not only preserves law and order but establishes a new "limited" governance that frees the other mandates for their proper and just functioning. As DeJonge suggests, it aims at a "violent restoration" of the mandates.[64]

The problem with this narration is it exaggerates the government's mandate by centering on the notion of preservation in explicating the mandates instead of centering Bonhoeffer's pronounced emphasis on reconciliation. While Wolf Krötke is certainly correct that speaking of one account of the mandates is impossible, Bonhoeffer nevertheless affirms consistently that the origin and formation of the mandates is always the activity of God.[65] This remains true even when Bonhoeffer wavers between grounding the mandates in creation or eschaton, since the emphasis on God's creative and reconciling Word remains at the center.[66] Even in the government's task of restraining evil in the *saeculum*, Bonhoeffer nevertheless emphasizes that its origin and authorization are only in Christ.[67] Hence Bonhoeffer vigorously affirms that there is no right to revolution, since this implies that the origin of politics is in violent human activity from below rather than a gift from above (*oben*), indicated in Bonhoeffer's preference for the language of government (*Obrigkeit*) over state (*Staat*).[68]

In "Christ, Reality, and the Good," Bonhoeffer notably emphasizes that the government's task is not creative or generative like the other mandates, but only preservative. The delimitation of its task is precisely in preserving space for the well functioning of the other mandates, but it is incapable of restoring or

---

61. Lovin, "Becoming Responsible in Christian Ethics," 394–5.
62. Green, "Pacifism and Tyrannicide," 45.
63. DBWE 16:590.
64. DeJonge, *Bonhoeffer on Resistance*, 155.
65. Wolf Krötke, "Dietrich Bonhoeffers Verständnis des Staates," in *Dem Rad in die Speichen fallen*, 314–15.
66. Bonhoeffer grounds the mandates in creation more clearly in "State and Church" (DBWE 16:511, 518–19); in eschaton more clearly in "Personal and Objective Ethics" (DBWE 16:550).
67. DBWE 16:510–13.
68. DBWE 16:502, 525.

6. The Dismantling, Reconciliation, and Future of the Law

establishing the other mandates—it acknowledges and protects them through the sword, but its origin and authorization stem from elsewhere: "Government itself cannot produce life or values. It is not creative."[69] Even the government is not generative of its own source, depending upon the church as its "hidden center" to hear and receive its authorization in the Christ-event.[70] It is for this reason that the retrieval of Bonhoeffer's language of "orders of preservation" to describe the mandates possesses the danger of overstatement, since it ultimately prioritizes the preservative function of the government as constitutive of the mandates as a whole, thus ignoring the generative and creative character of the other three mandates.

The shortcoming of the common narration of the borderline case is it asserts that the sword can generate a new peaceable politics. When law and order disintegrate and the other mandates fragment, violence is narrated as the generative means of establishing a new politics that restores the mandates of family, work, and church. One can hear echoes of Arendt's notion of *homo faber* in this narration where the "idea" of the mandates is realized or fabricated through the application of force.[71] This comes through in Rasmussen's suggestion that "[Bonhoeffer] is carefully crafting a rare exception to nonviolent means whereby carefully constrained use of deadly violence is, under the circumstances, the only route left for reinstating nonviolent means themselves as the normal and normative course and practice."[72] The instrumental character of violence comes to the fore in this narration with the gap between preserving and constituting violence being revealed to be nonexistent. One of the ironies of this narration is that it inadvertently continues to affirm the absolute character of the government's mandate by assuming that the other mandates depend ultimately upon its violence for their restoration. The result is that the conspiratorial violence of the borderline case is actually complicit in the violence of the totalitarian order, since violence remains the originating and preserving principle of the emerging order.

The fiction of violence terminating in peaceful politics comes under question at this point, since it is difficult to imagine exceptional violence not becoming the norm in the new regime, thus initiating a similarly fragmented and conflicted politics under a different name. This is the impulse that emerges when Bonhoeffer suggests in "State and Church" that any resistance is complicit with and thus inseparable from the guilt of the order that it stands against:

> Because in all decisions of the state the historical entanglement in the guilt of the past is incalculably large, it is for the most part not possible to judge the

---

69. DBWE 6:70. In "State and Church," Bonhoeffer can also say: "Government keeps what is created in its order but cannot itself produce life; it is not creative" (DBWE 16:518); and later: "that means government possesses for this realm only regulative but not constitutive significance" (DBWE 16:520).
70. DBWE 12:326.
71. Arendt, *The Human Condition*, 153–9.
72. Rasmussen, "Response," 170.

legitimacy of a single decision. Here the venture of responsibility must be risked.... Even where the guilt of government is blatantly obvious, the guilt that gave rise to this guilt may not be disregarded.[73]

This consideration is intensified when one observes that the resistance circle was not only "tainted" through the means of violence in the coup d'état but also by their thorough participation in the violence and *ethos* of National Socialism. As Victoria Barnett observes, the conspiracy circle included enthusiastic anti-Semites (e.g., von Hase and Canaris) as well as war criminals who oversaw widescale massacres (e.g., General Alexander von Falkenhausen and Reich Criminal Police Commissioner Arthur Nebe).[74] There is a sense that the complicity and conflicts that characterize the conspiracy circle entered their very selves. It is difficult to imagine how the violence enacted by the conspiracy circle would not somehow enter into and determine the politics that follow thereafter, exacerbating the conflicts found between the varying mandates. It is this very phenomenon of irresolvable conflict that commentators have identified as mundane within contemporary society.[75]

A differing narration of the borderline case emerges in light of the *limits* of violence. Contrary to the pacifist impulse, the limit is not between nonviolence and violence, which can imply the total deactivation of violence before the politics of peace, dismissing the place of the sword in Bonhoeffer's account of the mandates. It is rather the limit between the restraining and preserving task of the government and the renewal and empowerment of political life by the Spirit. The preventative character of the government's task cannot provide the sufficient conditions for free political action, since it is only capable of restraining behavior, not empowering free action in the fullness of life.[76] It works by inspiring fear of judgment by enacting punishment, which can foreclose, rather than open, avenues for liberated action. At its best, it restrains injustice, but at its worst it stunts free action in the name of safeguarding civil and moral behavior. While violent overthrow may judge the excesses of wicked governance through its "total removal," it cannot produce the renewal of the mandates.[77] Whatever violence accomplishes in the borderline situation, it nevertheless awaits a renewal and peace that comes *extra nos*. As Bonhoeffer argues in "Christ and Peace": "There are no possibilities at the human level to organize or build for peace."[78] There is a limit to the possibilities of the government's task as there is a limit to all the mandates.

---

73. DBWE 16:517–18.

74. Victoria Barnett, "Bonhoeffer and the Conspiracy," in *The Oxford Handbook on Dietrich Bonhoeffer*, 74.

75. Lovin, *Christian Realism and the New Realities*, 202; Puffer, "The 'Borderline Case' in Bonhoeffer's Political Theology," 267–9.

76. DBWE 16:590.

77. DBWE 16:532.

78. DBWE 12:260.

The continuing task and limits of violence remain an important theme when Bonhoeffer turns in "Heritage and Decay" to the dangerous possibility of a "final fall into the abyss" in political life. Bonhoeffer, there, describes the twofold action of church and government in expectation of a miracle that renews political life:

> Only two things can prevent the final fall into the abyss: the miracle of a new awakening of faith; and the power that the Bible calls "the restrainer," κατεχων (2 Thess. 2:7), that is, the ordering power, equipped with great physical strength, which successfully stands in the way of those who would throw themselves into the abyss. The miracle is the rescuing act of God that reaches in from above, beyond all historical calculations and probabilities, and creates new life out of nothingness—that is, the resurrection from the dead. The "restraining power" (*das Aufhaltende*) is the force that is made effective within history by God's rule of the world, which sets limits to evil. The "restrainer" (*der Aufhaltende*) itself is not God and is not without guilt, but God uses it to protect the world from disintegration. The place where God's miracle is proclaimed is the church. The "restraining force" is the ordering power of the state. As different as they are in essence, they move close to each other in the face of threatening chaos, and the hatred of the destructive powers directs itself as a deadly enemy to both of them alike.[79]

What is striking in Bonhoeffer's formulation is not so much the coordination of restraint and proclamation, but the gap that remains between them even in their moving closer together. For whatever the restrainer can accomplish, it cannot enact the miracle of faith that renews political life, saving it from its descent into the abyss. It would be a mistake, however, to conceive of proclamation in an instrumental sense as well. The empowerment and fulfillment of the church's task is a divine gift in the order of miracle, too.[80] The point is that the renewal and reformation of political life is not antithetical to the restraint and judgment of evil through violence, but a gap nevertheless exists between the immanent disposal of totalitarian politics through violence and the emergence of a "miraculous" new politics on a differing basis. This is the limit (*Grenz*) of violence before the miraculous activity of God in the borderline case (*Grenzfall*). While the borderline case is entangled in violence that begets violence, it also directs persons to pray for and expect the renewal of the mandates in the miracle of God's activity that founds and renews a peaceable politics and ethics.

---

79. DBWE 6:131–2.

80. As Bonhoeffer says in "Protestantism without Reformation": "The freedom of the church is not where it has possibilities, but only where the gospel is truly effective in its own power to create space for itself on earth, even and especially when there are no such possibilities for the church" (DBWE 15:448).

The Reconciliation of Politics and Ethics

Discussions pertaining to the exception do not always carefully distinguish what sort of exception is being invoked. The exception can be a moral or a political concept with both senses often converging in a singular discourse. As elucidated in Chapter 4, Bonhoeffer's employment of the logic of *necessitá* in "History and the Good [2]" draws the two senses together, speaking of the transgression of moral precepts as well as the "irrational" act beyond positive law that nevertheless serves political life. Necessity puts the moral and the political in conflict with one another, contributing to the conflicted conscience of the one who must act. The conspirators, therefore, testify to the experience of conflict, since venturing into the mire of political conspiracy afflicted the moral conscience. Ernst Wolf has suggested that there is a precedent for this conflicted conscience in German ecclesial thought paradigmatic of the era insofar as the church abdicated its political witness to the state *en toto* (even becoming subservient to the state in an Erastian sense), preoccupying itself solely with moral proclamation. This imbalanced attention led to an underdeveloped or even nonexistent ethics of resistance among the conspiracy circle, contributing to their tortured moral consciences.[81]

While there is an undeniable fidelity to aspects of "History and Good [2]" and the testimony of the conspirators in the common narration, Bonhoeffer also described the necessary interconnection and cohesion between politics and ethics on various occasions, particularly in his writings during the conspiracy period. In numerous places, Bonhoeffer affirms the unity and mutual inflection of the political and the ethical. In "Personal and Objective Ethics," Bonhoeffer states that Christian ethics not only address "worldly orders and conditions" but also set the limits of political life in the form of Decalogue: "The Decalogue is the framework within which a free obedience becomes possible in worldly life."[82] Bonhoeffer also describes the church's proclamation to the world as proceeding on the basis of the Decalogue, which "negatively defines the limits" of authentic and free political life.[83] There is no "double morality" for the church and world. As the two tables of the Decalogue belong together, so, too, are the Decalogue and Sermon on the Mount equally binding for all, calling for obedience and faith in all realms of life.[84] Bonhoeffer's most memorable development of this notion appears in his account of the Ethical that stands at the limits of free political life, which Bonhoeffer ultimately identifies as the law.[85] What emerges in these pivotal texts is that the Decalogue relates intimately to the formation and sustenance of political life, demonstrating how moral limits encompass the political and how truly political

---

81. DBWE 6:292. Wolf, "Political and Moral Motives behind the Resistance," 193–234.

82. DBWE 16:541, 548. Bonhoeffer repeats this claim regarding the Decalogue in "On the Possibility of the Church's Message to the World" (DBWE 6:358–61). See also DBWE 16:531.

83. DBWE 6:360.

84. DBWE 6:357.

85. DBWE 6:386-7.

acts are by definition affirmations of the Decalogue and not transgressions of it. This is the origin of Bonhoeffer's counterintuitive claim that valid state violence can be obedience to the Sermon on the Mount and the fifth commandment.[86] The unity of God's law affirms the coordination of the moral and political.

Commentators often recognize both the testified experience of conflict between the moral and the political in the borderline case as well as their unity and integration under the rubric of God's commandment, often negotiating them through an employment of the concept of tyrannicide. The moral and the political offer integrated guidance in the tyrannicide framework: where the political law offers guidance on when it is lawful to remove the tyrant, the moral law disciplines as well as discloses the nature of political violence. Its appeal for commentators is its seeming ability to provide a language that captures the complexity of the multiple demands of the exception under a single rubric.

Nevertheless, one of the curious elements of the tyrannicide framework is its ambivalent use of the term "exception." It is often assumed that tyrannicide is a synonym for the exception, but what exactly the exception is and how it relates to or expresses God's commandment is often left unstated.[87] Accentuating this lacuna is perhaps the most curious element of this narration of tyrannicide: it tends to describe not the command for tyrannicide itself or the character of the exception, but the discernment of the situation within which tyrannicide finds instantiation. In other words, it implicitly narrates the borderline case as the condition of the commandment, positioning tyrannicide as a last resort that is fitting for the circumstances. If the commandment is particular and concrete, requiring obedience, the primary element of discernment is upon the *quaestio facti*, the question of whether the situation for tyrannicide has actually emerged. This remains true in realist readings as well, since the gap between reality and the higher law requires an attentiveness to the circumstances and the "realistic" possibilities available therein.[88] The character of the exception remains ambiguous in this narration of tyrannicide because attention has been shifted to the circumstances within which tyrannicide becomes necessary rather than attending to the exceptional form of God's concrete commandment. The borderline case is made the condition for the exception.

This fixation on whether the conditions for tyrannicide have emerged cannot but occlude any emphasis on the temporality of God's command in visitation. It instead de-temporalizes the moment by treating it as an assemblage of circumstances within which God's command requires obedience. What results is an insufficient

---

86. DBWE 16:548–9; DBWE 6:359.

87. For instance, the subheading to the tyrannicide discussion for Green reads: "Tyrannicide—the Exception" (Green, "Pacifism and Tyrannicide," 41). And de Gruchy: "In so doing [Bonhoeffer] wedged open 'the way for the exception,' which in his case was tyrannicide" (De Gruchy, *Bonhoeffer and South Africa*, 96).

88. This is how Lovin reads Bonhoeffer's account of responsibility, see Lovin, *Christian Realism and the New Realities*, 194–6.

accounting of the historicity and freedom of God's command in the moment, thus expounding tyrannicide in a mode akin to procedural reason or the negotiation of positive law.[89] In the political sense, the tyrannicide discussion is kept within the orbit of the just war tradition, since it assumes that what is exceptional is primarily the circumstances, rather than the means of judgment that remains, in fact, quite ordinary. In the moral sense, the tyrannicide discussion is kept within the orbit of casuistic ethics as primacy is given to delineating the character and application of moral law by way of hard moral cases.

Instead of narrating the borderline case as the condition for the command, I argue it is truer to Bonhoeffer's theological argument to narrate the borderline case as a moment when God elicits the command beyond human expectation and the determinations of the moment. Such a reading disaggregates the borderline case from the command, so allowing for a mutual inflection between them.[90] In this narration, the borderline case is initially understood as a moment when persons encounter the inadequacies of their ethical and political concepts to address its challenges, inadequacies that contribute to the dissolution of concrete political life.[91] It is the rising to visibility of intractable problems that threaten generative human action, prompting the experience of conflict that raises the question of Psalm 11:3—"If the foundations are destroyed, what can the righteous do?" When God presents the command, however, the character of the borderline case is altered, since God's command limits, illuminates, and renews both the situation and the ethical and political therein. God's action in the form of the command performs this task in two ways.

First, the command discloses and overcomes the aberrations of political and ethical schemas that contribute to the emergence of the borderline case, establishing the ethical limits of fruitful political life in their place. It delimits the negative limits of political life in the Ethical. Second, the command in the borderline case also encounters persons as a gift that liberates persons for creative human action and surprising articulations of the law. While the command initially encounters one in the imperative mood, the liberating aspect of the command encounters one in the jussive mood.[92] "God's commandment is permission. It is distinguished from all human laws in that it commands freedom. It proves itself as God's commandment in that it eliminates this contradiction, in that the impossible becomes possible, and in that it really commands what lies beyond anything that

---

89. Smith, *Weird John Brown*, 103–21.

90. Puffer, "Taking Exception," 492.

91. DBWE 6:367; DBWE 16:530.

92. For a reading of Bonhoeffer's theology and ethics in a grammatical key, see David F. Ford, *Self and Salvation: Being Transformed* (Cambridge: Cambridge University Press, 2009), 253–65 and Plant, *Dietrich Bonhoeffer*, 118–25. On God's permissive command expressed in the jussive mood in the creation narratives in Genesis, see Katherine Sonderegger, *Systematic Theology: The Doctrine of God*, Vol. 1 (Minneapolis: Fortress Press, 2015), 302–3.

can be commanded, namely, freedom."⁹³ Hence the form of the command in the borderline case is utterly dissimilar to positive law in not merely generating an ethics and politics typified by the enactment or enforcement of a code in various cases.⁹⁴ It commands freedom beyond legislation. In this sense, the form of the command in the borderline case is itself an exception, transforming ethical and political law as one knows it.

To emphasize this permissive and liberating work of the command offers a more positive reading of Bonhoeffer's engagement in conspiratorial activity. While the imperatival force of the command sets itself against the political excesses of National Socialism, revealing the aberrations and illegitimacy of totalitarian rule, the freedom of the command liberates the conspiracy circle for a differing mode of resistance that not merely obeys or enforces the imperative of the law, but prayerfully awaits and boldly grasps after God's permissive command in resistance. The conspiracy is an affirmation of the gap between the imperatival force of God's command against unjust authority as well as—and at the same time—an act of free resistance within God's permissive command. In one sense, this act stands at the limit of the historical forms of the ethical and political, since it emerges in the midst of their disintegration. But in another sense, it witnesses to the center of human life from which the ethical and political emanate insofar as God's commandment liberates persons to participate in the formation of human life today.⁹⁵ As Bonhoeffer summarizes this relation in "History and Good [2]:" "In rendering obedience, human beings observe God's Decalogue, in exercising freedom, they create new decalogues (Luther)."⁹⁶

Imagining Politics after the Exception

"The ultimately responsible question is not how I extricate myself heroically from a situation but [how] the coming generation is to go on living."⁹⁷ The quotation from "After Ten Years" is renowned by admirers of Bonhoeffer for directing attention away from oneself to the younger generation and away from the present moment toward the future. The theme permeates Bonhoeffer's late theology, reflecting his concern for the future of society, politics, and the fullness of human life with

---

93. DBWE 6:382.
94. Smith, *Weird John Brown*, 108–13.
95. "The commandment of God revealed in Jesus Christ embraces life as a whole. It does not merely guard, like the ethical, the boundaries of life that must not be crossed, but it is at the same time the center and fullness of life. It is not only ought, but also allowed. It not only prohibits, but also liberates us for authentic life and for unreflective doing" (DBWE 6:381).
96. DBWE 6:288.
97. DBWE 8:42.

God and neighbor.[98] In a pragmatic sense, Bonhoeffer is consistently reflecting on the form and organization of the West after totalitarianism. This desire to participate in the rebuilding of Germany led him to return in 1939, and it cannot be forgotten that Bonhoeffer wrote *Ethics* for the West as it emerges into a postwar era that both reclaims its heritage and creatively organizes itself in unprecedented ways.[99] Within these texts and others from the era, Bonhoeffer is attempting to articulate concrete steps and measures that will aid the transition to this unknown future from a moment of unparalleled historical crisis. As Bonhoeffer says in his unfinished pulpit pronouncement for after the coup: "God sets before us an unprecedented task."[100]

This sense of concretely attending to the future is certainly prominent in the famous quote from "After Ten Years," but there is also a sense that responsible action hopes for a future beyond what was then (and is now) presently conceivable. Bonhoeffer indicates that the future might be the sort of thing for which one cannot prepare but for which one can only witness in symbolic action and faith. It is in this sense that Bonhoeffer draws on the prophetic witness of Jeremiah in his late theology, reflecting on the possibility of new life in the face of immanent and total destruction. As Bonhoeffer writes in "After Ten Years":

> What remains for us is only the very narrow path, sometimes barely discernible, of taking each day as if it were the last and yet living it faithfully and responsibly as if there were yet to be a great future. "Houses and fields and vineyards shall again be bought in this land," Jeremiah is told to proclaim—in paradoxical contradiction to his prophecies of woe—just before the destruction of the holy city; in light of the utter deprivation of any future, those words were a divine sign and a pledge of a great, new future. To think and to act with an eye on the coming generation and to be ready to move on without fear and worry—that is the course that has, in practice, been forced upon us.[101]

One can hear in Bonhoeffer's reflections a sense that by paradoxically living "as if" there is no tomorrow and "as if" there is a future filled with promise, one is acting for the younger generation through the mode of witness. Whether Bonhoeffer intended it or not, the notion of living "as if" echoes Paul's reflection on *hōs me* in 1 Corinthians 7, which subverts the present order through its action in expectancy of the eschatological future. Such action lives intentionally at the juncture between present and future, sensing that the new is coming but unable to realize it through one's action or speech. Bonhoeffer can thus suggest from prison that "we sense

---

98. DBWE 16:220, 528–39, 572–9; DBWE 8:330, 359–60, 377–90, 409, 499–506.
99. DBWE 6:10.
100. DBWE 16:572.
101. DBWE 8:50. There are also Bonhoeffer's reflections in prison on Jeremiah 27 (DBWE 8:389) and 45 (DBWE 8:150, 306, 361, 486).

something totally new and revolutionary, but we cannot yet grasp it and express it."[102]

There are two distinct threads that emerge in Bonhoeffer's reflections upon acting for the future. There is a thread that attempts to avoid arbitrariness and fantasy by acting toward concrete and "realistic" ends for the good of the younger generation, and there is a thread that eagerly witnesses to a future beyond the horizon of human possibilities through its symbolic action. One could, perhaps, hear echoes of the relation between the ultimate and penultimate in these threads insofar as concrete penultimate action is oriented toward and in service to the ultimate, but cannot in the end bring about the ultimate, since it comes by its own accord in its own time. By following the language of "Ultimate and Penultimate Things," one can sense that the two distinct threads belong together, since their uncoupling can lead to two extremes: the first can err toward compromise and the latter toward radicalism.[103]

But when one considers what it means to act toward the future in such an extraordinary moment, it becomes difficult to affirm that Bonhoeffer's action actually aimed toward "realistic" ends. Every attempt seems to have failed in achieving its desired result. The coded letter to the allies in the review of Paton's book achieved no affect within Allied governments, even with the appeals of Bishop George Bell.[104] The various coup attempts failed for one reason or another, and it led Bonhoeffer ultimately to prison and to his untimely death. And even if the coup succeeded, it is questionable (if not entirely doubtful) whether the Allied governments would cooperate with the emergent German government that emerged thereafter.[105] When reflecting on the various conspiracy efforts, one can hear echoes of Barth's charge that while the participants have all his "human sympathy," the resistance efforts nevertheless seemed "hopelessly passé" and "a dead end which did not seem to offer any light of promise for the future."[106] And yet, Bonhoeffer's activity and theological efforts have had an important effect on the younger generations, spurring fruitful theological reflection and inspiring liberating political action in unexpected places. One could say that Bonhoeffer served the younger generation, but not in the ways he expected. The effects of his actions are not the ones he intended. "Here," as Jane Bennett suggests in a different context, "causality is more emergent than efficient, more fractal than linear."[107]

---

102. DBWE 8:389.
103. DBWE 6:153–7.
104. DBWE 16:528–39. On this episode, see Dramm, *Dietrich Bonhoeffer and the Resistance*, 113–18.
105. Wolf, "Political and Moral Motives behind the Resistance," 196.
106. Quoted in DBWE 16:286 from Karl Barth and Carl Zuckmayer, *Late Friendship: The Letters of Karl Barth and Carl Zuckmayer*, trans. Geoffrey W. Bromiley (Grand Rapids: Eerdmans, 1982), 67.
107. Jane Bennett, *Vibrant Matter: A Political Ecology of Things* (Durham: Duke University Press, 2010), 33.

A consistent theme within this book is the attempt to trouble the notion that Bonhoeffer or the conspiracy circle could "reasonably" plan for a future after totalitarianism. The purpose of this critique is not to chastise the conspiracy circle for trying despite the odds but to question the more prominent notion that individuals can consistently anticipate and achieve the desired ends of their actions. Following the compelling critique of Esther Reed, it challenges the common narration of responsible action being performed by the sovereign "I" who can reliably anticipate and trace the consequences of their action. The movement of an "agent-act-consequence" causality is neither linear nor traceable, and this invites different narrations of responsible action and its ability to effect the future.[108] While there are situations and contexts where the movement of linear "agent-act-consequence" causality is valid, there are times and places where it is not. For Reed, it is the realities of global capitalism, whereas for this book it is the uniqueness of the exception as a time out of joint. It is in light of this claim paired with Bonhoeffer's statements about action for future generations that the question is raised: What does it mean to act meaningfully for the future in the extraordinary moment when the future remains an utterly unknown quantity beyond human control?

One could perhaps answer that Bonhoeffer's concrete attempts were generative as acts of political imagination.[109] By acting as if there was a great future and by planning for that future with concrete proposals, Bonhoeffer affirms the contingency and finitude of the present, bolstering hope-filled acts of resistance. Such action affirms that the present state of affairs is not immutable, and that God's future is full of promise beyond what one can see. It directs the imagination toward a theologically informed political life utterly distinct from totalitarianism, marked by reconciliation and Christological presence in its various activities and institutional forms. Its concrete reflections are couched in the hope of Christ, and this has real political effect whether these imaginative reflections are realized or not.

Nevertheless, the notion of imagination is necessarily limited by one's available conceptuality and background. Persons lack the requisite perspective to imagine the new since they are determined and situated within the old. Whatever they imagine may be different than the current state of affairs, but it will work within the histories, narratives, and communities within which it is fostered, and this can open as well as foreclose possibilities. The issue, in short, is that persons cannot adequately imagine the new or the future, since it is beyond their purview, beyond the possibilities of political life determined by violence. The ability to imagine novel political alternatives can seem impossible in the face of totalizing political

---

108. Reed, *The Limit of Responsibility*, 1–46.

109. On the politically generative role of imagination in Bonhoeffer, see Torbjörn Johannsen, "Prophetic Existence and the Power of the Imaginary as an Aspect of Political Theology: Dietrich Bonhoeffer and the Sunken World of the Prophets," in *Dem Rad in die Speichen fallen*, 287–300.

6. The Dismantling, Reconciliation, and Future of the Law

life. Thomas Lynch presses this point in an apocalyptic idiom when he emphasizes that the "demand for alternatives assumes the ability to know what should be hoped for and, indeed, how best to hope."[110] This is what the theology of crisis pressed in asserting the incommensurability of the present age with the *eschatos*, since the new order is utterly different from the present as "the overturning or rupture of all systems."[111] The imagination always faces a limit, and what limit is unsurpassable like the future that belongs to God?

Bonhoeffer's theology has an obvious affinity with apocalyptic theology, and he was certainly under the sway of the theology of crisis in his early career. Bonhoeffer, however, describes God's inbreaking not only as the negation of the present order; it also has a positive content that is founded upon and concretized in reconciliation, testified to and made present in the reading and proclamation of the Scriptures. The Word *extra nos* forms the political imaginary as a Word founded in the beginning but approaches from the eschaton in the ascended Christ. As Bonhoeffer suggests in his lecture, "Contemporizing New Testament Texts," the future confronts and determines the present in the proclamation of Scripture:

> "Contemporization" thus means an orientation toward this *future*, to this *outside*—and it is a disastrous mix-up between present and past to believe that one can define the present as something that resides *within itself* and *bears its own criterion within itself*. The criterion of the authentic present resides outside that present itself, resides in the future, in Scripture and in the word of Christ attested there.[112]

The impetus of Bonhoeffer's claim is that the future comes in the Scriptural sermon and reorients as well as determines the present, offering a language and imagery to orient oneself toward the future that has paradoxically become present. It is in this sense that the sermon is a politically potent act that is always capable of surprise, always capable of breaking the present open to God's future, opening the imagination to glimpse beyond one's immediate purview the coming Kingdom of God. The sermon is not merely a symbolic act that points to "what ought to be," but it is a proclamation of a divine call and reality made present in the moment—the future encounters the present in the Scriptural sermon and points to the reality of reconciliation from which a new language and political imaginary can emerge.

The centrality of Scripture in imagining and acting toward the future emerges even when the church's proclamation falters. Indeed, one perceives that Bonhoeffer's various reflections on "prayer and action" for the future are informed by Scripture—most obviously through the witness of Jeremiah in "After Ten Years." Such action is not arbitrary or fanatical even though it is not always reasonable,

---

110. Thomas Lynch, *Apocalyptic Political Theology: Hegel, Taubes, Malabou* (London: Bloomsbury Academic, 2019), 130.
111. Wolfe, "The Eschatological Turn in German Philosophy," 56.
112. DBWE 14:418.

since it responds to and images through prayer and action the reality of divine reconciliation to which Scripture testifies. The potency of this action when speech falters is precisely that it orients itself to a future it cannot directly anticipate or manipulate. It participates in its emergence, but it also remains surprised by the effects that emerge therefrom. This is captured in the syntagm "prayer and action" insofar as while both elements maintain their integrity, they nevertheless converge and overlap with prayer as a mode of action and action as a mode of prayer. Both are oriented to God's good works, which renew the world and Christian speech in unforeseen ways. "All Christian thinking, talking, and organizing must be born anew, out of that prayer and action."[113] This emphasis remains central in any theology of the exception—decision begets speech, but not in ways directly anticipatable. Its causality is nonlinear, ever open to the miraculous inbreaking of God that sets all things in a different light, including the political imagination. It responds to the present in expectation of God's future coming near to the point of intersection. This can beget more "measured" and modest political imaginaries as perceived in Bonhoeffer's *Ethics* or it can beget more radical imaginaries as perceived in Bonhoeffer's late "Outline for a Book."[114] And such action leaves itself open to taking unanticipated effect, prompting the political imaginaries of the younger generation in directions beyond what the author or original actor intended. In a certain sense, this is what this book has pursued at every stage—a reading of Bonhoeffer's life and thought that attends to what has come before, but open to differing effects that illuminate Bonhoeffer's theology today. It echoes Benjamin's contention that historical records are not objective datum, but locations where divine presence flits by in the moment of danger.[115] The same remains true of both past and future, since their capturing remains in the mode of gift, rising up unexpectedly in the face of great peril and trial.

---

113. DBWE 8:389.
114. DBWE 8:499–505.
115. See Theses 5 and 6 in Benjamin, "Theses on the Philosophy of History," 198–9.

CONCLUSION

The central impulse of this book has been to think after the exception in its historicity. The exception is principally not an ethical or a political concept, but a moment in history that impinges upon both ethics and politics. I argue that this impulse is native to Bonhoeffer's theology, particularly in the texts most often associated with the exception in his corpus. Bonhoeffer consistently narrates human activity, ethics, and politics in light of God's revelation that contextualizes them, thus echoing the negating power of the theology of crisis. At the same time, Bonhoeffer also affirms that in the exception God initiates new modes of free action in ethical and political life. The exception is not a mere gap or interlude in history, but an adventitious moment of divine dismantlement and reconstitution. The exception is akin to the miracle by renewing and unveiling free human life in unanticipatable and extraordinary ways. The transformation of individual and communal action exceeds the immanent possibilities of history. The impetus of transformation remains outside of human control; it *befalls* humanity in the moment.

The convergence of history and revelation in the narration of the exception is not only in God's decision to bind Godself to history, revealing and implanting Christ therein and thereby reconstituting history through Christ. The convergence is likewise in the way that both history and revelation contextualize human action, accentuating the passivity of persons to the determinations of history (time) and divine action (eternity). Reading the exception in its historicity decenters the person in its narration; the "agent" does not "act into" the situation, subtly implying their stable and coherent view of the situation from a respectable distance. Likewise, the emphasis on its historicity also refuses to narrate the moment as a challenge that one can mitigate or overcome through one's ingenuity or political *virtú*. The exception is instead a moment that disarms the strengths and resources of human action as in the moment of temptation. The one who undergoes the exception cannot achieve a "bird's eye view" of the situation, nor can one adequately deliberate upon, anticipate, or perform a good action that overcomes its challenges. The moment overwhelms the individual, calling for a response to its impossible demands, demonstrating the weakness and vulnerability of human reasoning and action to external forces.

The exception not only decenters human action but also judges human action. Bonhoeffer remains incisive in his ability to discern and uncover the subtle modes of self-justification and self-serving violence that attach to prominent modes of ethical and political rationalization. Bonhoeffer further captures how the determinations of sin extend through all human action and reality, revealing how the machinations of totalitarianism are always closer at hand than one imagines or hopes. The danger of a successful coup is that it merely propagates the violence of totalitarianism in the "new" politics that emerges from it, and there is good reason to perceive this impulse following into present democratic regimes as well.[1] The exception, then, reveals how human action is disempowered and beholden to the powers of sin and death. It is for this reason that Bonhoeffer asserts that the only secure hope for good historical action is God's sovereign action beyond the possibilities of this age. As Bonhoeffer states in "History and Good [1]": "Free action, as it determines history recognizes itself ultimately as being God's action, the purest activity as passivity."[2]

Converse to what one might expect, the emphasis on passivity and disarming human action does not entail the impotency of human action. For divine action in Bonhoeffer's idiom liberates good human action in history, liberating one from the determinations of sin for free action in and before Christ. The confession of passivity before God's action neither entails an acceptance of political realism—a confession that the good act is impossible, leading to an acceptance of "realistic" and guilt-inducing violence. The confession is rather a positive mode of perception grounded in the event of liberation which reframes human action within the good purposes of God. In the face of the "impossible" situation, God liberates a person to perceive and act into the moment in freedom from the determinations of law and circumstance. But, as argued in Chapter 5, the free action undetermined by law does not entail freedom *from* the law, it only entails a different and fecund relation to the law. The exception initiates a political community formed within the law in the shared experience of liberation, opening political life to the renewal of the Spirit. Indeed, the exception invites creative reflection upon the law and its articulation in light of the moment, remaining open to surprising and unforeseen aspects of God's commandment that were obscured or previously distorted. In short, the exception not only displays the limits and impotencies of the prevailing frame of reference but bursts it open, enabling persons to hear and respond anew to God's command and promise in history. The exception invites new articulations and practices of the law in and through the various mandates.

Responding to Hermeneutic Questions in the Discourse on the Exception

The entry point to the argument of this book was an engagement with the prevailing discourse on the exception in Bonhoeffer studies. Chapter 1 summarized this discourse while elucidating key interpretive decisions that contribute to the varied readings and divergences on the topic. The result of this summation was

---

1. Agamben, *Homo Sacer*, 119–26.
2. DBWE 6:226.

the articulation of a number of interpretive questions upon which the dividing lines between readings are formed. While Chapter 2 answered the questions about the (dis)continuity of Bonhoeffer's corpus and the coherence of Bonhoeffer's life and thought, the other questions raised in Chapter 1 remain unanswered, though evoked at other junctures of the text. In seeking to make a clear contribution to the dialogue on Bonhoeffer and the exception, I now venture an answer to the remaining questions.

One question overarching the book is whether one discerns or decides upon the exception, whether the "ultimate" criterion of action is objective, public, and reasonable or subjective, private, and fanatical. I questioned the adequacy of this binary in Chapters 4 and 5, since it centers on the individual agent and their deliberative processes and capacities, rather than on the character of the moment and God's action therein. One of the by-products of this binary is that it assumes that one can isolate the "agent" from the moment, since the agent acts into the moment as the terminus of a deliberative process, thus centering narration on one's interpretation of the moment that leads to action that, when successful, changes the course of history. The emphasis on the historicity of the exception undercuts the binary of decision or discernment by beginning with the *passivity* of the individual who responds to rather than interprets or deliberates over the moment. This liberates the notion of responsibility for a genuine responsiveness to God and neighbor in the simplicity of action (Chapter 4).

To be clear, the emphasis on passivity is not the total abdication of intentional human action for the future (which implies some notion of deliberation and reasoning) but only its reframing and relativization.[3] The person always acts toward the future in prayer and action, seeking to participate in the good activity of God in history, even when the future is beyond one's ability to anticipate and achieve. The exception disarms the notion that one can reasonably anticipate and form the future through their action without abandoning responsible action for the future or condemning human action to senselessness (Chapter 6). As I argue in Chapter 5, one continues to discern the will of God, the character of the moment, and the character of one's action in the exception, but this discernment is often a posteriori. Clarity about and a narration of the moment are gifts often, but not necessarily, received after the fact, though these, too, are always partial and piecemeal with the ultimate ground of decision hidden from all except God. The ground of good historical action is not within the person, but in the God who guides history. This same impulse led to the conclusions of Chapter 2: the coherence and continuity of Bonhoeffer's fragmentary life and thought are not intrinsic to Bonhoeffer, but hidden in God alone and gifted to persons in history.

The refusal to dichotomize decision and discernment raises sharp questions of the presumption that Bonhoeffer's resistance thought is best understood within the tyrannicide tradition, since tyrannicide readings are often invoked to rebut readings of Bonhoeffer that seem to court fanatical and irrational violence. In these

---

3. Carr, *Time, Narrative, and History*, 31–41.

approaches, tyrannicide is positioned as action in accordance with the circumstances (discernment) rather than enthusiastic action against reality (decision). Green exemplifies this approach by arguing that Bonhoeffer intentionally develops his resistance account against the background of the tyrannicide tradition in order to critically undermine spurious employments of Bonhoeffer by contemporary figures like George W. Bush or Paul Hill. A more promising approach from someone who affirms the tyrannicide reading is Larry Rasmussen, who describes tyrannicide as a fitting label for Bonhoeffer's thought after the fact, coalescing what remains fragmentary in Bonhoeffer's corpus. The benefit of Rasmussen's approach is that he captures how the moment required decision before Bonhoeffer could articulate a coherent rationale for action. As Rasmussen is fond of repeating: "Bonhoeffer did not have time."[4] While I diverge from Rasmussen regarding the adequacy of the tyrannicide framework (Chapter 6), his post-eventual ascription provides space for unforeseen and novel summations of Bonhoeffer's fragmentary theology, recognizing that summarizing Bonhoeffer's thought as exception or tyrannicide is not necessarily violent even if it is a post-eventual descriptor. This impulse is behind contemporary readings that continue to search with Bonhoeffer for a language to describe the character of good action in moments of crisis when prevailing political and ethical frameworks seem to fall short. Bonhoeffer's corpus thus remains open to creative readings beyond his original "intentions" without necessarily becoming violent appropriations. Just like my interpretation of the commandment of God in the jussive mood (Chapter 6), Bonhoeffer's texts remain open to creative readings beyond the existing interpretive paradigms or strictures of historical context while nevertheless remaining in relation to both.

This openness of Bonhoeffer's texts to unforeseen readings coheres well with my understanding of the traditioned character of Bonhoeffer's thought. While agreeing with DeJonge that Bonhoeffer's thought is irreducibly Lutheran, the Lutheranism I perceive has a different character.[5] Whereas DeJonge tends to read Bonhoeffer as a stable, coherent, and systematic thinker through the Lutheran confessions, I read Bonhoeffer as an open-ended, experimental, and occasional thinker like the early Luther. Put differently, I read Bonhoeffer as formed less by the systematization of Lutheran theology in form and content and formed more by the urgency and often paradoxical formulations of the early Luther. This mode of theological expression arises when one is seized by God, propelling one to witness to God's liberating activity with urgency. This urgency is perceivable in the Pauline epistles, Luther's "The Freedom of the Christian," Kierkegaard's account of the moment, and Barth's *Römerbrief*.[6]

---

4. Rasmussen, "Response," 165.

5. One could say that Bonhoeffer, following Mawson, is Lutherish rather than Lutheran. Mawson, "Lutheran or Lutherish?"

6. "We [Bonhoeffer and Barth] stand in the tradition of Paul, Luther, Kierkegaard, in the tradition of genuine Christian thinking" (DBWE 10:463).

There is an apocalyptic impulse ingredient to this account of tradition that remains open to unforeseen developments beyond the possibilities and internal development of the tradition, often incorporating and discarding elements from other sources in the creative development of a tradition. This account perceives that between the gaps and indeterminacies of a tradition, responsible and creative readings emerge that put past articulations in a different light. It is for this reason that my assertion that Bonhoeffer's resistance thought is unsystematic and varied is unproblematic, since it remains open for other interpretive possibilities within a traditioned discourse initiated within the experience of grace. It likewise identifies with greater ease different influences and voices behind Bonhoeffer's accounts that exceed the immanent frame of Lutheran theology while nevertheless remaining Lutheran in character. The tradition, in short, does not violently appropriate other thinkers in their employment but remains vulnerable to other voices, prompting a development of the tradition through responsiveness to voices beyond it.

The susceptibility and vulnerability of a tradition is ingredient to the responsible hermeneutic of South African readers of Bonhoeffer summarized in Chapter 1. The benefit of the South African reading over the American readings of the "Bonhoeffer moment" is that the former reflects the vulnerability and passivity of the contemporary reader undergoing the claims of Bonhoeffer. Whereas the American readings center on the interpretive possibilities of appropriating Bonhoeffer and his context today, keeping the interpreter at the center of the debate as in the binary of decision and discernment, the South African hermeneutic emphasizes the passivity of the reader to Bonhoeffer's contemporary yet elusive voice that bursts out of the determinations of history (whether his historical context or our own) by speaking in an unforeseen yet fecund manner. This mode of reading affirms not only the historical situatedness of reading Bonhoeffer but also that Bonhoeffer's voice emerges most perspicuously in a fleeting moment—in a time when everything is out of joint. The settled terms of discourse in Bonhoeffer studies are thereby ruptured, opening new avenues for Bonhoeffer to speak with urgency, inviting new and imaginative modes of action beyond the determinations of the age in the freedom of God. It is in this sense that Bonhoeffer himself remains an exception, resisting the domestication of historicizing readings.

Can One Speak of the Exception in Bonhoeffer?

Is it appropriate to speak of the exception in Bonhoeffer? The question has lingered through the course of the text, emerging at different junctures only for an answer to be delayed in the course of its argument. The warrant for the delay is that I do not claim that the exception is native to Bonhoeffer's texts, I only claim that it is the entry point into a discourse on Bonhoeffer's texts, providing a set of questions to interrogate Bonhoeffer while thinking with him. The term has proved valuable in its flexibility, allowing for a wide engagement with the Bonhoeffer corpus that does not limit itself to the texts where Bonhoeffer speaks explicitly in the language of exception. I have chosen to follow the language of exception throughout the book while recognizing that it may prove unfruitful in the end. The question about whether the exception is an appropriate language, however, can be delayed no longer, requiring an answer (or decision) since the end of the project is now at hand.

Before moving toward an answer to the question, one must affirm the idiosyncrasies of Bonhoeffer's thought in comparison to the broader discourse on the exception. As much as Bonhoeffer's thought may hold resonances to readings of the exception in the vein of Schmitt and Kierkegaard, his thought diverges from them in important respects, too. It is for this reason that I attend directly to Bonhoeffer's texts rather than performing a comparative analysis, since this reduces the possibility of importing the conceptuality of another onto Bonhoeffer's texts in creating a synthesis. One may charge that the reading I offer is also determined by my starting point of Bonhoeffer's account of history. I would respond that since the starting point emerged from the reading of the texts themselves, this does not reflect a determination but an intuition—one that proceeds on the basis of an insight that may end in places that one did not anticipate. This remains true in the writing of this book. The themes and interlocuters who emerged were not the ones that were initially in mind, and the conclusions reached in the final chapters were unexpected. The course undertaken reflects a key supposition about exceptions themselves: the discourse is always open to unexpected turns that surprise all who are involved.

One of the more surprising conclusions is that there are strong reasons both to reject and adopt the language of exception in Bonhoeffer. A negative answer suggests itself when one considers that Bonhoeffer rarely speaks of a moment that demands an exception to or suspension of God's commandment. As explicated in Chapter 6, Bonhoeffer affirms the presence and continuity of God's commandment in history, which includes the Sermon on the Mount, creation, and the Decalogue. The experience of ethical conflict, further, does not entail an actual transgression of the command as much as a transgression of entities that have achieved an independence *from* God's command through sin, revealing that the exception is not in relation to God's commandment but to the abstractions and deficiencies that originate in the incursion of sin. It is in this light that Bonhoeffer's declaration that justification is the end of ethics is wholly appropriate as well as his declaration that the politics of this age must acquiesce to the coming Kingdom of God. The exception is characterized by the effects of the fall in a moment when God's commandment is present but obscured, requiring the disciple to seek after it in prayer and action, mirroring the moment of temptation as a surrender before God in expectation of divine deliverance. Indeed, one may suggest that the exception is an extension of the moment of temptation, reflected in Bonhoeffer's description of the moment of the command's obscuration as a severe trial (*Anfechtung*).[7] The commandment of God does not mirror the form of positive law, possessing discrete parts that can be pitted against one another, making the appellation exception

---

7. DBWE 15:523.

harder to maintain. While the law can address a person in the imperative mood, it also encounters one in the jussive mood, reflecting the permissive and expansive character of God's command that liberates free action. The exception, in this sense, cannot properly be an exception, since it is not an exception to a rule.

A positive answer suggests itself when one reads the exception not as an ethical or juristic concept but as a moment that "stands apart" from the continuous flow of time (Chapters 3 and 4). From the human perspective, the exception is an event that is discontinuous from what precedes it and follows thereafter. It is, in Rasmussen's idiom, an epochal break in time.[8] It refuses reduction to historical cause and effect or generalization on a transtemporal or a priori basis. The moment disorients all who undergo it, thus the emphasis on human passivity. From the divine perspective revealed in Christ, the exception is an adventitious moment of divine action that liberates and renews human activity and thought (Chapters 4 and 5). The exception, echoing Schmitt and more foundationally Kierkegaard, is in the order of miracle. It affirms that while the exception is always in relation to the ordinary, it is not explicable on the basis of the ordinary. It instead explicates the ordinary on its own extraordinary basis. The exception properly understood is not the destruction of what has come before, but the renewal of the world that is continuous with God's superabundant activity in the beginning (Chapter 3). It is for these reasons that the language of exception is wholly appropriate.

One might resist a positive answer since the exception seems a term bound for misrepresentation given its prevailing connotations of lawbreaking, arbitrariness, irrationality, enthusiasm, and authoritarianism. The book has vigorously defended the exception against these charges at various stages (Chapters 3, 5, and 6), but one might wonder whether the term is damned to carry this legacy. Is it, then, worth maintaining this language even with an account of the exception centered on its historicity and divine action? I venture to maintain the language of exception in spite of its dangers and shortcomings. The language of exception best captures the illusiveness and singularity of the event that resists generalization, the primacy of freedom before God over the determinations of law in the narration of human action, and the character of God's creative and liberating act as nothing short of an exception (Jn 8:32). The exception, further, witnesses to the possibility of new and unexpected avenues of discourse and action even in the most hopeless of times when our future seems all but sealed for destruction. This affirmation is provisional insofar as all summarizing concepts invite challenge and reformulation. This answer cannot be a final word in the discourse, but it represents an attempt to think with Bonhoeffer in hoping for the unexpected and new today.

---

8. Larry Rasmussen, "The Ethics of Responsible Action," in *The Cambridge Companion to Dietrich Bonhoeffer*, ed. John W. de Gruchy (Cambridge: Cambridge University Press, 1995), 206.

BIBLIOGRAPHY

Agamben, Giorgio. *Homo Sacer: Sovereign Power and Bare Life*. Translated by Daniel Heller-Roazen. Stanford: Stanford University Press, 1998.
Agamben, Giorgio. *State of Exception*. Translated by Kevin Attell. Chicago: University of Chicago Press, 2005.
Aquinas, Thomas. *Summa Theologiae*. 61 Vols. Cambridge: Blackfriars, 1964–81.
Arendt, Hannah. *Eichmann in Jerusalem: A Report on the Banality of Evil*. Middlesex: Penguin Books, 1964.
Arendt, Hannah. *Origins of Totalitarianism*. London: Penguin Random House, 2017.
Arendt, Hannah. *The Human Condition*. Chicago: The University of Chicago Press, 1958.
Barth, Karl. *Church Dogmatics*. 4 Vols. Edited by Geoffrey W. Bromiley and T. F. Torrance. New York: T&T Clark, 2009.
CD II/2: *Church Dogmatics*. Volume II/2. *The Doctrine of God*. Edited by G. W. Bromiley and T. F. Torrance. New York: T&T Clark, 2009.
CD III/4: *Church Dogmatics*. Volume III/4. *The Doctrine of Creation*. Edited by Geoffrey W. Bromiley and T. F. Torrance. New York T&T Clark, 2009.
Barth, Karl and Carl Zuckmayer. *Late Friendship: The Letters of Karl Barth and Carl Zuckmayer*. Translated by Geoffrey W. Bromiley. Grand Rapids: Eerdmans, 1982.
Bartholomew, Ryan. *Kierkegaard's Indirect Politics: Interludes with Lukács, Schmitt, Benjamin and Adorno*. Amsterdam: Brill, 2014.
Benjamin, Walter. *Illuminations*. Edited by Hannah Arendt. Translated by Harry Zohn. New York: Mariner Books, 2019.
Benjamin, Walter. "The Critique of Violence (1921)." In *Walter Benjamin: Selected Writings, Volume 1: 1913–1926*, edited by Marcus Bollock and Michael W. Jennings. Translated by Edmund Jephcott, 236–52. London: Harvard University Press, 1996.
Bennett, Jane. *Vibrant Matter: A Political Ecology of Things*. Durham: Duke University Press, 2010.
Bethge, Eberhard. *Dietrich Bonhoeffer: Theologian, Christian, Contemporary*. Translated by Peter Eric Mosbacher, Betty Ross, Frank Clarke, and William Glen-Doepel. London: Collins, 1970.
Bethge, Eberhard. *Exile and Martyr*. Edited by John de Gruchy. New York: The Seabury Press, 1976.
Bethge, Eberhard. *Friendship and Resistance: Essays on Dietrich Bonhoeffer*. Grand Rapids: Eerdmans Publishing Co., 1995.
Bonhoeffer, Dietrich. *Dietrich Bonhoeffer Werke*. Edited by Eberhard Bethge et al. 17 Vols. Munich: Chr. Kaiser/Gütersloher Verlagshaus, 1986-99.
DBW 1: *Sanctorum Communio: Eine dogmatische Untersuchung zur Soziologie der Kirche*. Edited by Joachim von Soosten. Munich: Gütersloher Verlaghaus, 1986.

DBW 2: *Act und Sein: Transzendentalphilosophie und Ontologie in der systematischen Theologie*. Edited by Hans-Richard Reuter. Munich: Güterloher Verlagshaus, 1988.

DBW 3: *Schöpfung und Fall*. Edited by Martin Rüter and Isle Tödt. Munich: Gütersloher Verlagshaus, 1989.

DBW 4: *Nachfolge*. Edited by Martin Kuske and Isle Tödt. Munich: Gütersloher Verlagshaus, 1989.

DBW 5: *Gemeinsames Leben: Das Gebetbuch der Bibel*. Edited by Gerhard Ludwig Müller and Albrecht Schönherr. Munich: Gütersloher Verlagshaus, 1987.

DBW 6: *Ethik*. Edited by Isle Tödt, Heinz Eduard Tödt, Ernst Feil, and Clifford Green. Munich: Gütersloher Verlagshaus, 1992.

DBW 7: *Fragmente aus Tegel*. Edited by Renate Bethge and Isle Tödt. Munich: Gütersloher Verlagshaus, 1994.

DBW 8: *Widerstand und Ergebung: Briefe und Aufzeichnungen aus der Haft*. Edited by Christian Gremmels, Eberhard Bethge, and Renate Bethge. Munich: Gütersloher Verlagshaus, 1998.

DBW 9: *Jugend und Studium 1918–1927*. Edited by Hans Pfeifer. Munich: Gütersloher Verlagshaus, 1992.

DBW 10: *Barcelona, Berlin, Amerika 1928–1931*. Edited by Reinhard Staats and Hans Christoph von Hase. Munich: Gütersloher Verlagshaus, 1992.

DBW 11: *Ökumene, Universität, Pfarramt 1931–1932*. Edited by Eberhard Amelung and Christoph Strohm. Munich: Gütersloher Verlagshaus, 1994.

DBW 12: *Berlin 1932–1933*. Edited by Carsten Nicolaisen and Ernst-Albert Scharffenorth. Munich: Güterloher Verlaghaus, 1997.

DBW 13: *London 1933–1935*. Edited by Hans Goedeking, Martin Heimbucher, and Hans-Walter Schleicher. Munich: Gütersloher Verlagshaus, 1994.

DBW 14: *Illegale Theologenausbildung: Finkenwalde 1935–1937*. Edited by Otto Dudzus and Jürgen Henkys. Munich: Gütersloher Verlagshaus, 1996.

DBW 15: *Illegale Theologenausbildung: Sammelvikariate 1937–1940*. Edited by Dirk Schulz. Munich: Gütersloher Verlagshaus, 1998.

DBW 16: *Konspiration und Haft 1940–1945*. Edited by Jørgen Glenthøj, Ulrich Kabitz, and Wolf Krötke. Munich: Gütersloher Verlagshaus, 1996.

Bonhoeffer, Dietrich. *Dietrich Bonhoeffer Works*. Edited by Victoria Barnett, Wayne Whitson Floyd Jr., and Barbara Wojhoski. 17 vols. Minneapolis: Fortress Press, 1996–2013.

DBWE 1: *Sanctorum Communio: A Theological Study of the Sociology of the Church*. Edited by Clifford J. Green. Translated by Reinhard Krauss and Nancy Lukens. Minneapolis: Fortress Press, 1998.

DBWE 2: *Act and Being: Transcendental Philosophy and Ontology in Systematic Theology*. Edited by Wayne Whitson Floyd, Jr. Translated by H. Martin Rumscheidt. Minneapolis: Fortress Press, 1996.

DBWE 3: *Creation and Fall*. Edited by John W. de Gruchy. Translated by Douglas Stephen Bax. Minneapolis: Fortress Press, 1997.

DBWE 4: *Discipleship*. Edited by Geffrey B. Kelly and John D. Godsey. Translated by Barbara Green and Reinhard Krauss. Minneapolis: Fortress Press, 2001.

DBWE 5: *Life Together: The Prayerbook of the Bible*. Edited by Geffrey B. Kelly. Translated by Daniel W. Bloesch and James H. Burtness. Minneapolis: Fortress Press, 1996.

DBWE 6: *Ethics*. Edited by Clifford J. Green. Translated by Reinhard Krauss, Charles C. West, and Douglas W. Stott. Minneapolis: Fortress Press, 2005.

DBWE 7: *Fiction from Tegel Prison*. Edited by Clifford J. Green. Translated by Nancy Lukens. Minneapolis: Fortress Press, 1999.

DBWE 8: *Letters and Papers from Prison*. Edited by John W. de Gruchy. Translated by Isabel Best, Lisa E. Dahill, Reinhard Krauss, and Nancy Lukens. Minneapolis: Fortress Press, 2009.
DBWE 9: *The Young Bonhoeffer: 1918–1927*. Edited by Paul Duane Mathey, Clifford J. Green, and Marshall D. Johnson. Translated by Mary C. Nebelsick with Douglas W. Stott. Minneapolis: Fortress Press, 2003.
DBWE 10: *Barcelona, Berlin, New York: 1928–1931*. Edited by Clifford J. Green. Translated by Douglas W. Stott. Minneapolis: Fortress Press, 2008.
DBWE 11: *Ecumenical, Academic, and Pastoral Work: 1931–1932*. Edited by Victoria J. Barnett, Mark S. Brocker, and Michael B. Lukens. Translated by Anne Schmidt-Lange, with Isabel Best, Nicolas Humphrey, and Marion Pauck. Minneapolis: Fortress Press, 2012.
DBWE 12: *Berlin: 1932–1933*. Edited by Larry L. Rasmussen. Translated by Isabel Best and David Higgins. Minneapolis: Fortress Press, 2009.
DBWE 13: *London: 1933–1935*. Edited by Keith Clements. Translated by Isabel Best. Minneapolis: Fortress Press, 2007.
DBWE 14: *Theological Education at Finkenwalde: 1935–1937*. Edited by H. Gaylon Barker and Mark S. Brocker. Translated by Douglas W. Stott. Minneapolis: Fortress Press, 2013.
DBWE 15: *Theological Education Underground: 1937–1940*. Edited by Victoria J. Barnett. Translated by Victoria J. Barnett, Claudia D. Bergmann, and Peter Frick, with Scott A. Moore. Minneapolis: Fortress Press, 2012.
DBWE 16: *Conspiracy and Imprisonment: 1940–1945*. Edited by Mark S. Brocker. Translated by Lisa E. Dahill. Minneapolis: Fortress Press, 2006.
ZN: *Zettelnotizen für eine "Ethik"*. Edited by Ilse Tödt. Gütersloh: Kaiser, 1993.
Bonhoeffer, Dietrich and Maria von Wedemeyer. *Love Letters from Cell 92*. Edited by Ruth-Alice von Mismarck and Ulrich Kabitz. Translated by John Brownjohn. London: HarperCollins Publishers, 1994.
Brock, Brian. "Bonhoeffer and the Bible in Christian Ethics: Psalm 119, The Mandates, and Ethics as a 'Way.'" *Studies in Christian Ethics* 18, no. 3 (2005): 7–29.
Brown, Petra. *Bonhoeffer: God's Conspirator in a State of Exception*. Switzerland: Palgrave MacMillan, 2019.
Brown, Petra. "Bonhoeffer, Schmitt, and the State of Exception." *Pacifica* 26, no. 3 (2013): 246–64.
Butler, Judith. *Giving an Account of Oneself*. New York: Fordham University Press, 2005.
Carr, David. *Time, Narrative, and History*. Bloomington: Indiana University Press, 1986.
Clark, Adam and Michael Mawson, eds. *Ontology and Ethics: Bonhoeffer and Contemporary Scholarship*. Eugene: Pickwick Publications, 2013.
Cone, James. *A Black Theology of Liberation: Fortieth Anniversary Edition*. Mary Knoll: Orbis Books, 2018.
Courtenay, William. "Nominalism and Late Medieval Religion." In *The Pursuit of Holiness in Late Medieval and Renaissance Religion*, edited by Charles Trinkaus and Heiko A. Oberman, 26–59. Leiden: Brill, 1974.
Dahill, Lisa. *Reading from the Underside of Selfhood: Bonhoeffer and Spiritual Formation*. Eugene: Pickwick Publications, 2008.
DeCort, Andrew D. *Bonhoeffer's New Beginning: Ethics After Desolation*. Minneapolis: Fortress Press, 2018.
De Graff, Guido. *Politics in Friendship: A Theological Account*. London: Bloomsbury T&T Clark, 2014.

De Gruchy, John. *Bonhoeffer and South Africa: Theology in Dialogue*. Grand Rapids: Eerdmans Publishing, 1984.
De Gruchy, John. *Bonhoeffer's Questions: A Life-Changing Conversation*. Minneapolis: Fortress Press, 2019.
De Keijzer, Josh. "Revelation as Being: Bonhoeffer's Appropriation of Heidegger's Ontology." *The Journal of Religion* 98, no. 3 (2018): 348–70.
DeJonge, Michael. *Bonhoeffer on Resistance: The Word Against the Wheel*. Oxford: Oxford University Press, 2018.
DeJonge, Michael. "Bonhoeffer's Non-Commitment to Nonviolence: A Response to Stanley Hauerwas." *Journal of Religious Ethics* 44, no. 2 (2016): 278–94.
DeJonge, Michael. *Bonhoeffer's Reception of Luther*. Oxford: Oxford University Press, 2017.
DeJonge, Michael. *Bonhoeffer's Theological Formation*. Oxford: Oxford University Press, 2012.
DeJonge, Michael. "How to Read Bonhoeffer's Peace Statements: Or, Bonhoeffer was a Lutheran and Not an Anabaptist." *Theology* 118, no. 3 (2015): 162–71.
DeJonge, Michael. "Race is an *Adiaphoron*: The Place of Race in Bonhoeffer's 1933 Writings." *Evangelische Theologie* 80, no. 4 (2020). https://doi.org/10.14315/evth-2020-800406.
DeJonge, Michael and Clifford Green, eds. *Luther, Bonhoeffer, and Public Ethics: Reforming The Church of the Future*. New York: Lexington Books, 2018.
Derrida, Jacques. *Politics of Friendship*. Translated by George Collins. London: Verso, 1997.
Derrida, Jacques. *The Beast and the Sovereign*. 2 Vols. Edited by Geoffrey Bennington and Peggy Kamuf. Chicago: University of Chicago Press, 2009.
De Wilde, Marc. "Violence in the State of Exception: Reflections on Theologico-Political Motifs in Benjamin and Schmitt." In *Political Theologies: Public Religions in a Post-Secular World*, edited by Hent de Vries and Lawrence E. Sullivan, 188–200. New York: Fordham Press, 2006.
Dramm, Sabine. *Dietrich Bonhoeffer and the Resistance*. Minneapolis: Fortress Press, 2009.
Duns Scotus, John. *Duns Scotus on the Will and Morality*. Edited by William A. Frank. Selected and translated by Alan B. Wolter, O.F.M. Washington DC: Catholic University of America Press, 1997.
Dupré, Louis. *The Enlightenment and the Intellectual Foundations of Modern Culture*. New Haven: Yale University Press, 2004.
Eberhardt, Kai-Ole. "Das Geheimnis des Waltens Gottes in der Geschichte: Providenz und Ethik in Dietrich Bonhoeffers Glaubenssätzen von 1942." *Kirchliche Zeitgeschichte* 31, no. 1 (2018): 221–44.
Elshtain, Jean Bethke. "Reflection on the Problem of 'Dirty Hands.'" In *Torture: A Collection*, edited by Sanford Levinson, 77–89. Oxford: Oxford University Press, 2006.
Elshtain, Jean Bethke. *Sovereignty: God, State, and Self*. New York: Basic Books, 2008.
Emerton, David. *God's Church-Community: The Ecclesiology of Dietrich Bonhoeffer*. London: Bloomsbury T&T Clark, 2020.
Evans, Stephen C. "Is the Concept of an Absolute Duty Toward God Morally Unintelligible?" In *Kierkegaard's Fear and Trembling: Critical Appraisal*, edited by Robert L. Perkins, 141–51. Eugene: Wipf and Stock Publishers, 2009.
Falque, Emmanuel. *Crossing the Rubicon: The Borderlands of Philosophy and Theology*. Translated by Reuben Shank. New York: Fordham University Press, 2016.
Feil, Ernst. *The Theology of Dietrich Bonhoeffer*. Translated by Martin Rumscheidt. Minneapolis: Fortress Press, 1985.

Floyd Jr., Wayne Whitson and Charles Marsh, eds. *Theology and the Practice of Responsibility: Essays on Dietrich Bonhoeffer*. Valley Forge: Trinity Press, 1994.

Ford, David F. *Self and Salvation: Being Transformed*. Cambridge: Cambridge University Press, 2009.

Fowl, Stephen and L. Gregory Jones. *Reading in Communion: Scripture and Ethics in the Christian Life*. Eugene: Wipf and Stock Publishers, 1998.

French, David. "How Should One Resist the Trump Administration?" *New York Times*. Published on February 14, 2017. https://www.nytimes.com/2017/02/14/opinion/how-should-one-resist-the-trump-administration.html.

Frick, Peter, ed. *Bonhoeffer and Interpretive Theory: Essays on Methods and Understanding*. Frankfurt am Main: Peter Lang GmbH, 2013.

Frick, Peter, ed. *Bonhoeffer's Intellectual Formation: Theology and Philosophy in His Thought*. Tübingen: Mohr Siebeck, 2008.

Gadamer, Hans-Georg. *Truth and Method*. Translated by Joel Weinsheimer and Donald G. Marshall. London: Bloomsbury Publishing, 2013.

Gides, David M. *Pacifism, Just War, and Tyrannicide: Bonhoeffer's Church-World Theology and His Changing Forms of Political Thinking and Involvement*. Eugene: Pickwick Publications, 2011.

Gingle, Dallas. "Justification and Judgments: Walzer, Bonhoeffer, and the Problem of Dirty Hands." *Journal of the Society of Christian Ethics* 37, no. 1 (2017): 83–99.

Green, Clifford. *Bonhoeffer: A Theology of Sociality*. Grand Rapids: William B. Eerdmans Publishing Co., 1999.

Green, Clifford. "Pacifism and Tyrannicide: Bonhoeffer's Christian Peace Ethic." *Studies in Christian Ethics* 18, no. 3 (2005): 31–47.

Green, Clifford. "Peace Ethic or "Pacifism?" An Assessment of *Bonhoeffer the Assassin*." *Modern Theology* 31, no. 1 (January 2015): 201–8.

Green, Clifford. "Review of *Dietrich Bonhoeffer: Reality and Resistance*." *Conversations in Religion and Theology* 6, no. 2 (2008): 155–73.

Green, Clifford and Guy C. Carter, eds. *Interpreting Bonhoeffer: Historical Perspectives | Emerging Issues*. Minneapolis: Fortress Press, 2013.

Griffin, Leslie. "The Problem of Dirty Hands." *The Journal of Religious Ethics* 31 (1989): 31–61.

Grøn, Arne. "Time and History." In *The Oxford Handbook of Kierkegaard*, edited by John Lippitt and George Pattison, 273–91. Oxford: Oxford University Press, 2013.

Gutiérrez, Gustavo. *The Power of the Poor in History*. Translated by Robert McAfee. Mary Knoll: Orbis Books, 1983.

Hale, Lori Brandt and Reggie Williams. "Is this a Bonhoeffer Moment?" *Sojourners*. Published February, 2018. https://sojo.net/magazine/february-2018/bonhoeffer-moment.

Hauerwas, Stanley. "Dietrich Bonhoeffer." In *The Blackwell Companion to Political Theology*, edited by Peter Scott and William T. Cavanaugh, 136–49. Maiden: Blackwell Publishing, 2004.

Hauerwas, Stanley. *Performing the Faith: Bonhoeffer on Truth and Politics*. Grand Rapids: Brazos Press, 2004.

Haynes, Stephen R. *The Battle for Bonhoeffer: Debating Discipleship in the Age of Trump*. Grand Rapids: Eerdmans, 2018.

Haynes, Stephen R. *The Bonhoeffer Phenomenon: Portraits of a Protestant Saint*. Minneapolis: Fortress Press, 2004.

Hays, Richard. *The Moral Vision of the New Testament*. San Francisco: Harper, 1996.

Heidegger, Martin. *Being and Time*. Translated by John Macquarrie and Edward S. Robinson. London: HarperCollins, 2008.

Heuser, Stefan. "The Cost of Citizenship: Disciple and Citizen in Bonhoeffer's Political Ethics." *Studies in Christian Ethics* 18, no. 3 (2005): 49–69.

Janicaud, Dominique et al., *Phenomenology and the "Theological Turn": The French Debate*. Translated by Bernard G. Prusak. New York: Fordham University Press, 2000.

Johnson, Keith L. and Timothy Larson, eds. *Bonhoeffer, Christ, and Culture*. Edited by Keith L. Johnson and Timothy Larson. Downers Grove: InterVarsity Press, 2013.

Kahn, Paul W. *Political Theology: Four New Chapters on the Concept of Sovereignty*. New York: Columbia University Press, 2012.

Kaiser, Joshua. *Becoming Simple and Wise: Moral Discernment in Dietrich Bonhoeffer's Vision of Christian Ethics*. Eugene: Pickwick Publications, 2015.

Kant, Immanuel. "Idea for a Universal History with a Cosmopolitan Aim." In *Immanuel Kant: Anthropology, History, and Education*, edited by Günter Zöller and Robert B. Louden, translated by Allen W. Wood. *The Cambridge Edition of the Works of Immanuel Kant*, 108–20. Cambridge: Cambridge University Press, 2007.

Kant, Immanuel. *Practical Philosophy*. Edited and translated by Mary J. Gregor. *The Cambridge Edition of the Works of Immanuel Kant*, 605–15. Cambridge: Cambridge University Press, 1996.

Kelly, Geffrey B. and F. Burton Nelson. *The Cost of Moral Leadership: The Responsibility of Dietrich Bonhoeffer*. Grand Rapids: Eerdmans Publishing House, 2020.

Kierkegaard, Søren. *Either/Or II*. Edited by Howard V. Hong and Edna H. Hong. Princeton: Princeton University Press, 1987.

Kierkegaard, Søren. *Fear and Trembling*. Edited by C. Stephen Evans and Sylvia Walsh. Translated by Sylvia Walsh. Cambridge: Cambridge University Press, 2011.

Kierkegaard, Søren. *Fear and Trembling and Repetition*. Edited and translated by Howard V. Hong and Edna H. Hong. Princeton: Princeton University Press, 1983.

Kierkegaard, Søren. *Furcht und Zittern/ Wiederholung*, 2nd ed. Jena: Eugen Diederichs, 1909.

Kierkegaard, Søren. *Philosophical Fragments*. Edited and translated by Howard V. Hong and Edna H. Hong. Princeton: Princeton University Press, 1985.

Kierkegaard, Søren. *The Concept of Anxiety: A Simple Psychologically Orienting Deliberation on the Dogmatic Issue of Hereditary Sin*. Edited and translated by Reidar Thomte. Princeton: Princeton University Press, 1980.

Kierkegaard, Søren. *Works of Love*. Edited and translated by Howard V. Hong and Edna H. Hong. Princeton: Princeton University Press, 1995.

Kim, Isaac. "The Limits of Bonhoefferian Responsibility: On Jean Bethke Elshtain's (Mis) use of Bonhoeffer." *Political Theology* 20, no. 3 (2019): 262–79.

Kirkpatrick, Matthew. *Attacks on Christendom in A World Come of Age: Kierkegaard, Bonhoeffer, and the Question of "Religionless Christianity"*. Eugene: Pickwick Publications, 2011.

Kirkpatrick, Matthew, ed. *Engaging Bonhoeffer: The Impact and Influence of Bonhoeffer's Life and Thought*. Minneapolis: Fortress Press, 2016.

Kolb, Robert. *Martin Luther and the Enduring Word of God: The Wittenberg School and Its Scripture-Centered Proclamation*. Grand Rapids: Baker Academic, 2016.

Koopman, Nico and Robert Vosloo, eds. *Reading Bonhoeffer in South Africa after the Transition to Democracy: Selected Essays*. Berlin: Peter Lang, 2020.

Krötke, Wolf. *Barmen—Barth—Bonhoeffer: Beiträge zu einer zeitgemäßen christozentrischen Theologie*. Bielefeld: Luther-Verlage, 2009.

Krötke, Wolf. *Karl Barth and Dietrich Bonhoeffer: Theologians for a Post-Christian World*. Translated by John Burgess. Grand Rapids: Baker Academic, 2019.
Latmiral, Gaetano. "Letter to Professor Gerhard Leibholz, June 3, 1946." *Dietrich Bonhoeffer Yearbook / Jahrbuch 2003* 1 (2003): 27–31.
Locke, John. *Two Treatises of Government*. Edited by Peter Laslett. Cambridge: Cambridge University Press, 1960.
Lovin, Robin W. "Becoming Responsible in Christian Ethics." *Studies in Christian Ethics* 22, no. 4 (2009): 389–98.
Lovin, Robin W. *Christian Realism and the New Realities*. Cambridge: Cambridge University Press, 2008.
Löwith, Karl. *Meaning in History*. Chicago: The University of Chicago Press, 1949.
Luther, Martin. *Luther's Works*. Edited by Jaroslav Pelikan and Helmut T. Lehmann. 56 Vols. Philadelphia: Fortress Press; St. Louis: Concordia Publishing House, 1955–86.
LW 26: *Lectures on Galatians 1935: Chapters 1–4*. St. Louis: Concordia Publishing House, 1963.
LW 31: *Career of the Reformer I*. Philadelphia: Fortress Press, 1959.
LW 33: *Career of the Reformer III*. Philadelphia: Fortress Press, 1957.
LW 46: *Christian in Society III*. Philadelphia: Fortress Press, 1967.
Lynch, Thomas. *Apocalyptic Political Theology: Hegel, Taubes, Malabou*. London: Bloomsbury Academic, 2019.
Machiavelli, Niccolò. *Discourses on Livy*. Translated by Harvey C. Mansfield and Nathan Tarcov. Chicago: The University of Chicago Press, 1996.
Machiavelli, Niccolò. *The Prince*. Edited and translated by Peter Bondanella. Oxford: Oxford University Press, 2005.
Marion, Jean-Luc. *Being Given: Toward a Phenomenology of Givenness*. Translated by Jeffrey L. Kosky. Stanford: Stanford University Press, 2002.
Marion, Jean-Luc. *In the Self's Place: The Approach of Saint Augustine*. Translated by Jeffrey L. Kosky. Stanford: Stanford University Press, 2012.
Marquard, Odo. *Farewell to Matters of Principle: Philosophical Studies*. Oxford: Oxford University Press, 1989.
Marsh, Charles. *Reclaiming Dietrich Bonhoeffer: The Promise of His Theology*. Oxford: Oxford University Press, 1997.
Marsh, Charles. *Strange Glory: A Life of Dietrich Bonhoeffer*. New York: Alfred A. Knoft, 2014.
Mauldin, Joshua T. "Interpreting the Divine Mandates in a Bonhoeffer Moment." *Political Theology* 20, no. 7 (2019): 574–94.
Mawson, Michael. *Christ Existing as Community*. Oxford: Oxford University Press, 2018.
Mawson, Michael. "Lutheran or Lutherish? Framing Bonhoeffer's Reception of Luther." *Modern Theology* 3, no. 2 (2019): 1–8.
Mawson, Michael and Philip G. Ziegler, eds. *Christ, Church, and World: New Studies in Bonhoeffer's Theology and Ethics*. London: T&T Clark, 2016.
Mawson, Michael and Philip G. Ziegler, eds.*The Oxford Handbook of Dietrich Bonhoeffer*. Oxford: Oxford University Press, 2019.
McBride, Jennifer. *The Church for the World: A Theology of Public Witness*. Oxford: Oxford University Press, 2014.
Meinecke, Friedrich. *Der Idee der Staatsräson in der Neueren Geschichte*. München und Berlin: Druck und Verlag von R. Oldenbourg, 1925.
Meinecke, Friedrich. *Die Deutsche Katastrophie: Betrachtungen und Erinnergungen*. Wiesbaden: Eberhard Brockhaus Verlag, 1946.

Meinecke, Friedrich. *Machiavellism: The Doctrine of Raison D'état and Its Place in Modern History*. Translated by Douglas Scott. London: Routledge and Kegan Paul, 1957.

Mengus, Raymond. "Dietrich Bonhoeffer and the Decision to Resist." *The Journal of Modern History* 64 (December 1992): S134–S146.

Metaxas, Eric. *Bonhoeffer: Pastor, Martyr, Prophet, Spy*. Nashville: Thomas Nelson, 2010.

Metaxas, Eric. "Should Christians Vote for Trump." *Wall Street Journal*. Published on October 12, 2016. https://www.wsj.com/articles/should-christians-vote-for-trump-1476294992.

Michelfelder, Diane and Richard E. Palmer, eds and trans. *Dialogue and Deconstruction: The Gadamer-Derrida Encounter*. New York: SUNY Press, 1989.

Mjaaland, Marius Timmann. "Sovereignty and Submission: Luther's Political Theology and the Violence of Christian Metaphysics." *Studies in Christian Ethics* 31, no. 4 (2018): 435–51.

Moberly, Jennifer. "'Felicity to the Original Text'? The Translation of Bonhoeffer's *Ethics*." *Studies in Christian Ethics* 22, no. 3 (2009): 336–56.

Moberly, Jennifer. *The Virtue of Bonhoeffer's Ethics: A Study in Dietrich Bonhoeffer's Ethics in Relation to Virtue Ethics*. Eugene: Pickwick Publications, 2013.

Moses, John A. *The Reluctant Revolutionary: Dietrich Bonhoeffer's Collision with Prusso-German History*. Oxford: Berghahn Books, 2014.

Müller, Hanfried. *Von der Kirche zur Welt: Ein Beitrag zu der Beziehung des Wortes Gottes auf die societas in Dietrich Bonhoeffers theologischer Entwicklung*. Leipzig: Koehler & Amelang, 1961.

Nation, Mark Thiessen and Stanley Hauerwas, "'A Pacifist and Enemy of the State:' Bonhoeffer's Journal to Nonviolence." *ABC Religion and Ethics*. Published on April 19, 2018. https://www.abc.net.au/religion/a-pacifist-and-enemy-of-the-state-bonhoeffers-journey-to-nonviol/10094798.

Nation, Mark Thiessen, Anthony G. Siegrist, and Daniel P. Umbel. *Bonhoeffer the Assassin? Challenging the Myth, Recovering His Call to Peacemaking*. Grand Rapids: Baker Academic, 2013.

Niebuhr, H. R. *The Responsible Self: An Essay in Christian Moral Philosophy*. Louisville: Westminster John Knox Press, 1999.

Nielson, Kirsten Bush, Ralf Karolus Wüstenberg, and Jens Zimmermann, eds. *Dem Rad in die Speichen fallen: Das Politische in der Theologie Dietrich Bonhoeffers | A Spoke in the Wheel: The Political Theology of Dietrich Bonhoeffer*. München: Gütersloher Verlagshaus, 2013.

Nietzsche, Friedrich. *Beyond Good and Evil*. Edited by Rolf-Peter Horstmann. Translated by Judith Norman. Cambridge: Cambridge University Press, 2012.

Nissen, Ulrik B. "Dietrich Bonhoeffer: A Journey from Pacifism to Resistance." In *Christianity and Resistance in the 20th Century: From Kaj Munk and Dietrich Bonhoeffer to Desmond Tutu*, edited by Søren Dosenrode, 147–74. Leiden: Brill, 2008.

Oakley, Francis. "Voluntarist Theology and Early-Modern Science: The Matter of Divine Power, Absolute and Ordained." *History of Science* 56, no. 1 (2018): 72–96.

O'Donovan, Oliver. *Finding & Seeking*. Volume 2 of *Ethics as Theology*. Cambridge: William B. Eerdmans Publishing Company, 2014.

O'Donovan, Oliver. *Resurrection and Moral Order: An Outline for Evangelical Ethics*, 2nd ed. Grand Rapids: William B. Eerdmans Publishing Company, 1994.

O'Donovan, Oliver. *The Desire of the Nations*. Cambridge: Cambridge University Press, 1996.

Ott, Heinrich. *Reality and Faith: The Theological Legacy of Dietrich Bonhoeffer*. Translated by Alex A. Morrison. Philadelphia: Fortress Press, 1971.
Palmisano, Trey. *Peace and Violence in the Ethics of Dietrich Bonhoeffer: An Analysis of Method*. Eugene: Wipf and Stock, 2016.
Pangritz, Andreas. *Karl Barth in the Theology of Dietrich Bonhoeffer*. Translated by Barbara and Martin Rumscheidt. Grand Rapids: William B. Eerdmans Publishing Company, 2000.
Paulson, Steven D. *Doing Lutheran Theology*. New York: T&T Clark, 2011.
Peck, William J., ed. *New Studies in Bonhoeffer's Ethics*. New York: The Edwin Mellon Press, 1987.
Picht, Georg and Winston Davis, trans. "The Concept of Responsibility: Introduction and Translation." *Religion* 28, no. 2 (1998): 190–203.
Plant, Stephen. *Dietrich Bonhoeffer*. Continuum: London, 2004.
Puffer, Matthew. "Election in Bonhoeffer's *Ethics*: Discerning a Late Revision." *International Journal of Systematic Theology* 14, no. 3 (2012): 255–76.
Puffer, Matthew. "Taking Exception to the *Grenzfall*'s Reception: Revisiting Karl Barth's Ethics of War." *Modern Theology* 28, no. 3 (2012): 478–502.
Puffer, Matthew. "Three Rival Versions of Moral Reasoning: Interpreting Bonhoeffer's Ethics of Lying, Guilt, and Responsibility." *Harvard Theological Review* 112, no. 2 (2019): 160–83.
Radler, Karola S. *"Decision" in the Thought of Dietrich Bonhoeffer and Carl Schmitt: A Comparative Study*. Dissertation. Stellenbosch University, 2019.
Ramsey, Paul. *Deeds and Rules in Christian Ethics*. New York: Scribner, 1967.
Ramsey, Paul. "The Case of the Curious Exception." In *Norm and Context in Christian Ethics*, edited by Gene H. Outka and Paul Ramsey, 67–135. London: SCM Press, 1968.
Rasmussen, Larry. *Dietrich Bonhoeffer: His Significance for North Americans*. Minneapolis: Fortress Press, 1990.
Rasmussen, Larry. *Dietrich Bonhoeffer: Reality and Resistance*. Nashville: Abingdon Press, 1972.
Rasmussen, Larry. "The Ethics of Responsible Action." In *The Cambridge Companion to Dietrich Bonhoeffer*, edited by John W. de Gruchy, 206–25. Cambridge: Cambridge University Press, 1995.
Reed, Esther. *The Limit of Responsibility: Dietrich Bonhoeffer's Ethics for a Globalizing Era*. London: Bloomsbury T&T Clark, 2018.
Ricoeur, Paul. *The Just*. Translated by David Pellauer. Chicago: The University of Chicago Press, 1995.
Ritter, Gerhard. *Die Dämonie der Macht: Betrachtungen über Geschichte und Wesen des Machtproblems in politischen Denke der Neuzeit*. Stuttgart: H. R. C. Hannsmann, 1947.
Ritter, Gerhard. *Machtstaat und Utopie: vom Streit um die Dämonie der Macht seit Machiavelli und Morus*. München: Oldenbourg, 1940.
Robinson, David S. *Christ and Revelatory Community in Bonhoeffer's Reception of Hegel*. Tübingen: Mohr Siebeck, 2018.
Romano, Claude. *Event and World*. Translated by Shane Mackinlay. New York: Fordham University Press, 2009.
Schliesser, Christine. *Everyone Who Acts Responsibly Becomes Guilty: Bonhoeffer's Concept of Accepting Guilt*. London: Westminster John Knox Press, 2008.
Schlingensiepen, Ferdinand. *Dietrich Bonhoeffer, 1906–1945: Martyr, Thinker, Man of Resistance*. Translated by Isabel Best. London: Bloomsbury, 2009.

Schmitt, Carl. *Political Theology: Four Chapters on the Concept of Sovereignty*. Translated by George Schwab. Chicago: University of Chicago Press, 2005.

Schmitt, Carl. *The Concept of the Political*. Translated by George Schwab. Chicago: The University of Chicago Press, 2007.

Schmitt, Carl. "Zu Friedrich Meineckes 'Idee der Staatsräson.'" *Archiv für Sozialwissenschaft und Sozialpolitik* 56, no. 1 (1926): 226–35.

Schmitz, Florian. *"Nachfolge": Zur Theologie Dietrich Bonhoeffers*. Göttingen: Vandenhoeck & Ruprecht GmbH, 2013.

Schoebert, Wolfgang. "The Concept of Responsibility: Dilemma and Necessity." *Studies in Christian Ethics* 22, no. 4 (2009): 423–41.

Sigurdson, Ola. "'Theology in the Middle of Things': Existential Preconditions of Systematic Theology." *International Journal of Systematic Theology* 22, no. 4 (2020): 473–93.

Smith, Ronald Gregor, ed. *World Come of Age: A Symposium on Dietrich Bonhoeffer*. London: Collins, 1967.

Smith, Ted A. *The New Measures: A Theological History of Democratic Practice*. Cambridge: Cambridge University Press, 2007.

Smith, Ted A. *Weird John Brown: Divine Violence and the Limits of Ethics*. Stanford: Stanford University Press, 2015.

Sonderegger, Katherine. *Systematic Theology: The Doctrine of God*. Volume 1. Minneapolis: Fortress Press, 2015.

Taubes, Jacob. *The Political Theology of Paul*. Translated by Dana Hollander. Stanford: Stanford University Press, 2004.

Tietz, Christiane. *Theologian of Resistance: The Life and Thought of Dietrich Bonhoeffer*. Translated by Victoria J. Barnett. Minneapolis: Fortress Press, 2016.

Tietz, Christiane and Jens Zimmermann, eds. *Bonhoeffer, Religion and Politics: 4th International Bonhoeffer Colloquium*. Berlin: Peter Lang, 2012.

Tödt, Heinz Edward. *Authentic Faith: Bonhoeffer's Theological Ethics in Context*. Edited by Ernst-Albert Scharffenorth. Translated by David Stassen and Isle Tödt. Cambridge: William B. Eerdmans Publishing Co, 2007.

Tooze, Adam. *Shutdown: How Covid Shook the World's Economy*. New York: Viking, 2021.

Van den Heuvel, Stephen. *Bonhoeffer's Christocentric Theology and Fundamental Debates in Environmental Ethics*. Eugene: Pickwick Publications, 2017.

Verhagen, Koert. "God, the Middle Term: Bonhoeffer, Kierkegaard, and Christ's Mediation in *Works of Love*." *Religions* 11, no. 78 (2020). doi:10.3390/rel11020078.

Vosloo, Robert. "Bonhoeffer, our Contemporary? Engaging Bonhoeffer on Time, the Times, and Public Theology." *The Bonhoeffer Legacy: An International Journal* 5, no. 2 (2018): 19–36.

Vosloo, Robert. "Dietrich Bonhoeffer's Reformation Day Sermons and Performative Remembering." *Theology Today* 74, no. 3 (2017): 252–62.

Vosloo, Robert. "The Feeling of Time: Bonhoeffer on Temporality and the Fully Human Life." *Scriptura* 99 (2008): 337–49.

Vosloo, Robert. "Time Out of Joint and Future-Oriented Memory: Engaging Dietrich Bonhoeffer in the Search for a Way to Deal Responsibly with the Ghosts of the Past." *Religions* 8, no. 42 (2017): 1–9.

Walzer, Michael. "The Problem of Dirty Hands." *Philosophy and Public Affairs* 2, no. 2 (1973): 160–80.

Wannenwetsch, Bernd. *Political Worship*. Oxford: Oxford University Press, 2004.

Wannenwetsch, Bernd. "'Responsible Living' or 'Responsible Self'? Bonhoefferian Reflections on a Vexed Moral Notion." *Studies in Christian Ethics* 18, no. 3 (2005): 125–40.
Wannenwetsch, Bernd, ed. *Who Am I? Bonhoeffer's Theology Through His Poetry*. London: T&T Clark, 2009.
Webster, John. *Word and Church: Essays in Church Dogmatics*. London: T&T Clark, 2016.
Williams, Reggie. "Bonhoeffer and King: Christ the Moral Arc." *Black Theology* 9, no. 3 (2011): 356–69.
Williams, Reggie. *Bonhoeffer's Black Jesus: Harlem Renaissance Theology and an Ethic of Resistance*. Waco: Baylor University Press, 2014.
Williams, Rowan. *Christ: The Heart of Creation*. London: Bloomsbury, 2018.
Willis, Jenkins and Jennifer McBride, eds. *Bonhoeffer and King: Their Legacies and Import for Christian Social Thought*. Minneapolis: Fortress Press, 2010.
Winter, Yves. *Machiavelli and the Orders of Violence*. Cambridge: Cambridge University Press, 2018.
Winter, Yves. "Necessity and Fortune: Machiavelli's Politics of Nature." In *Second Nature: Rethinking the Natural Through Politics*, edited by Crina Archer, Laura Ephraim, and Lida Maxwell, 26–45. New York: Fordham University Press, 2013.
Wolf, Ernst, "Political and Moral Motives Behind the Resistance." In *The German Resistance to Hitler*, edited by Walter Schmitthenner and Hans Buchheim, translated by Peter and Betty Ross, 193–234. London: B. T. Batsford Ltd, 1970.
Wolfe, Judith. "The Eschatological Turn in German Philosophy." *Modern Theology* 35, no. 1 (2019): 55–70.
Wüstenberg, Ralf. *A Theology of Life: Dietrich Bonhoeffer's Religionless Christianity*. Translated by Douglas W. Scott. Grand Rapids: W. B. Eerdmans, 1998.
Yelle, Robert A. *Sovereignty and the Sacred: Secularism and the Political Economy of Religion*. Chicago: University of Chicago Press, 2019.
Zahl, Simeon. "Non-Competitive Agency and Luther's Experiential Argument Against Virtue." *Modern Theology* 35, no. 2 (2019): 199–222.
Ziegler, Philip G. "Dietrich Bonhoeffer—An Ethics of God's Apocalypse?" *Modern Theology* 23, no. 4 (2007): 579–94.
Ziegler, Philip G. "Graciously Commanded: Dietrich Bonhoeffer and Karl Barth on the Decalogue." *Scottish Journal of Theology* 71, no. 2 (2018): 127–41.
Ziegler, Philip G. "'Tempted for our Sake'—Bonhoeffer on Christ's Temptation." In *Polyphonie der Theologie: Verantwortung und Widerstand in Kirche und Politik*, edited by Matthias Grebe, 391–402. Stuttgart: Kohlhammer, 2019.
Ziegler, Philip G. "Witness to Christ's Dominion: The Political Service of the Church." *Theology* 116, no. 5 (2013): 323–31.
Zimmermann, Jens. *Dietrich Bonhoeffer's Christian Humanism*. Oxford: Oxford University Press, 2019.
Zimmermann, Jens and Brian Gregor, eds. *Being Human, Becoming Human: Dietrich Bonhoeffer and Social Thought*. Cambridge: James Clarke & Co., 2010.

INDEX

Note: Page numbers followed by "n" refer to notes.

"absolute demand" (*absoluten Forderung*)   65, 67
Act and Being   48, 57
adventitious liberation   116–22
"After Ten Years"   6, 23, 49, 54–5, 101, 112 n.2, 157, 158, 161
Agamben, Giorgio   18
Althaus, Paul   81
Anabaptist readings of Bonhoeffer's resistance thought   24–31
"anxiety" (*Angst*)   65, 67
apocalyptic theology   161
Arendt, Hannah   140
  on *homo faber*   151
  The Origins of Totalitarianism   115
  on totalitarianism   111
authoritarianism   169

Barnett, Victoria   152
Barth, Karl   23
  Römerbrief   166
"Basic Questions of a Christian Ethic"   68, 81
Bell, George   28, 133, 159
Bethel Confession   120 n.34
Bethge, Eberhard   38, 136, 146
"Bible Study on Temptation"   11, 61, 76, 77
Bloomquist, Karen   15
Bonhoeffer moment   14–17, 19, 167
Bonhoeffer's life   39–60
  fragmentariness of   43–7
  hermeneutic implications of   57–8
Bonhoeffer's thought   39–60
  fragmentariness of   47–56
  hermeneutic implications of   58–60
  narration of   49–50

Bonhoeffer's writings, fragmentary form of   47–9
borderline case (*Grenzfall*)   5, 12, 32, 47, 50, 51, 55, 56, 58, 84–6, 91, 94, 95, 105, 135, 144 n.30
  multiple rationales in late resistance thought   50–6
  reconciliation in   145–57
Brown, Petra   14, 32, 34–7, 88, 97, 123

"The Character and Ethical Consequences of Religious Determinism"   70–1
"Christ, Reality, and the Good"   82, 98, 150–1
"Christ and Peace"   152
"The 'Christian' and the 'Ethical' as a Topic"   5, 51, 137 n.6, 141
Christian Realism   32
"The Church and the Jewish Question"   29–30
"Church and World I"   147
church sectarianism   22
civil disobedience   15
civil rights movement   24
community   5, 26, 33, 48, 51, 62, 67–9, 120, 140–2, 147, 150
  church   25, 82, 109 n.77, 148
  political   36, 119, 121, 132, 164
"Concerning the Christian Concept of God"   69
conspiracy, as repentance   132–4
conspiracy plot   1, 9, 26–7, 46–7, 132–4, 152, 154–7
"Contemporizing New Testament Texts"   161

Index

Courtenay, William 72 n.52
Creation and Fall 61, 73–5

Decalogue 136, 142–5, 154, 155
defenseless venture, freedom of 87
De Graff, Guido 133–4
de Gruchy, John 16–17, 19
DeJonge, Michael 14, 37, 47, 150, 166
    Lutheran reading of Bonhoeffer 24–5, 27–31
"destruction" (*Destruktion*) 139 n.14
discernment (*prüfen*) 11, 14, 34, 49, 56, 59, 87, 88, 97, 112, 124, 125, 147, 155, 165–7
    of creation 82
    as a "last principle" 125–32
    of the moment 36
    moral 52
    question of decision vs. 36–7, 106, 165–6
Discipleship 10, 17, 22, 24, 25, 27, 30, 34, 35, 37, 65 n.19, 75, 95 n.35, 104 n.67, 109 n.77, 111, 116, 119, 120, 122–7, 132
divine voluntarism 72–6

Eberhardt, Kai-Ole 101, 102
Elshtain, Jean Bethke 91
"Essay on the Sense of Time" 45
eternity 18, 98, 130, 163
ethics
    "Church and World I" 147
    of commandment 23
    of everyday life 23
    of extremity 23
    history and 61, 65, 69–72
    necessity and *necessitá* 92–4
    nonfoundational 140–2
    peace 27
    political 25, 26
    reconciliation of 154–7
    in revelation 69–72
    "Ultimate and Penultimate Things" 130, 138, 159
Ethics
    "The 'Christian' and the 'Ethical' as a Topic" 5, 51
    "Ethics as Formation" 95 n.35, 128

"God's Love and the Disintegration of the World" 51, 52, 55, 56, 95 n.35, 98, 125, 129
"History and Good [1]" 71
"History and Good [2]" 5, 6, 21, 22, 33, 34, 51, 52, 54–6, 83–110, 154
"Natural Life" 6, 27–8, 50, 51, 145
"Ethics as Formation" 95 n.35, 128 n.57
exception (*Ausnahme*)
    Bonhoeffer's theology, appropriate to reflect on 5–8
    borderline case (*Grenzfall*) 5, 12, 32, 47, 50, 51, 55, 56, 58, 84–6, 94, 95, 105, 135, 144 n.30, 145–57
    in contemporary theology 13–38
    creation of 72–6
    history and 8–10
    in moral and political theology 2–5
    necessity and *necessitá* 3, 5, 11, 21, 25, 27, 34–6, 51, 53, 54, 73, 83, 84, 86, 88–99, 102–4, 110, 121, 122, 125, 128, 137, 142, 147, 148, 154
    responsible action in 85–8
    state of exception (*Ausnahmezustand*) 4, 34, 35
    ultima ratio 5, 22, 34, 53, 83–7, 91, 92, 134
extraordinary (*außerordentliche*) 34–5
extraordinary freedom, politics of 111–34
    adventitious liberation 116–22
    totalitarianism, annihilation of freedom in 112–16
    undetermined political freedom 116–22

fanaticism 88, 124
Feil, Ernst 42, 47, 56
Floyd, Wayne Whitson, Jr. 49
Franz, Markus 40–1
freedom 105–6
    political, undetermined 116–22
    in totalitarianism, annihilation of 112–16
    undetermined 123–32
"The Freedom of the Christian" 166
free venture, of responsible individual or fanatic 32–7
French Revolution 113, 114

friendship 119–22, 134
"The Führer and the Individual in the Younger Generation" 112

Gadamer, Hans-Georg 16, 139 n.14
"God's Love and the Disintegration of the World" 51, 52, 55, 56, 95 n.35, 98, 125, 129
Great War 115
Green, Clifford 14, 25, 150
   on tyrannicide 20–2

Hauerwas, Stanley 14
   Anabaptist reading of Bonhoeffer 24–6, 28
   Performing the Faith: Bonhoeffer and the Practice of Nonviolence 25
Haynes, Stephen 14
   The Bonhoeffer Phenomenon 13
Heidegger, Martin 10
   Being and Time 139 n.14
"Heritage and Decay" 113, 115, 153
hermeneutical circle 17
history
   and ethics 61, 65, 69–72
   and the exception 8–10
   and the moment 11, 61–82
   moment of temptation 76–80, 101, 163, 168
   necessity and *necessità* 90–2, 103
   to political orders, relation of 80–2
   and providence 8 n.35, 78, 80, 101, 102, 104
   undoing of 69–72
"History and Good [1]" 71, 164
"History and Good [2]" 5, 6, 21, 22, 33, 34, 51, 52, 54–6, 83–110, 154
   distancing from *necessità* 94–8
   emphasizing history in 98–103
   narrating the exception in 104–10
   necessità, logic and tension of 88–94
   responsible action in the exception 85–8
Hobbes, Thomas 35
Holl, Karl 73 n.60

ideological determination 117–19
"The Individual and the Führer" 114, 115
individualism 72, 113

irrationality 34, 88, 169
Iwand, Hans-Joachim 20

Jaspers, Karl 35

Kaiser, Joshua
   Becoming Simple and Wise 127
Kant, Immanuel 55
Kierkegaard, Søren 166, 169
   Fear and Trembling 3, 11, 61, 65, 67–9, 75, 80, 131
   Philosophical Fragments 117 n.24
   Repetition 3
   resonances in *der Augenblick* 65–9
Klapproth, Erich 74–5
Krötke, Wolf 136, 150

Latmiral, Gaetano 30 n.95
law 5, 8, 123, 135–45
   as creation and Decalogue, path of 142–5
   natural 136
   positive 136, 144 n.32
   and promise, distinction between 99
   public 4
   timefullness of 136–40
Letters and Papers from Prison 79 n.83
   Widerstand und Ergebung 79 n.83
liberalism 113
Lovin, Robin 32–4, 36, 37, 88
Luther, Martin
   The Bondage of the Will 70, 103 n.64
Lutheran
   readings of Bonhoeffer's resistance thought 24–31
   theology 14, 24–31, 74 n.64, 84, 98, 99, 102, 103, 166, 167
Lutheran Church 148
Lutheranism 166
Lynch, Thomas 161

Machiavelli, Niccolò
   on necessity and *necessità* 3, 5, 11, 21, 25, 27, 34–6, 51, 53, 54, 73, 83, 84, 86, 88–99, 102–4, 110, 121, 122, 125, 128, 137, 142, 147, 148, 154
   The Prince 89
   ultima ratio 5, 22, 34, 53, 83–7, 91, 92, 134

MacIntyre, Alasdair   28 n.87
McKenny, Gerald   108
mandates, the   10, 12, 32, 34, 36, 37, 80, 81, 105, 110, 120–2, 132, 141–3, 164
   conflict between   33
   critique of   33
   intrinsic laws of   88
   language of   7, 82
   reconciliation of   149–53
   relationship between   135, 146
Marion, Jean-Luc   129
Massenmachiavellismus   93
material determination   117–18
Mawson, Michael
   Christ Existing as Community   62 n.2
meditation   140–2
Meinecke, Friedrich   89, 93
Messianic Time   18
Metaxas, Eric   15
moment (*Augenblick*), the
   of exception   135–45
   history and   11, 61–82
   of temptation   76–80, 101, 163, 168
moral theology, exception in   2–5
Müller, Hanfried   146

Nation, Mark   14
   Anabaptist reading of Bonhoeffer   24–5
   Bonhoeffer the Assassin?   26–7
National Socialism   93, 112 n.5, 115, 119, 152, 157
"Natural Life"   6, 27–8, 50, 51, 145
"necessary emergency situations" (*notwendige Ausnahmezustände*)   5
necessity and *necessitá*   3, 5, 11, 25, 34–6, 51, 53, 54, 73, 84, 99, 110, 121, 125, 128, 137, 142, 147, 148, 154
   distancing from   94–8
   ethics   92–4
   historical   90–2, 103
   human   21, 86, 104
   logic and tension of   88–94
   political   21, 83, 86, 88, 91–2, 122
   unconditional   27
Niebuhr, H. Richard   34 n.109
   The Responsible Self   96

"Night Voices"   45–7
nominalism   72 n.52
nonviolence   15, 26, 151, 152

O'Donovan, Oliver   3
Operation Seven   1
orders of creation   72, 80, 81, 149 n.60
orders of preservation   75, 80, 81, 143, 149, 151

pacifism   10, 15, 26, 27
paradoxical obedience   3, 124–5
passive suffering   22
Paulson, Steven   123
peace ethic   27
Peck, William   41 n.10
penultimate and ultimate, relationship between   33–4
"'Personal' and 'Objective' Ethics"   82, 154
personhood   62, 65
phenomenology   9–10
political and politics
   after the exception   157–62
   enemy love and friendship in   119–22
   ethics   25, 26
   freedom, undetermined   116–22
   necessity and *necessitá*   21, 83, 86, 88, 91–2, 122
   orders, relation of history to   80–2
   realism   91, 145, 164
   reconciliation   154–7
   theology, exception in   2–5
   violence   155
polycrisis   2
"A Position Paper on State and Church"   6, 82, 133 n.81, 151–2
"Protestantism without Reformation"   153 n.80
Puffer, Matthew   51–2, 55, 56

Rasmussen, Larry   14, 25, 151
   Reality and Resistance   22
   on tyrannicide   20, 23–4
reconciliation
   in borderline case (*Grenzfall*)   145–57
   of church and world   146–9
   of mandates   149–53
   of politics and ethics   154–7

Reed, Esther   95, 160
representative action (*Stellvertretung*)   85, 108
responsibility   10, 21, 22, 26, 32–4, 62–4, 80, 84–6, 93–7, 106, 107, 113, 133 n.81, 152, 165
   ethical   72 n.54
   necessitá in   97
responsible action   85–8
   defenseless venture, freedom of   87
   state and   86
   structure of   105–10
   tensions and polarities in   88
"Revelation"   63
Ritter, Gerhard   89
Romano, Claude   9

Sanctorum Communio   61, 62, 65, 67, 68, 72 n.54, 73, 77, 80
Schmitt, Carl   35, 169
   on state of exception (*Ausnahmezustand*)   4
Seeberg, Reinhold   81
Siegrist, Anthony G.
   Bonhoeffer the Assassin?   26–7
simple obedience   11, 110–12, 124, 125, 130, 131–2
Sittenlehre   137
Sittlichkeit   66
Smith, Ted   118
Spielraum   122
"Stations on the Way to Freedom"   58 n.79
structure of responsible life   21, 85, 96, 99, 105–10
   moment of   76–80, 101, 163, 168
   primordial   78

temptation
   Akedah   75
   Anfechtung   139, 168
theology of crisis   11, 69, 138, 161, 163
three estates (*Stände*)   32
Tooze, Adam   2
totalitarianism   93, 111, 119, 158, 160, 164
   annihilation of freedom in   112–16
   definition of   112 n.3

transgression   2, 3, 93, 108, 124, 143, 154, 155, 168
tyrannicide   4–5, 14, 19–24, 27, 155, 156, 165, 166

Ulrich, Hans   134
ultima ratio   5, 22, 34, 53, 83–7, 91, 92, 134
"Ultimate and Penultimate Things"   130, 138, 159
Umbel, Daniel P.
   Bonhoeffer the Assassin?   26–7

vicarious representative action (*Stellvertretung*)   21, 62, 85, 107–9
Vietnam War   24
Vilmar, August Friedrich Christian   76 n.75
violence   21, 26, 27, 35, 36, 82, 88, 91, 95, 97, 103, 120, 122, 123, 134, 150–3, 160, 163, 164
   extremity of   92
   fanatical   15, 20, 36, 165
   force of   92
   Gewalt   92
   irrational   165
   necessity of   11, 84, 92, 94
   political   155
   religious   34
Vosloo, Robert   18–19
   "Bonhoeffer, Our Contemporary?"   18

Walzer, Michael   91
Wannenwetsch, Bernd   107
"What Does It Mean to Tell the Truth?"   7, 55–6
"Who Am I?"   43–4, 57
Wolf, Ernst   20

Yoder, John Howard   25, 28 n.83

Zerstörung   139 n.14
Ziegler, Philip G.   107, 149
Zimmermann, Jens
   Bonhoeffer's Christian Humanism   128–9

www.ingramcontent.com/pod-product-compliance
Lightning Source LLC
Chambersburg PA
CBHW051524230426
43668CB00012B/1735